Financial Accounting

Study Guide
Fifth Edition

Belverd E. Needles, Jr.
DePaul University

Edward H. Julius
California Lutheran University

Houghton Mifflin Company   **Boston**   **Toronto**
Geneva, Illinois   Palo Alto   Princeton, New Jersey

Sponsoring Editor: Karen Natale
Associate Sponsoring Editor: Margaret Monahan
Senior Manufacturing Coordinator: Priscilla Bailey
Marketing Manager: Karen Natale

Cover Design: Edda V. Sigurdardottir
Cover Image: Timothy Hursley/The Arkansas Office, Inc.

Copyright © 1995 by Houghton Mifflin Company. All rights reserved.

No part of this work may be reproduced or transmitted in any form or by any means, electronic or mechanical, including photocopying and recording, or by any information storage or retrieval system without the prior written permission of Houghton Mifflin Company unless such copying is expressly permitted by federal copyright law. Address inquiries to College Permissions, Houghton Mifflin Company, 222 Berkeley Street, Boston, MA 02116-3764.

Printed in the U.S.A.

ISBN: 0-395-71049-9

456789-CS-98 97

Contents

To the Student		v

Chapter

1	Uses of Accounting Information and the Basic Financial Statements	1
2	Measuring Business Transactions	13
3	Measuring Business Income	25
4	Completing the Accounting Cycle	37
5	Accounting for Merchandising Operations	47
6	Financial Reporting and Analysis	61
7	Short-Term Liquid Assets	71
8	Inventories	87
9	Long-Term Assets	95
10	Current Liabilities and the Time Value of Money	109
11	Long-Term Liabilities	123
12	Contributed Capital	135
13	Retained Earnings and Corporate Income Statements	147
14	The Statement of Cash Flows	159
15	Financial Statement Analysis	169
16	International Accounting and Intercompany Investments	177

Appendix

B	The Merchandising Work Sheet and Closing Entries	189
C	Special-Purpose Journals	195
D	Accounting for Unincorporated Businesses	201
E	Overview of Governmental and Not-for-Profit Accounting	205
F	Accounting for Bond Investments	209

Specimen Financial Statements: The Coca-Cola Company   211

Answers   245

To the Student

This self-study guide is designed to help you improve your performance in your first accounting course. You should use it in your study of *Financial Accounting, Fifth Edition,* by Needles.

Reviewing the Chapter

This section of each chapter summarizes in a concise but thorough manner the essential points related to the chapter's learning objectives. Each integrated learning objective is restated and its page references given for easier cross-referencing to the text. All key terms are covered in this section. Where applicable, a summary of journal entries introduced in the chapter also is presented.

Testing Your Knowledge

Each chapter contains a matching quiz of key terms, a short-answer section, true-false statements, and multiple-choice questions to test your understanding of the learning objectives and vocabulary in the chapter. This Study Guide also contains eight crossword puzzles to test your knowledge of key terms.

Applying Your Knowledge

An important goal in learning accounting is the ability to work exercises and problems. In this section of each chapter, you can test your ability to apply two or three of the new principles introduced in the chapter to "real-life" accounting situations.

Specimen Financial Statements

The financial report section from the 1991 Annual Report of the Coca-Cola Company is provided as a real example of the financial statements of a major corporation. This complete set of financial statements together with management's discussion and analysis, notes to the financial statements, report of the independent auditors, and other information are provided for you to see the end product of the accounting process. They can be used by instructors and students for discussion and illustration of the concepts, techniques, and statements presented in *Financial Accounting, Fifth Edition.*

Answers

The Study Guide concludes with answers to all questions, exercises, problems, and crossword puzzles. All answers are cross-referenced to the learning objectives in the chapter.

B.E.N.
E.H.J.

CHAPTER 1 USES OF ACCOUNTING INFORMATION AND THE BASIC FINANCIAL STATEMENTS

REVIEWING THE CHAPTER

Objective 1: Define *accounting*, **identify business goals and activities, and describe the role of accounting in making informed decisions (pp. 3–7).**

1. **Accounting** is an information system that measures, processes, and communicates financial information about an identifiable economic entity. It provides information that is essential for decision making. **Bookkeeping,** a small but important aspect of accounting, is the mechanical and repetitive recordkeeping process.

2. A **business** is an economic unit that sells goods and services at prices that will provide an adequate return to its owners. For a business to survive, management must make satisfactory earnings to hold investment capital (called **profitability**) and must keep sufficient funds on hand to pay debts as they fall due (called **liquidity**). The company also has other goals, such as improving its products and expanding operations. It is management that directs the company toward these goals by making decisions.

3. Businesses pursue their goals by engaging in financing, investing, and operating activities.
   a. **Financing activities** are needed to obtain funding for the business, and include such activities as issuing stocks and bonds and repaying creditors.
   b. **Investing activities** consist of spending the funds raised, and include activities such as buying and selling land, buildings, and equipment.
   c. **Operating activities** involve the everyday sale of goods and services as well as the related everyday activities.

4. A distinction is usually made between **management accounting,** which focuses on information for internal users, and **financial accounting,** which involves the preparation, reporting, analysis, and interpretation of accounting information in reports for external users. These reports are called **financial statements.**

5. The **computer** is an electronic tool that rapidly collects, organizes, and communicates vast amounts of information. The computer does not take the place of the accountant. However, the accountant must understand how it operates because it is an integral part of the accounting information system.

6. A **management information system (MIS)** is an information network that takes in all major functions (called *subsystems*) of a business. The accounting information system is the financial hub of the management information system.

Objective 2: Identify the many users of accounting information in society (pp. 7–10).

7. There are basically three groups that use accounting information: management, outsiders with a direct financial interest, and outsiders with an indirect financial interest.

a. As already stated, **management** steers a business toward its goals by making the business's important decisions.
b. Present or potential investors and present or potential creditors are considered outside users with a direct financial interest in a business. Most businesses publish financial statements that report their profitability and financial position. Investors use these financial statements to assess the strength or weakness of the company, whereas creditors examine the financial statement to determine the company's ability to repay debts on time.
c. Society as a whole, through government officials and public groups, can be viewed as an accounting information user with an indirect financial interest in a business. Specifically, such users include tax authorities, regulatory agencies, economic planners, and other groups (such as labor unions and financial analysts).

8. The **Securities and Exchange Commission (SEC)** is an agency of the federal government set up by the U.S. Congress to protect the public by regulating the issuing, buying, and selling of stocks.

9. Managers within government and within not-for-profit organizations such as hospitals, universities, professional organizations, and charities also make extensive use of financial information.

Objective 3: Explain the importance of business transactions, money measure, and separate entity to accounting measurement (pp. 10–12).

10. To make an accounting measurement, the accountant must answer the following basic questions:
    a. What is measured?
    b. When should the measurement be made?
    c. What value should be placed on what is measured?
    d. How should what is measured be classified?

11. Accounting is concerned with measuring transactions of specific business entities in terms of money.
    a. **Business transactions** are economic events that affect the financial position of a business. Business transactions can involve an exchange of value (for example, sales, borrowings, and purchases) or a nonexchange (for example, the physical wear and tear on machinery, and losses due to fire or theft).
    b. The **money measure** concept states that business transactions should be measured in terms of money. Financial statements are normally prepared in terms of the monetary unit of the business's country (dollars, pesos, etc.). When transactions occur between countries with differing monetary units, the amounts must be translated from one currency to another, using the appropriate **exchange rate.**
    c. For accounting purposes, a business is treated as a **separate entity,** distinct from its owners, creditors, and customers.

Objective 4: Describe the corporate form of business organization (pp. 12–16).

12. The three basic forms of business organization are sole proprietorships, partnerships, and corporations. Accountants recognize each form as an economic unit separate from its owners. A **sole proprietorship** is a business owned by one person, a **partnership** is a business owned by two or more persons, and a **corporation** is a business owned by stockholders but managed by a board of directors.

13. The corporation is the dominant form of American business because it makes possible the accumulation of large quantities of capital. The stockholders of a corporation are liable only to the extent of their investment, and ownership (evidenced by **shares of stock**) can be transferred without affecting operations.
    a. Before a corporation may do business, it must apply for and obtain a charter from the state. The state must approve the **articles of incorporation,** which describe the basic purpose and structure of the proposed corporation.
    b. Management of a corporation consists of the board of directors, who determine corporate policy, and the officers, who carry on the daily operations. The board is elected by the stockholders, and the officers are appointed by the board.
    c. Some specific duties of the board of directors are to (a) declare dividends, (b) authorize contracts, (c) determine executive salaries, (d) arrange major loans with banks, and (e) appoint an **audit committee** to serve as a channel of communication between the corporation and the independent auditors. Management's primary means of reporting the corporation's financial position and results of operations is its annual report.

Objective 5: Define *financial position*, state the accounting equation, and show how they are affected by simple transactions (pp. 16–23).

14. Every transaction affects a firm's financial position. **Financial position** is shown by a balance sheet, so called because the two sides or parts of the balance sheet must always equal each other. In a sense, the balance sheet presents two ways of viewing the same business: the left side shows the assets (resources) of the business, whereas the right side shows who provided the assets. Providers consist of owners (listed under "owners' equity") and creditors (represented by the listing of "liabilities"). Therefore, it is logical that the total dollar amount of assets must equal the total dollar amount of liabilities and owners' equity. This is the **accounting equation.** It is formally stated as

    Assets = liabilities + owners' equity

    Other correct forms are

    Assets − liabilities = owners' equity

    Assets − owners' equity = liabilities

15. **Assets** are the economic resources of a business. Examples of assets are cash, accounts receivable, inventory, buildings, equipment, patents, and copyrights.

16. **Liabilities** are debts of the business. Examples of liabilities are money borrowed from banks, amounts owed to creditors for goods bought on credit, and taxes owed to the government.

17. **Owners' equity** represents the claims by the owners of a business to the assets of the business. It equals the residual interest in assets after deducting the liabilities. Because it is equal to assets minus liabilities, owners' equity is said to equal the **net assets** of the business.

18. The owners' equity of a corporation is called **stockholders' equity** and consists of contributed capital and retained earnings. **Contributed capital** represents the amount invested by the owners, whereas **retained earnings** (broadly) represent the accumulation of the profits and losses of a company since its inception, less total dividends declared. **Dividends** are distributions of assets to stockholders from past earnings; they appear in the statement of retained earnings.

19. Retained earnings are affected by three types of transactions. **Revenues,** which result when services have been provided, increase retained earnings. **Expenses,** which represent costs of doing business, decrease retained earnings, as do dividends. When revenues exceed expenses, a **net income** results. When expenses exceed revenues, however, a **net loss** has been suffered.

20. Every transaction changes the balance sheet in some way. In practice, companies do not prepare a new balance sheet after each transaction. However, it is important for accounting students to understand the exact effect of each transaction on the parts of the balance sheet.

21. Although every transaction changes the balance sheet, the accounting equation always remains in balance. In other words, dollar amounts may change, but assets must always equal liabilities plus owners' equity.

22. **Accounts** are used by accountants to accumulate amounts produced from like transactions.

Objective 6: Identify the four basic financial statements (pp. 23–26).

23. Accountants communicate information through financial statements. The four principal statements are the balance sheet, income statement, statement of retained earnings, and statement of cash flows.

24. Every financial statement has a three-line heading. The first line gives the name of the company. The second line gives the name of the statement. The third line gives the relevant dates (the date of the balance sheet or the period of time covered by the other three statements).

25. The **income statement,** whose components are revenues and expenses, is perhaps the most important financial statement. Its purpose is to measure the business's success or failure in earning an income over a given period of time.

26. The **statement of retained earnings** is a labeled calculation of the changes in retained earnings (defined in paragraph 18) during the accounting period. Retained earnings at the beginning of the period is the first item on the statement, followed by an addition for net income or a deduction for net loss and a deduction for dividends declared. The ending retained earnings figure that results is transferred to the stockholders' equity section of the balance sheet.

27. The **balance sheet** shows the financial position of a business on a certain date. The resources owned by the business are called assets; debts of the business are called liabilities; and the owners'

financial interest in the business is called **owners' equity**.

28. The **statement of cash flows** shows much information that is not present in the balance sheet or income statement. This statement discloses all the business's operating, investing, and financing activities during the accounting period. As discussed, in part, in paragraph 3, operating activities consist mainly of receipts from customers and payments to suppliers and others in the ordinary course of business. Investing activities might include selling a building or investing in stock. Financing activities might include issuing stock or paying dividends. The statement's bottom line will indicate the net increase or decrease in cash during the period.

Objective 7: State the relationship of generally accepted accounting principles (GAAP) to financial statements and the independent CPA's report, and identify the organizations that influence GAAP (pp. 26–28).

29. Accounting theory provides the reasoning behind and framework for accounting practice. **Generally accepted accounting principles (GAAP)** are the set of guidelines and procedures that constitute acceptable accounting practice at a given time. The set of GAAP changes continually as business conditions change and practices improve.

30. The financial statements of publicly held corporations are audited by licensed professionals, called **certified public accountants (CPAs),** to ensure the quality of those statements. Before an **audit** can take place, however, the CPA must be independent of the client (without financial or other ties). On completion of the audit, the CPA reports on whether or not the audited statements "present fairly, in all material respects" and are "in conformity with generally accepted accounting principles."

31. The **Financial Accounting Standards Board (FASB)** is the authoritative body for development of GAAP. This group is separate from the AICPA and issues Statements of Financial Accounting Standards.

32. The **American Institute of Certified Public Accountants (AICPA)** is the professional association of CPAs. Its senior technical committees help influence accounting practice.

33. The Securities and Exchange Commission (SEC) is an agency of the federal government. It has the legal power to set and enforce accounting practices for companies whose securities are traded by the general public.

34. The **Governmental Accounting Standards Board (GASB)** was established in 1984 and is responsible for issuing accounting standards for state and local governments.

35. The **International Accounting Standards Committee (IASC)** is responsible for developing worldwide accounting standards. To date, it has approved more than thirty such standards, which have been translated into six languages.

36. The **Internal Revenue Service (IRS)** enforces and interprets the set of rules that govern the assessment and collection of federal income taxes.

Objective 8: Define *ethics* and describe the ethical responsibilities of accountants (pp. 29–30).

37. **Ethics** is a code of conduct that applies to everyday life. **Professional ethics** is the application of a code of conduct to the practice of a profession. The accounting profession has developed such a code, intended to guide the accountant in carrying out his or her responsibilities to the public. In short, the accountant must act with integrity, objectivity, independence, and due care.
    a. **Integrity** means that the accountant is honest, regardless of consequences.
    b. **Objectivity** means that the accountant is impartial in performing his or her job.
    c. **Independence** is the avoidance of all relationships that could impair the objectivity of the accountant, such as owning stock in a company he or she is auditing.
    d. **Due care** means carrying out one's responsibilities with competence and diligence.

38. The **Institute of Management Accountants** has adopted a code of professional conduct of competence, confidentiality, integrity, and objectivity.

TESTING YOUR KNOWLEDGE

*Matching**

Match each term with its definition by writing the appropriate letter in the blank.

1. Accounting
2. Bookkeeping
3. Computer
4. Management information system (MIS)
5. Management accounting
6. Financial accounting
7. Accounting equation
8. Dividend
9. Certified public accountant (CPA)
10. Sole proprietorship
11. Partnership
12. Corporation
13. Generally accepted accounting principles (GAAP)
14. Balance sheet
15. Income statement
16. Statement of retained earnings
17. Statement of cash flows
18. Separate entity
19. Money measure
20. Asset
21. Liability
22. Owners' equity
23. Contributed capital

a. A debt of a business
b. A business owned by stockholders but managed by a board of directors
c. A distribution of earnings to stockholders
d. The standard that all business transactions should be measured in terms of money
e. The statement that shows the financial position of a company on a certain date
f. The repetitive recordkeeping process
g. An economic resource of a business
h. An information system that measures, processes, and communicates economic information
i. A business owned and managed by two or more persons
j. An expert accountant licensed by the state
k. Representation on the balance sheet of stockholders' investments in a corporation
l. The statement that shows a company's profit or loss over a certain period of time
m. The statement that discloses the operating, investing, and financing activities during the period
n. The branch of accounting concerned with providing external users with financial information needed to make decisions
o. An electronic tool that processes information rapidly
p. The balance sheet section that represents the owners' economic interest in a company
q. The statement that shows the changes in the Retained Earnings account during the period
r. The information network that links a company's functions together
s. Assets = liabilities + owners' equity
t. The accounting concept that treats a business as distinct from its owners, creditors, and customers
u. The guidelines that define acceptable accounting practice at a given point in time
v. A business owned and managed by one person
w. The branch of accounting concerned with providing managers with financial information needed to make decisions

---

**Note to student:* The matching quiz might be completed more efficiently by starting with the definition and searching for the corresponding term.

Short Answer

Use the lines provided to answer each item.

1. On the lines that follow, insert the correct heading for the annual income statement of Alpha Corporation on June 30, 19xx.

   _____
   _____
   _____

2. Briefly distinguish between bookkeeping and accounting.

   _____
   _____
   _____

3. Briefly define the terms below, all of which relate to the accountant's Code of Professional Conduct.

   a. Integrity _____
      _____

   b. Objectivity _____
      _____

   c. Independence _____
      _____

   d. Due care _____
      _____

4. What three broad groups use accounting information?

   _____
   _____
   _____

5. What two objectives must be met for a company to survive?

   _____
   _____

6. List the four principal financial statements and state briefly the purpose of each.

   Statement

   a. _____
      _____

   b. _____
      _____

   c. _____
      _____

   d. _____
      _____

   Purpose

   a. _____
      _____

   b. _____
      _____

   c. _____
      _____

   d. _____
      _____

True-False

Circle T if the statement is true, F if it is false. Please provide explanations for false answers, using the blank lines at the end of the section.

T F 1. Financial position can best be determined by referring to the income statement.

T F 2. The IRS is responsible for interpreting and enforcing GAAP.

T F 3. One form of the accounting equation is assets − liabilities = owners' equity.

T F 4. Revenues have the effect of increasing owners' equity.

T F 5. The existence of Accounts Receivable on the balance sheet indicates that the company has one or more creditors.

T F 6. When expenses exceed revenues, a company has suffered a net loss.

T F 7. The measurement stage of accounting involves preparation of the financial statements.

T F 8. Dividends appear as a deduction in the income statement.

T F 9. The current authoritative body dictating accounting practice is the FASB.

T F 10. A sole proprietor is personally liable for all debts of the business.

T F 11. The statement of cash flows would disclose whether or not land was purchased during the period.

T F 12. The statement of retained earnings links a company's income statement to its balance sheet.

T F 13. The IASC is responsible for setting guidelines for state and local governments.

T F 14. A corporation is managed directly by its stockholders.

T F 15. Generally accepted accounting principles are not like laws of math and science; they are guidelines that define correct accounting practice at the time.

T F 16. Net assets equal assets plus liabilities.

T F 17. The major sections of a balance sheet are assets, liabilities, owners' equity, revenues, and expenses.

T F 18. A business transaction must always involve an exchange of money.

T F 19. A management information system deals not only with accounting, but with other activities of a business as well.

T F 20. The income statement is generally considered to be the most important financial statement.

T F 21. A business should be understood as an entity that is separate and distinct from its owners, customers, and creditors.

T F 22. Economic planners are accounting information users with a direct financial interest.

T F 23. The essence of an asset is that it is expected to benefit future operations.

Uses of Accounting Information and the Basic Financial Statements

Multiple Choice

Circle the letter of the best answer.

1. Which of the following accounts would *not* appear on the balance sheet?
   a. Wages Expense
   b. Common Stock
   c. Notes Receivable
   d. Wages Payable

2. Companies whose stock is publicly traded must file financial statements with the
   a. FASB.
   b. GASB.
   c. SEC.
   d. AICPA.

3. One characteristic of a corporation is
   a. unlimited liability of its owners.
   b. the ease with which ownership is transferred.
   c. ownership by the board of directors.
   d. dissolution upon the death of an owner.

4. Which of the following statements does *not* involve a distinct period of time?
   a. Income statement
   b. Balance sheet
   c. Statement of cash flows
   d. Statement of retained earnings

5. The principal purpose of an audit by a CPA is to
   a. express an opinion on the fairness of a company's financial statements.
   b. detect fraud by a company's employees.
   c. prepare the company's financial statements.
   d. assure investors that the company will be profitable in the future.

6. Collection on an account receivable will
   a. increase total assets and increase total owners' equity.
   b. have no effect on total assets, but will increase total owners' equity.
   c. decrease both total assets and total liabilities.
   d. have no effect on total assets, liabilities, or owners' equity.

7. In a partnership,
   a. profits are always divided equally among partners.
   b. management consists of the board of directors.
   c. no partner is liable for more than a proportion of the company's debts.
   d. dissolution results when any partner leaves the partnership.

8. Which of the following is *not* a major account heading in the balance sheet or income statement?
   a. Accounts Receivable
   b. Owners' Equity
   c. Liabilities
   d. Revenues

9. Payment of a liability will
   a. decrease total liabilities and decrease total owners' equity.
   b. decrease total assets and increase total owners' equity.
   c. decrease total assets and decrease total liabilities.
   d. have no effect on total assets, liabilities, or owners' equity.

10. The purchase of an asset for cash will
    a. increase total assets and increase total owners' equity.
    b. increase total assets and increase total liabilities.
    c. increase total assets and decrease total liabilities.
    d. have no effect on total assets, liabilities, or owners' equity.

11. Which of the following is *not* an activity listed in the statement of cash flows?
    a. Investing Activities
    b. Funding Activities
    c. Operating Activities
    d. Financing Activities

APPLYING YOUR KNOWLEDGE

Exercises

1. Lindlay Steel, Inc., always publishes annual financial statements. This year, however, it has suffered a huge loss and is trying to keep this fact a secret by refusing anyone access to its financial statements. Why might each of the following nevertheless insist upon seeing Lindlay's statements?

   a. Potential investors in Lindlay

   b. The Securities and Exchange Commission

   c. The bank, which is considering a loan request by Lindlay

   d. Present stockholders of Lindlay

   e. Lindlay's management

2. Randi Corporation had assets of $100,000 and liabilities of $70,000 at the beginning of the year. During the year assets decreased by $15,000 and stockholders' equity increased by $20,000. What is the amount of liabilities at year end?

   $_____

3. Following are the accounts of Acme TV Repair Corporation as of December 31, 19xx.

Accounts Payable	$ 1,300
Accounts Receivable	1,500
Building	10,000
Cash	?
Common Stock	14,500
Equipment	850
Land	1,000
Retained Earnings	3,000
Truck	4,500

   Using this information, prepare a balance sheet *in good form.* (You must derive the dollar amount for Cash.)

   Acme TV Repair Corporation
   Balance Sheet
   December 31, 19xx

   Assets

   Liabilities

   Stockholders' Equity

4. Following are the transactions for Johnson Paints, Inc., for the first month of operations.
   a. Walt and Carol Johnson invested $20,000 cash in the newly formed corporation.
   b. Purchased paint supplies and equipment for $650 cash.
   c. Purchased a company truck on credit for $5,200.
   d. Received $525 for painting a house.
   e. Paid one-half of the amount due on the truck previously purchased.
   f. Billed a customer $150 for painting his garage.
   g. Paid $250 for one month's rental of the office.
   h. Received full payment from the customer whose garage was painted (transaction f).

i. Sold a company ladder for $20. The buyer said he would pay next month.
j. The company declared and paid a $200 cash dividend.

In the table below, show the effect of each transaction on the balance sheet accounts by putting the dollar amount, along with a plus or minus, under the proper account. Determine the balance in each account at month's end. As an example, transaction *a* has already been recorded.

	Assets					Liabilities	Stockholder's Equity	
Transaction	Cash	Accounts Receivable	Supplies and Equipment	Trucks	Accounts Payable	Common Stock	Retained Earnings
a	+$20,000					+$20,000	
b							
c							
d							
e							
f							
g							
h							
i							
j							
Balance at end of month							

Crossword Puzzle for Chapter 1

ACROSS

2. Accounting mainly for external use
5. _____ proprietorship
8. Resources of a company
10. One to whom another is indebted
11. _____ sheet
13. Professional organization of accountants
14. The language of business
15. IRS's concern
17. Measure of debt-paying ability
18. Data-generating network
19. Separate _____ concept

DOWN

1. See 3-Down
3. With 1-Down, income statement measure
4. Independent CPA activity
6. Measure of business performance
7. Form of business organization
9. Regulatory agency of publicly held corporations
11. Recorder of business transactions
12. Debt of a company
16. Ownership in a company

Uses of Accounting Information and the Basic Financial Statements

CHAPTER 2 MEASURING BUSINESS TRANSACTIONS

REVIEWING THE CHAPTER

Objective 1: Explain, in simple terms, the generally accepted ways of solving the measurement issues of recognition, valuation, and classification (pp. 52–53).

1. Before recording a business transaction, the accountant must determine three things:
   a. When the transaction should be recorded (the **recognition** issue)
   b. What value to place on the transaction (the **valuation** issue)
   c. How the components of the transaction should be categorized (the **classification** issue)

2. A sale is recognized (entered in the accounting records) when the title to merchandise passes from the supplier to the purchaser, regardless of when payment is made or received. This point of sale is referred to as the **recognition point.**

3. The **cost principle** states that the dollar value (**cost**) of any item involved in a business transaction is its original cost (also called *historical cost*). Generally, any change in value after the transaction is not reflected in the accounting records.

Objective 2: Describe the chart of accounts and recognize commonly used accounts (pp. 53–58).

4. Every business transaction is classified in a filing system consisting of accounts. An account is the basic storage unit for accounting data. Each asset, liability, component of owner's equity, revenue, and expense has a separate account.

5. All of a company's accounts are contained in a book or file called the **general ledger** (or simply the *ledger*). Each account appears on a separate page, and the accounts generally are in the following order: assets, liabilities, stockholders' equity, revenues, and expenses. A list of the accounts with their respective account numbers, called a **chart of accounts,** is presented at the beginning of the ledger for easy reference.

6. Although the accounts used by companies will vary, there are some that are common to most businesses. Some typical assets are Cash, Notes Receivable, Accounts Receivable, Prepaid Expenses, Land, Buildings, and Equipment. Some typical liabilities are Notes Payable, Accounts Payable, and Mortgage Payable.

7. The stockholders' equity section of a corporation's balance sheet contains a common stock account and a retained earnings account. Common stock represents the amount of capital invested by stockholders, whereas retained earnings represent cumulative profits and losses, less cumulative dividends declared. Dividends are distributions of assets (generally cash) to stockholders and may be declared only when sufficient retained earnings (and cash) exist.

8. A separate account is kept for each type of revenue and expense. The exact revenue and expense accounts used will vary, depending on the type of

business and the nature of its operations. Revenues cause an increase in retained earnings, whereas expenses cause a decrease.

Objective 3: Define *double-entry system* and state the rules for double entry (pp. 58–62).

9. The **double-entry system** of accounting requires that for each transaction there must be one or more accounts debited and one or more accounts credited, and that total dollar amounts of debits must equal total dollar amounts of credits.

10. An account in its simplest form, a **T account,** has three parts:
    a. A title that expresses the name of the asset, liability, or stockholders' equity account
    b. A left side, which is called the **debit** side
    c. A right side, which is called the **credit** side

11. At the end of an accounting period, **balances** (also known as *account balances*) are calculated in order to prepare the financial statements. If using T accounts, there are three steps to follow in determining these account balances:
    a. Foot (add up) the debit entries. The **footing** (total) should be made in small numbers beneath the last entry.
    b. Foot the credit entries.
    c. Subtract the smaller total from the larger. A debit balance exists when total debits exceed total credits; a credit balance exists when the opposite is the case.

12. To determine which accounts are debited and which are credited in a given transaction, one uses the following rules:
    a. Increases in assets are debited.
    b. Decreases in assets are credited.
    c. Increases in liabilities and stockholders' equity are credited.
    d. Decreases in liabilities and stockholders' equity are debited.
    e. Revenues, common stock, and retained earnings increase stockholders' equity, and are therefore credited.
    f. Dividends and expenses decrease stockholders' equity, and are therefore debited.

13. Transactions may be analyzed and processed by executing the following five steps:
    a. Determine the effect (increase or decrease) of the transaction on assets, liabilities, and stockholders' equity accounts. Each transaction should be supported by a **source document,** such as an invoice or canceled check.
    b. Apply the rules of double entry.
    c. Enter the transaction (record the entry) into the journal.
    d. Post the journal entry to the general ledger.
    e. Prepare the trial balance.

Objective 4: Apply the steps for transaction analysis and processing to simple transactions (pp. 62–68).

14. To record a transaction, one must (a) obtain a description of the transaction, (b) determine which accounts are involved and what type each is (for example, asset or revenue), (c) determine which accounts are increased and which are decreased, and (d) apply the rules stated in paragraph 12 a–f.

Objective 5: Record transactions in the general journal (pp. 69–70).

15. As transactions occur, they are recorded initially and chronologically in a book called the **journal.** The **general journal** is the simplest and most flexible type of journal. Each transaction **journalized** (recorded) in the general journal contains (a) the date, (b) the account names, (c) the dollar amounts debited and credited, (d) an explanation, and (e) the account numbers, if the transaction has been posted. A line should be skipped after each **journal entry,** and more than one debit or credit can be entered for a single transaction (called a **compound entry**).

Objective 6: Post transactions from the general journal to the ledger (pp. 70–71).

16. The general journal records details of each transaction; the results of these details are summarized in the general ledger which updates each account. Each day's journal entries must be posted to the appropriate account in **ledger account form. Posting** is a transferring process that results in an updated balance for each account. The dates and amounts are transferred from the journal to the ledger, and new account balances are calculated. The Post. Ref. columns are used for cross-referencing between the journal and the ledger.

Objective 7: Prepare a trial balance and describe its value and limitations (pp. 71–74).

17. Periodically, the accountant must double-check the equality of the total of debit and credit balances in the ledger. This is done formally by means of a **trial balance.** A normal balance is

determined by whether an account is increased by entries to the debit side or by entries to the credit side. The side on which increases are recorded dictates what is considered the **normal balance.** For example, asset accounts have a normal debit balance.

18. If the trial balance does not balance, one or more errors have been made in the journal, ledger, or trial balance. The accountant must locate the errors to put the trial balance in balance. It is important to know, however, that it is possible to make errors that would not cause the trial balance to be out of balance (that is, errors that cannot be detected through the trial balance).

19. Ruled lines appear in financial reports before each subtotal, and a double line customarily is placed below the final amount. Although dollar signs are required in financial statements, they are omitted in journals and ledgers. On paper with ruled columns, commas and periods are omitted, and a dash frequently is used to designate zero cents.

Summary of Journal Entries Introduced in Chapter 2

A. (L.O. 4) Cash   XX (amount invested)
        Common Stock   XX (amount invested)
           Investment of cash into business by owners

B. (L.O. 4) Prepaid Rent   XX (amount paid)
        Cash   XX (amount paid)
           Advance payment for rent

C. (L.O. 4) Art Equipment   XX (purchase price)
        Cash   XX (amount paid)
           Purchase of art equipment for cash

D. (L.O. 4) Office Equipment   XX (purchase price)
        Cash   XX (amount paid)
        Accounts Payable   XX (amount to be paid)
           Purchase of office equipment, partial payment made

E. (L.O. 4) Art Supplies   XX (purchase price)
        Office Supplies   XX (purchase price)
        Accounts Payable   XX (amount to be paid)
           Purchase of art and office supplies on credit

F. (L.O. 4) Prepaid Insurance   XX (amount paid)
        Cash   XX (amount paid)
           Advance payment for insurance coverage

G. (L.O. 4) Accounts Payable   XX (amount paid)
        Cash   XX (amount paid)
           Payment on a liability

H. (L.O. 4) Cash   XX (amount received)
        Advertising Fees Earned   XX (amount earned)
           Received payment for services rendered

I. (L.O. 4) Office Wages Expense   XX (amount incurred)
        Cash   XX (amount paid)
           Recorded and paid wages for the period

J. (L.O. 4) Cash   XX (amount received)
        Unearned Art Fees   XX (amount received)
           Received payment for services to be performed

K. (L.O. 4) Accounts Receivable   XX (amount to be received)
        Advertising Fees Earned   XX (amount earned)
           Rendered service, payment to be received at later time

L. (L.O. 4) Utility Expense   XX (amount incurred)
        Cash   XX (amount paid)
           Recorded and paid utility bill

M. (L.O. 4) Telephone Expense   XX (amount incurred)
           Accounts Payable   XX (amount to be paid)
               Recorded telephone bill, payment to be made at later time

N. (L.O. 4) Dividends   XX (amount paid)
           Cash   XX (amount paid)
               Declared and paid a dividend

TESTING YOUR KNOWLEDGE

Matching

Match each term with its definition by writing the appropriate letter in the blank.

_____ 1. Original (historical) cost
_____ 2. Account
_____ 3. Debit
_____ 4. Credit
_____ 5. Account balance
_____ 6. Ledger
_____ 7. Posting
_____ 8. Prepaid expenses
_____ 9. Accounts Payable
_____ 10. Common Stock
_____ 11. Retained Earnings
_____ 12. Double-entry system
_____ 13. Trial balance
_____ 14. Journal
_____ 15. Post. Ref.
_____ 16. Footing
_____ 17. Compound entry
_____ 18. Unearned revenue
_____ 19. Dividends

a. Transferring data from the journal to the ledger
b. The amount in an account at a given point in time
c. An entry with more than one debit or credit
d. A distribution of assets to stockholders, resulting from profitable operations
e. A procedure for checking the equality of debits and credits in the ledger accounts
f. A record that occupies a page of the ledger
g. The book that contains all of a company's accounts
h. Adding up
i. A liability arising when payment is received prior to the performance of services
j. Cumulative profits and losses, less dividends declared
k. The proper valuation to place on a business transaction
l. Amounts owed to others
m. Amounts paid in advance for goods or services
n. The book of original entry
o. The right side of a ledger account
p. The column in the journal and ledger that provides for cross-referencing between the two
q. The left side of a ledger account
r. The method that requires both a debit and a credit for each transaction
s. The account that represents ownership in a corporation

Short Answer

Use the lines provided to answer each item.

1. List the five steps that must be executed to analyze and process transactions.

   _____

   _____

   _____

   _____

   _____

2. Given the following journal entry, indicate which part of the entry applies to each measurement issue listed.

   July 14   Cash   150
                   Accounts Receivable   150
                   Collection on account

   a. Recognition issue _____

   b. Valuation issue _____

   c. Classification issue _____

3. Describe a transaction that would require a debit to one asset and a credit to another asset.

   _____

   _____

4. Describe a transaction that would require a debit to a liability and a credit to an asset.

   _____

   _____

5. List the three account types that affect the retained earnings account.

   _____

   _____

   _____

True-False

Circle T if the statement is true, F if it is false. Please provide explanations for the false answers, using the blank lines at the end of the section.

T F 1. A sale should be recorded on the date of payment.

T F 2. *Historical cost* is another term for *original cost*.

T F 3. There must be a separate account for each asset, liability, component of stockholders' equity, revenue, and expense.

T F 4. The credit side of an account implies something favorable.

T F 5. In a given account, total debits must always equal total credits.

T F 6. Management can determine cash on hand quickly by referring to the journal.

T F 7. The number and titles of accounts vary among businesses.

T F 8. Promissory Note is an example of an account title.

T F 9. Prepaid expenses are classified as assets.

T F 10. Increases in liabilities are indicated with a credit.

T F 11. In all journal entries, at least one account must be increased and another decreased.

T F 12. Journal entries are made after transactions have been entered into the ledger accounts.

T F 13. In the journal, all liabilities and stockholders' equity accounts must be indented.

T F 14. A debit is never indented in the journal.

T F 15. Posting is the process of transferring data from the journal to the ledger.

T F 16. The Post. Ref. column of a journal or ledger should be empty until posting is done.

T F 17. In practice, the ledger account form is used, but the T account form is not.

T F 18. The chart of accounts is a table of contents to the general journal.

Measuring Business Transactions

T F 19. Unearned Revenue has a normal debit balance.

T F 20. Retained Earnings is a cash account placed in the asset section of the balance sheet.

T F 21. The Common Stock account represents stockholders' investments, but not corporate profits and losses.

Multiple Choice

Circle the letter of the best answer.

1. Which of the following is *not* considered in initially recording a business transaction?
   a. Classification
   b. Recognition
   c. Summarization
   d. Valuation

2. When a liability is paid, which of the following is true?
   a. Total assets and total liabilities remain the same.
   b. Total assets and total stockholders' equity decrease.
   c. Total assets decrease by the same amount that total liabilities increase.
   d. Total assets and total liabilities decrease.

3. Which of the following is *not* true about a proper journal entry?
   a. All credits are indented.
   b. All debits are listed before the first credit.
   c. An explanation is needed for each debit and each credit.
   d. A debit is never indented, even if a liability or owners' equity account is involved.

4. When an entry is posted, what is the last step to be taken?
   a. The explanation must be transferred.
   b. The account number is placed in the reference column of the ledger.
   c. The journal page number is placed in the reference column of the journal.
   d. The account number is placed in the reference column of the journal.

5. Which of the following errors will probably be disclosed by the preparation of a trial balance (i.e., would cause it to be out of balance)?
   a. Failure to post an entire journal entry (i.e., nothing is posted).
   b. Failure to record an entry in the journal (i.e., nothing is entered).
   c. Failure to post part of a journal entry.
   d. Posting the debit of a journal entry as a credit, and the credit as a debit.

6. When cash is received in payment of an account receivable, which of the following is true?
   a. Total assets increase.
   b. Total assets remain the same.
   c. Total assets decrease.
   d. Total assets and total owners' equity increase.

7. Which of the following is increased by debits?
   a. Dividends
   b. Unearned Revenue
   c. Mortgage Payable
   d. Retained Earnings

8. Which of the following accounts is an asset?
   a. Unearned Revenue
   b. Prepaid Rent
   c. Retained Earnings
   d. Fees Earned

9. Which of the following accounts is a liability?
   a. Interest Payable
   b. Interest Expense
   c. Interest Receivable
   d. Interest Income

10. A company that rents an office (i.e., a lessee or tenant) would never have an entry to which account for that particular lease?
    a. Prepaid Rent
    b. Unearned Rent
    c. Rent Payable
    d. Rent Expense

11. Which of the following accounts has a normal credit balance?
    a. Prepaid Insurance
    b. Dividends
    c. Sales
    d. Advertising Expense

APPLYING YOUR KNOWLEDGE

Exercises

1. Following are all the transactions of Pinnacle Printing, Inc. for the month of May. For each transaction, provide *in good form* the journal entries required. Use the journal provided on the following page.

   May 2 Pinnacle Printing, Inc., was granted a charter by the state, and investors contributed $28,000 in exchange for 2,800 shares of $10 par value common stock.

   3 Rented part of a building for $300 per month. Paid three months' rent in advance.

   5 Purchased a small printing press for $10,000 and photographic equipment for $3,000 from Irvin Press, Inc. Paid $2,000 and agreed to pay the remainder as soon as possible.

   8 Hired a pressman, agreeing to pay him $200 per week.

   9 Received $1,200 from Doherty's Department Store as an advance for brochures to be printed.

   11 Purchased paper for $800 from Pulp Supply Company. Issued Pulp a promissory note for the entire amount.

   14 Completed a $500 printing job for Sullivan Shoes. Sullivan paid for half, agreeing to pay the remainder next week.

   14 Paid the pressman his weekly salary.

   15 Paid Irvin Press, Inc., $1,000 of the amount owed for the May 5 transaction.

   18 Received remainder due from Sullivan Shoes for the May 14 transaction.

   20 A $700 cash dividend was declared and paid by the corporation.

   24 Received an electric bill of $45. Payment will be made in a few days.

   30 Paid the electric bill.

2. Following are three balance sheet accounts, selected at random from Holding Company's ledger. For each, determine the account balance.

Accounts Receivable		Accounts Payable	
2,000	1,000	1,200	4,200
750		2,000	

Cash	
15,000	1,000
4,000	1,200
	2,200

   a. Accounts Receivable has a (debit or credit) balance of $_____.

   b. Accounts Payable has a (debit or credit) balance of $_____.

   c. Cash has a (debit or credit) balance of $_____.

   (Continued on page 24)

Date		Description	Debit	Credit
May	2	Cash	28,000	
		Common Stock		28,000
		To record the stockholders' original investment		

3. Two journal entries are presented below. Post both entries to the ledger accounts provided. Only those accounts needed have been provided, and previous postings have been omitted to simplify the exercise.

\multicolumn{5}{c	}{General Journal}	Page 7
Date		Description	Post. Ref.	Debit	Credit
Apr.	3	Cash		1,000	
		Revenue from Services			1,000
		Received payment from Malden Company for services			
	5	Accounts Payable		300	
		Cash			300
		Paid Douglas Supply Company for supplies purchased on March 31 on credit			

Cash — Account No. 11

Date	Item	Post. Ref.	Debit	Credit	Balance Debit	Balance Credit

Accounts Payable — Account No. 21

Date	Item	Post. Ref.	Debit	Credit	Balance Debit	Balance Credit

Revenue from Services — Account No. 41

Date	Item	Post. Ref.	Debit	Credit	Balance Debit	Balance Credit

CHAPTER 3 MEASURING BUSINESS INCOME

REVIEWING THE CHAPTER

Objective 1: Define *net income* and its two major components, *revenues* and *expenses* (pp. 99–101).

1. Earning a **profit** is an important goal of most businesses. A major function of accounting is to measure and report a company's success or failure in achieving this goal. This is done by means of an income statement.

2. **Net income** is the net increase in stockholders' equity resulting from the operations of the company. Net income results when revenues exceed expenses, and a **net loss** results when expenses exceed revenues.

3. **Revenues** are the price of goods sold and services rendered during a specific period of time. Examples of revenues are Sales (the account used when merchandise is sold), Commissions Earned, and Advertising Fees Earned.

4. **Expenses** are the costs of goods and services used in the process of earning revenues. Examples of expenses are Telephone Expense, Wages Expense, and Advertising Expense.

5. Revenue and expense accounts are sometimes referred to as **temporary** (or *nominal*) **accounts** because they are temporary in nature. Their purpose is to record revenues and expenses during a particular accounting period. At the end of that period, their totals are transferred to the Retained Earnings account, leaving zero balances to begin the next accounting period.

6. Balance sheet accounts are sometimes referred to as **permanent** (or *real*) **accounts** because their balances can extend past the end of an accounting period. They are *not* set back to zero.

Objective 2a: Explain the difficulties of income measurement caused by the accounting period issue (p. 101).

7. The **periodicity** assumption (the solution to the **accounting period issue**) states that although measurements of net income for short periods of time are approximate, they are nevertheless useful to statement users. Income statement comparison is made possible through accounting periods of equal length. A **fiscal year** covers any twelve-month accounting period used by a company. Many companies use a fiscal year that corresponds to a calendar year, which is a twelve-month period that ends on December 31.

Objective 2b: Explain the difficulties of income measurement caused by the continuity issue (pp. 101–102).

8. Under the **going concern** assumption (the solution to the **continuity issue**), the accountant assumes that the business will continue to operate indefinitely, unless there is evidence to the contrary.

Objective 2c: Explain the difficulties of income measurement caused by the matching issue (pp. 102–103).

9. When the **cash basis of accounting** is used, revenues are recorded when cash is received, and expenses are recorded when cash is paid. This method, however, can lead to distortion of net income for the period.

10. According to the **matching rule,** revenues should be recorded in the period(s) in which they

are actually earned, and expenses should be recorded in the period(s) in which the expenses are incurred; the timing of cash payments or receipts is irrelevant.

Objective 3: Define *accrual accounting* **and explain two broad ways of accomplishing it (pp. 103–104).**

11. **Accrual accounting** consists of all techniques used to apply the matching rule. Specifically, it involves (1) recognizing revenues when earned (**revenue recognition**) and expenses when incurred, and (2) adjusting the accounts at the end of the period.

Objective 4: State four principal situations that require adjusting entries (pp. 104–105).

12. A problem arises when revenues or expenses apply to more than one accounting period. The problem is solved by making **adjusting entries** at the end of the accounting period. Adjusting entries allocate to the current period the revenues and expenses that apply to that period, deferring the remainder to future periods. A **deferral** is the postponement of the recognition of an expense already paid or of a revenue already received [see 13(a) and (b) below]. An **accrual** is the recognition of an expense or revenue that has arisen but has not yet been recorded [see 13(c) and (d) below].

13. Adjusting entries are required to accomplish several things:
    a. To divide recorded costs (such as the cost of machinery or prepaid rent) among two or more accounting periods.
    b. To divide recorded revenues (such as commissions collected in advance) among two or more accounting periods.
    c. To record unrecorded revenues (such as commissions earned but not yet billed to customers).
    d. To record unrecorded expenses (such as wages earned by employees after the last payday in an accounting period).

Objective 5: Prepare typical adjusting entries (pp. 105–114).

14. When an expenditure is made that will benefit more than just the current period, the initial debit is usually made to an asset account instead of to an expense account. Then, at the end of the accounting period, the amount that has been used up is transferred from the asset account to an expense account.

a. **Prepaid expenses,** like Prepaid Rent and Prepaid Insurance, are debited when they are paid for in advance.
b. An account for supplies, such as Office Supplies, is debited when supplies are purchased. At the end of the accounting period, an inventory of supplies is taken. The difference between supplies available for use during the period and ending inventory is the amount used up during the period.
c. A long-lived asset such as a building, trucks, or office furniture is debited to an asset account when purchased. At the end of each accounting period, an adjusting entry must be made to transfer a part of the original cost of each long-lived asset to an expense account. The amount transferred or allocated is called **depreciation** or *depreciation expense.*
d. The **Accumulated Depreciation account** is called a **contra account** because on the balance sheet it is subtracted from its associated asset account. Thus proper balance sheet presentation will show the original cost, the accumulated depreciation as of the balance sheet date, and the undepreciated balance (called **carrying value** or *book value*).

15. In making the adjusting entry to record depreciation, Depreciation Expense is debited and Accumulated Depreciation is credited.

16. Sometimes payment is received for goods before they are delivered or for services before they are rendered. In such cases, a liability account such as **Unearned Revenues** or Unearned Fees would appear on the balance sheet. This account is a liability because it represents revenues that still must be earned.

17. Often at the end of an accounting period, revenues have been earned but not recorded because no payment has been received. An adjusting entry must be made to record these **accrued** (unrecorded) **revenues.** For example, interest that has been earned might not be received until the next period. A debit must be made to Interest Receivable and a credit to Interest Income to record the current period's interest for the income statement. This entry will also record the asset for the balance sheet.

18. Similarly, expenses have often been incurred but not recorded in the accounts because cash has not yet been paid. An adjusting entry must be made to record these **accrued expenses.** For example, interest on a loan may have accrued that does not have to be paid until the next period. A debit to

Interest Expense and a credit to Interest Payable will record the current period's interest for the income statement. A similar adjusting entry would be made for estimated income taxes. These entries will also record the liabilities for the balance sheet.

Objective 6: Prepare financial statements from an adjusted trial balance (pp. 114–117).

19. After all the adjusting entries have been posted to the ledger accounts and new account balances have been computed, an **adjusted trial balance** should be prepared. If it is in balance, the adjusted trial balance is then used to prepare the financial statements.

Supplemental Objective 7: Analyze cash flows from accrual-based information (pp. 117–118).

20. Net income is best determined by applying accrual accounting, whereby revenues are recorded when earned and expenses when incurred. Liquidity, or the ability to pay debts when they fall due, relies upon cash flow (not accrual-based) information. Fortunately, cash receipts and payments can be calculated, given accrual-based net income and related information. The general rule for determining cash flow received from any revenue or paid for any expense (except depreciation) is to determine the potential cash payments or cash receipts and then deduct the amount not paid or received. For example, cash payments for rent would equal rent expense plus an increase (or minus a decrease) in prepaid rent occurring during the period.

Summary of Journal Entries Introduced in Chapter 3

A. (L.O. 5) Rent Expense   XX (amount expired)
        Prepaid Rent   XX (amount expired)
     Expiration of prepaid rent

B. (L.O. 5) Insurance Expense   XX (amount expired)
        Prepaid Insurance   XX (amount expired)
     Expiration of prepaid insurance

C. (L.O. 5) Art Supplies Expense   XX (amount consumed)
        Art Supplies   XX (amount consumed)
     Consumption of art supplies

D. (L.O. 5) Office Supplies Expense   XX (amount consumed)
        Office Supplies   XX (amount consumed)
     Consumption of office supplies

E. (L.O. 5) Depreciation Expense, Art Equipment   XX (amount allocated to period)
        Accumulated Depreciation, Art Equipment   XX (amount allocated to period)
     Depreciation recorded

F. (L.O. 5) Depreciation Expense, Office Equipment   XX (amount allocated to period)
        Accumulated Depreciation, Office Equipment   XX (amount allocated to period)
     Depreciation recorded

G. (L.O. 5) Unearned Art Fees   XX (amount earned)
        Art Fees Earned   XX (amount earned)
     Performance of service paid for in advance

H. (L.O. 5) Fees Receivable   XX (amount to be received)
        Advertising Fees Earned   XX (amount earned)
     Accrual of unrecorded revenue

I. (L.O. 5) Office Wages Expense   XX (amount incurred)
        Wages Payable   XX (amount to be paid)
     Accrual of unrecorded expense

J. (L.O. 5) Income Taxes Expense   XX (amount estimated)
        Income Taxes Payable   XX (amount estimated)
     Accrual of estimated income taxes

Cash Flow Formulas (S.O. 7)

Type of Account	Potential Payment or Receipt	Not Paid or Received	Result
Prepaid Expense	Ending Balance + Expense for the Period	− Beginning Balance	= Cash Payments for Expenses
Unearned Revenue	Ending Balance + Revenue for the Period	− Beginning Balance	= Cash Receipts from Revenues
Accrued Liability	Beginning Balance + Expense for the Period	− Ending Balance	= Cash Payments for Expenses
Accrued Receivable	Beginning Balance + Revenue for the Period	− Ending Balance	= Cash Receipts from Revenues

TESTING YOUR KNOWLEDGE

Matching

Match each term with its definition by writing the appropriate letter in the blank.

_____ 1. Net income
_____ 2. Revenues
_____ 3. Expenses
_____ 4. Expired cost
_____ 5. Unexpired cost
_____ 6. Temporary (nominal) accounts
_____ 7. Permanent (real) accounts
_____ 8. Fiscal year
_____ 9. Going concern assumption
_____ 10. Cash basis of accounting
_____ 11. Accrual accounting
_____ 12. Matching rule
_____ 13. Adjusting entry
_____ 14. Depreciation expense
_____ 15. Accumulated Depreciation
_____ 16. Contra account
_____ 17. Unearned revenue
_____ 18. Adjusted trial balance
_____ 19. Deferral
_____ 20. Accrual

a. All the techniques used to apply the matching rule
b. A liability that represents an obligation to deliver goods or render services
c. That portion of an asset that has not yet been charged as an expense
d. A general term for the price of goods sold or services rendered
e. The assumption that a business will continue indefinitely (solution to the continuity problem)
f. Accounts whose balances extend beyond the end of an accounting period
g. A method of determining whether accounts are still in balance
h. The idea that revenues are recorded (recognized) when earned and that expenses are recorded when incurred
i. The amount by which revenues exceed expenses (opposite of net loss)
j. An account that is subtracted from an associated account
k. Any twelve-month accounting period used by a company
l. An example of a contra account to assets
m. An end-of-period allocation of revenues and expenses relevant to that period
n. The cost of doing business
o. Recording revenues and expenses when payment is received or made
p. The expired cost of a plant asset for a particular accounting period
q. Accounts that begin each period with zero balances
r. A descriptive term for expense
s. Recognition of an expense or revenue that has arisen but has not yet been recorded
t. Postponement of the recognition of an expense already paid or of a revenue already received

Measuring Business Income

Short Answer

Use the lines provided to answer each item.

1. Briefly summarize the four situations that require adjusting entries.

2. Briefly explain the matching rule.

3. Define *depreciation* as the term is used in accounting.

4. Distinguish between prepaid expenses and unearned revenues.

True-False

Circle T if the statement is true, F if it is false. Please provide explanations for the false answers, using the blank lines at the end of the section.

T F 1. Accumulated Depreciation is a permanent account, whereas Depreciation Expense is a temporary account.

T F 2. Expired costs are listed in the income statement.

T F 3. A calendar year refers to any twelve-month period.

T F 4. The cash basis of accounting often violates the matching rule.

T F 5. Under the accrual basis of accounting, the timing of cash payments is vital for recording revenues and expenses.

T F 6. Adjusting entries must be made immediately after the financial statements are prepared.

T F 7. Prepaid insurance represents an unexpired cost.

T F 8. Office Supplies Expense must be debited for the amount in ending inventory of office supplies.

T F 9. Because Accumulated Depreciation appears on the asset side of the balance sheet, it has a debit balance.

T F 10. As a machine is depreciated, its accumulated depreciation increases and its unexpired cost decreases.

T F 11. Unearned Revenues is a contra account to Earned Revenues in the income statement.

T F 12. When an expense has accrued but payment has not yet been made, a debit is needed for the expense and a credit for Prepaid Expenses.

T F 13. The adjusted trial balance is the same as the trial balance, except that it has been modified by adjusting entries.

T F 14. If one has made a sale for which the money has not yet been received, one would debit Unearned Revenues and credit Earned Revenues.

T F 15. The original cost of a long-lived asset should appear on the balance sheet even after depreciation has been recorded.

T F 16. Adjusting entries help make financial statements comparable from one period to the next.

Multiple Choice

Circle the letter of the best answer.

1. Which of the following is an example of a temporary account?
   a. Prepaid Rent
   b. Unearned Revenues
   c. Wages Expense
   d. Accumulated Depreciation, Building

2. Depreciation does *not* apply to
   a. trucks.
   b. office supplies.
   c. machinery.
   d. office equipment.

3. An account called Unearned Fees is used when
   a. recorded costs must be divided among periods.
   b. recorded revenues must be divided among periods.
   c. unrecorded (accrued) expenses must be recorded.
   d. unrecorded (accrued) revenues must be recorded.

4. Depreciation best applies to
   a. recorded costs that must be divided among periods.
   b. recorded revenues that must be divided among periods.
   c. unrecorded expenses that must be recorded.
   d. unrecorded revenues that must be recorded.

5. Which of the following does *not* appear in the adjusted trial balance?
   a. Prepaid Insurance
   b. Unearned Management Fees
   c. Net Income
   d. Depreciation Expense

6. An adjusting entry made to record accrued interest on a note receivable due next year would consist of a debit to
   a. Cash and a credit to Interest Income.
   b. Cash and a credit to Interest Receivable.
   c. Interest Expense and a credit to Interest Payable.
   d. Interest Receivable and a credit to Interest Income.

7. The periodicity assumption solves the accounting period problem by recognizing that
   a. net income over a short period of time is a useful estimate.
   b. a business is likely to continue indefinitely.
   c. revenues should be recorded in the period earned.
   d. a twelve-month accounting period must be used.

8. Prepaid Rent is a(n)
   a. expense.
   b. contra account.
   c. liability.
   d. asset.

9. An adjusting entry would *never* be made to
   a. Unearned Revenue.
   b. Cash.
   c. Prepaid Advertising.
   d. Wages Expense.

APPLYING YOUR KNOWLEDGE

Exercises

1. On January 1, 19x1, Mass Transit Company began its business by buying a new bus for $24,000. One-eighth of the cost of the bus is depreciated each year. Complete *in good form* the balance sheet as of December 31, 19x3.

Mass Transit Company
Partial Balance Sheet
December 31, 19x3

Assets

Cash	$5,000
Accounts Receivable	3,000
Company Vehicles	
Total Assets	$ _____

---

2. For each set of facts, provide the dollar amount that would be recorded.
   a. The cost of supplies at the beginning of the period was $510. During the period, supplies that cost $800 were purchased. At the end of the period, supplies that cost $340 remained. Supplies Expense should be recorded for $_____.
   b. The company signed a lease for $14,000 on July 1, 19x1, to cover the four-year period beginning July 1, 19x1. How much Rent Expense should it record on December 31, 19x1? $_____
   c. The company was paid $600 in advance for services to be performed. By the end of the period, only one-fourth of it had been earned. How much of the $600 will appear as Unearned Revenues on the balance sheet? $_____

3. The facts that follow are based on Goodman Company's trial balance (shown below and at right). For each item, make the adjusting entry in the journal provided on the next page. Keep in mind that Goodman Company operates on the calendar year.
   a. Cost of supplies on hand, based on a physical count, is $375.
   b. Wages of $2,500 for the five-day workweek ($500 per day) are recorded and paid every Friday. December 31 falls on a Thursday.
   c. Services amounting to $600 were rendered during 19x1 for customers who had paid in advance.
   d. Five percent of the cost of buildings is taken as depreciation for 19x1.
   e. One-quarter of the prepaid advertising expired during 19x1.
   f. All of the insurance shown on the trial balance was paid for on July 1, 19x1, and covers the two-year period beginning July 1, 19x1.
   g. Work performed for customers that has not been billed or recorded amounts to $2,200.
   h. Accrued interest on a note payable amounts to $52. This interest will be paid when the note matures.
   i. Accrued income tax expense for the year amounts of $21,700. This amount will be paid early next year.

Goodman Company
Trial Balance
December 31, 19x1

	Debit	Credit
Cash	$ 77,300	
Notes Receivable	5,000	
Prepaid Advertising	8,000	
Prepaid Insurance	1,000	
Supplies	500	
Office Equipment	9,000	
Buildings	90,000	
Accumulated Depreciation, Buildings		$ 6,000
Notes Payable		1,500
Unearned Revenues		2,800
Common Stock		100,000
Dividends	13,000	
Revenues from Services		212,000
Wages Expense	118,500	
	$322,300	$322,300

Date	General Journal Description	Debit	Credit

4. At year-beginning and year-end, Doherty Industries had the following balance sheet balances:

	Jan. 1	Dec. 31
Wages Payable	$1,200	$3,700
Unearned Revenue	500	900
Prepaid Rent	2,400	1,800

In addition, the following figures were taken from the income statement:

Wages Expense	$ 8,700
Revenue from Services	35,000
Rent Expense	3,600

a. Cash paid for wages during the year = $_____.

b. Cash received for revenue during the year = $_____.

c. Cash paid for rent during the year = $_____.

Crossword Puzzle
for Chapters 2 and 3

ACROSS

1. An account that is subtracted from another
3. See 22-Down
6. Postponement of a revenue or expense
7. Journal column title (same as 2-Down)
9. Where accounts are kept
13. Source of revenues
16. Test of debit and credit equality (2 words)
18. Left side of journal or ledger
19. Monthly or yearly compensation
20. An asset that is not subject to depreciation
23. ____ bookkeeping (hyphenated)
24. Realize (revenues)

DOWN

1. Historical ____
2. Post. ____ column
4. Become an expense
5. Hourly or piecework-rate compensation
8. Income statement item
10. Opposite of nominal
11. Record transactions
12. Rule applied through accrual accounting
14. Right side of journal or ledger
15. Assignment of a dollar amount to
17. Recognition of unrecorded revenues or expenses
21. Written promise to pay
22. With 3-Across, the term accountants use to refer to profit

Measuring Business Income

CHAPTER 4 COMPLETING THE ACCOUNTING CYCLE

REVIEWING THE CHAPTER

Objective 1: State all the steps in the accounting cycle (pp. 143–145).

1. The steps in the **accounting cycle** are as follows:
   a. The transactions are analyzed from the source documents.
   b. The transactions are recorded in the journal.
   c. The entries are posted to the ledger.
   d. The accounts are adjusted at the end of the period to produce the adjusted trial balance.
   e. The revenue, expense, and dividends accounts are closed to conclude the current accounting period and prepare for the beginning of the new accounting period. Also, a post-closing trial balance is prepared.
   f. Financial statements are prepared from the adjusted trial balance.

Objective 2: Explain the purposes of closing entries (pp. 145–146).

2. **Closing entries** serve two purposes. First, they set the stage for the new accounting period by clearing revenue and expense accounts of their balances. (So that the Retained Earnings account can be updated, the Dividends account also is closed.) Second, they summarize the period's revenues and expenses by transferring the balance of revenue and expense accounts to the **Income Summary** account.

Objective 3: Prepare the required closing entries (pp. 146–150).

3. There are four closing entries, as follows:
   a. Revenue accounts are closed. This is accomplished with a compound entry that debits each revenue account for the amount required to give it a zero balance and credits its Income Summary for the revenue total. The Income Summary account exists only during the closing process and does not appear in the work sheet or in the financial statements.
   b. Expense accounts are closed. This is accomplished with a compound entry that credits each expense for the amount required to give it a zero balance, and debits Income Summary for the expense total.
   c. The Income Summary account is closed. After revenue and expense accounts have been closed, the Income Summary account will have either a debit balance or a credit balance. If a credit balance exists, then Income Summary must be debited for the amount required to give it a zero balance, and Retained Earnings is credited for the same amount. The reverse is done when Income Summary has a debit balance.
   d. The Dividends account is closed. This is accomplished by crediting Dividends for the amount required to give it a zero balance, and debiting Retained Earnings for the same amount. Note that the Income Summary account is not involved in this closing entry.

Objective 4: Prepare the post-closing trial balance (pp. 150–153).

4. After the closing entries are posted to the ledger, a **post-closing trial balance** must be prepared to verify again the equality of the debits and credits in the accounts. Only balance sheet accounts ap-

pear because all income statement accounts have zero balances at this point.

Supplemental Objective 5: Prepare reversing entries as appropriate (pp. 153–155).

5. At the end of each accounting period, the accountant makes adjusting entries to record accrued revenues and expenses. Many of the adjusting entries are followed in the next period by the receipt or payment of cash. Thus it would become necessary in the next period to make a special entry dividing amounts between the two periods. To avoid this inconvenience, the accountant can make **reversing entries** (dated the beginning of the new period). Reversing entries, though not required, allow the bookkeeper to simply make the routine bookkeeping entry when cash finally changes hands. Not all adjusting entries may be reversed. In the system we will use, only adjustments for accruals may be reversed. Deferrals may not.

Supplemental Objective 6: Prepare a work sheet (pp. 155–162).

6. Accountants use **working papers** to help organize their work and to provide evidence in support of the financial statements. The **work sheet** is one such working paper. It decreases the chance of overlooking an adjustment, acts as a check on the arithmetical accuracy of the accounts, and helps in preparing financial statements. The work sheet is never published but is a useful tool for the accountant.

7. The five steps in the preparation of the work sheet are as follows:
    a. Enter and total the account balances in the Trial Balance columns.
    b. Enter and total the adjustments in the Adjustments columns. (A letter identifies the debit and credit for each adjustment and can act as a key to a brief explanation at the bottom of the work sheet.)
    c. Enter (by means of **crossfooting**) and total the account balances as adjusted in the Adjusted Trial Balance columns.
    d. Extend (transfer) the account balances from the Adjusted Trial Balance columns to the Income Statement columns or the Balance Sheet columns (depending on which type of account is involved).
    e. Total the Income Statement columns and the Balance Sheet columns. Enter the net income or net loss in both pairs of columns (one will be a debit, the other a credit) as a balancing figure, and recompute the column totals.

Supplemental Objective 7: Use a work sheet for three different purposes (pp. 163–166).

8. Once the work sheet is completed, it can be used to (a) prepare the financial statements, (b) record the adjusting entries in the journal, and (c) record the closing entries in the journal, thus preparing the records for the new period.
    a. The income statement may be prepared from the information found in the work sheet's Income Statement columns. Calculations of the change in retained earnings for the period are shown in the statement of retained earnings. Information for this calculation may be found in the Balance Sheet columns of the work sheet (beginning retained earnings, net income, and dividends). The balance sheet may be prepared from information found in the work sheet's Balance Sheet columns and in the statement of retained earnings.
    b. Formal adjusting entries must be recorded in the journal and posted to the ledger so that the account balances on the books will agree with those on the financial statements. This is easily accomplished by referring to the Adjustments columns (and footnoted explanations) of the work sheet.
    c. Formal closing entries are entered into the journal and posted to the ledger, as explained in Objective 3. This is accomplished by referring to the work sheet's Income Statement columns (for the revenue and expense accounts) and its Balance Sheet columns (for the Dividends account).

Summary of Journal Entries Introduced in Chapter 4

A. (L.O. 3) Advertising Fees Earned   XX (current credit balance)
         Art Fees Earned   XX (current credit balance)
            Income Summary   XX (sum of revenue amounts)
               To close the revenue accounts

B. (L.O. 3) Income Summary   XX (sum of expense amounts)
         Office Wages Expense   XX (current debit balance)
         Utility Expense   XX (current debit balance)
         Telephone Expense   XX (current debit balance)
         Rent Expense   XX (current debit balance)
         Insurance Expense   XX (current debit balance)
         Art Supplies Expense   XX (current debit balance)
         Office Supplies Expense   XX (current debit balance)
         Depreciation Expense, Art Equipment   XX (current debit balance)
         Depreciation Expense, Office Equipment   XX (current debit balance)
         Income Taxes Expense   XX (current debit balance)
             To close the expense accounts

C. (L.O. 3) Income Summary   XX (current credit balance)
         Retained Earnings   XX (net income amount)
            To close the Income Summary account
            (profit situation)

D. (L.O. 3) Retained Earnings   XX (dividends for period)
         Dividends   XX (dividends for period)
            To close the Dividends account

E. (S.O. 5) Office Wages Expense   XX (amount incurred)
         Wages Payable   XX (amount to be paid)
            To accrue unrecorded wages

F. (S.O. 5) Wages Payable   XX (amount previously accrued)
         Office Wages Expense   XX (amount accrued this period)
         Cash   XX (amount paid)
            Paid wages; entry E above was *not* reversed

G. (S.O. 5) Wages Payable   XX (amount to be paid)
         Office Wages Expense   XX (amount incurred)
            Reversing entry for E above (assume Office Wages
            Expense had been closed at end of period)

H. (S.O. 5) Office Wages Expense   XX (amount paid)
         Cash   XX (amount paid)
            Paid wages; entry E above *was* reversed

I. (S.O. 5) Income Taxes Payable   XX (amount estimated)
         Income Taxes Expense   XX (amount estimated)
            To reverse adjusting entry for estimated income taxes

J. (S.O. 5) Advertising Fees Earned   XX (amount accrued)
         Fees Receivable   XX (amount accrued)
            To reverse adjusting entry for accrued fees receivable

Completing the Accounting Cycle

TESTING YOUR KNOWLEDGE

Matching

Match each term with its definition by writing the appropriate letter in the blank.

_____ 1. Post-closing trial balance
_____ 2. Working papers
_____ 3. Work sheet
_____ 4. Foot
_____ 5. Crossfooting
_____ 6. Reversing entry
_____ 7. Closing entries
_____ 8. Income Summary

a. An account used only during closing process
b. Add a column
c. The means of transferring net income or loss to the Retained Earnings account
d. A working paper that facilitates the preparation of financial statements
e. A final proof that the accounts are in balance
f. The opposite of an adjusting entry, journalized to facilitate routine bookkeeping
g. Documents that help accountants organize their work
h. Adding from left to right

Short Answer

Use the lines provided to answer each item.

1. What four accounts or kinds of accounts are closed out each accounting period?

2. List the five columnar headings of a work sheet in their proper order.

3. In general, what accounts appear in the post-closing trial balance? What accounts do *not* appear?

4. Briefly, explain the purpose of reversing entries.

5. The six steps in the accounting cycle are presented here in the wrong order. Place the numbers 1 through 6 in the spaces provided to indicate the correct order.

   _____ The entries are posted to the ledger.
   _____ The temporary accounts are closed.
   _____ The transactions are analyzed from the source documents.
   _____ The accounts are adjusted.
   _____ The transactions are recorded in the journal.
   _____ Financial statements are prepared from the adjusted trial balance.

True-False

Circle T if the statement is true, F if it is false. Please provide explanations for the false answers, using the blank lines at the end of the section.

T F 1. The work sheet is prepared before the formal adjusting entries have been made in the journal.

T F 2. Preparation of a work sheet helps reduce the possibility of overlooking an adjustment.

T F 3. Total debits will differ from total credits in the Balance Sheet columns of a work sheet by the amount of the net income or loss.

T F 4. The statement of retained earnings is prepared after the formal income statement, but before the formal balance sheet.

T F 5. The Income Summary account can be found in the statement of retained earnings.

T F 6. Closing entries convert real and nominal accounts to zero balances.

T F 7. When revenue accounts are closed, the Income Summary account will be credited.

T F 8. The Dividends account is closed to the Income Summary account.

T F 9. When the Income Summary account is closed, it always requires a debit.

T F 10. Reversing entries are never required.

T F 11. The work sheet is published with the balance sheet and income statement, as a supplementary statement.

T F 12. A key letter is needed in the Adjusted Trial Balance columns of a work sheet to show whether the entry is extended to the Balance Sheet columns or the Income Statement columns.

T F 13. If total debits exceed total credits (before balancing) in the Income Statement columns of a work sheet, that means that a net loss has occurred.

T F 14. The post-closing trial balance will contain the Dividends account.

T F 15. Reversing entries update the accounts at the end of the accounting period.

Completing the Accounting Cycle

Multiple Choice

Circle the letter of the best answer.

1. Which account will appear in the post-closing trial balance?
   a. Interest Income
   b. Income Summary
   c. Retained Earnings
   d. Dividends

2. Which of the following statements is true?
   a. Closing entries are prepared before formal adjusting entries.
   b. The work sheet is prepared after the post-closing trial balance.
   c. Formal adjusting entries are prepared before the work sheet.
   d. The financial statements are prepared before closing entries.

3. Reversing entries
   a. are dated as of the end of the period.
   b. are the opposite of adjusting entries.
   c. may be made for depreciation previously recorded.
   d. are the opposite of closing entries.

4. If total debits exceed total credits (before balancing) in the Balance Sheet columns of a work sheet,
   a. a net income has occurred.
   b. a net loss has occurred.
   c. a mistake has definitely been made.
   d. no conclusions can be drawn until the closing entries have been made.

5. Which of the following accounts would *not* be involved in closing entries?
   a. Unearned Commissions
   b. Retained Earnings
   c. Telephone Expense
   d. Dividends

6. When a net loss has occurred,
   a. all expense accounts are closed with debits.
   b. the Income Summary account is closed with a credit.
   c. the Dividends account is closed with a debit.
   d. all revenue accounts are closed with credits.

7. Which of the following is *not* an objective of closing entries?
   a. To transfer net income or loss into Retained Earnings
   b. To produce zero balances in all nominal accounts
   c. To update the revenue and expense accounts
   d. To be able to measure net income for the following period

8. A corporation began the accounting period with $50,000 in retained earnings, ended with $75,000 in retained earnings, and declared $30,000 in dividends. What was the corporation's net income or loss for the period?
   a. $55,000 net income
   b. $30,000 net loss
   c. $5,000 net loss
   d. $5,000 net income

APPLYING YOUR KNOWLEDGE

Exercises

1. Following are the accounts of a work sheet's Adjusted Trial Balance for the month of July. In the journal provided, make the necessary closing entries. All accounts have normal balances.

Accounts Payable	$ 1,000
Accounts Receivable	2,000
Cash	$13,500
Common Stock	10,000
Dividends	2,500
Rent Expense	500
Retained Earnings	3,000
Revenue from Services	4,700
Telephone Expense	50
Utility Expense	150

General Journal

Date	Description	Debit	Credit

2. Using the information from Exercise 1, complete the statement of retained earnings at the right.

Barrett's Fix-It Services, Inc.
Statement of Retained Earnings
For the Month Ended July 31, 19xx

Completing the Accounting Cycle

3. The following items *a* through *g* provide the information needed to make adjustments for Steve's Maintenance, Inc., as of December 31, 19xx. Complete the entire work sheet on the next page using this information. Remember to use key letters for each adjustment.
   a. On December 31, there is $200 of unexpired rent on the storage garage.
   b. Depreciation taken on the lawn equipment during the period amounts to $1,500.
   c. An inventory of lawn supplies shows $100 remaining on December 31.
   d. Accrued wages on December 31 amount to $280.
   e. Grass-cutting fees earned but as yet uncollected amount to $50.
   f. Of the $300 landscaping fees paid for in advance, $120 had been earned by December 31.
   g. Accrued income tax expense for the year amounts to $1,570. This amount will be paid early next year.

4. On December 1, Bowman Company borrowed $20,000 from a bank on a note for 90 days at 12 percent (annual) interest. Assuming that interest is not included in the face amount, prepare the following journal entries:
   a. December 1 entry to record the note
   b. December 31 entry to record accrued interest
   c. December 31 entry to close interest
   d. January 1 reversing entry
   e. March 1 entry to record payment of note plus interest.

General Journal				
Date		Description	Debit	Credit

Steve's Maintenance, Inc.
Work Sheet
For the Year Ended December 31, 19xx

Account Name	Trial Balance Debit	Trial Balance Credit	Adjustments Debit	Adjustments Credit	Adjusted Trial Balance Debit	Adjusted Trial Balance Credit	Income Statement Debit	Income Statement Credit	Balance Sheet Debit	Balance Sheet Credit
Cash	2,560									
Accounts Receivable	880									
Prepaid Rent	750									
Lawn Supplies	250									
Lawn Equipment	10,000									
Accum. Deprec., Lawn Equip.		2,000								
Accounts Payable		630								
Unearned Landscaping Fees		300								
Common Stock		5,000								
Retained Earnings		1,000								
Dividends	6,050									
Grass-Cutting Fees		15,000								
Wages Expense	3,300									
Gasoline Expense	140									
	23,930	23,930								
Rent Expense										
Depreciation Expense										
Lawn Supplies Expense										
Landscaping Fees Earned										
Wages Payable										
Income Taxes Expense										
Income Taxes Payable										
Net Income										

Completing the Accounting Cycle

CHAPTER 5 ACCOUNTING FOR MERCHANDISING OPERATIONS

REVIEWING THE CHAPTER

Objective 1: Identify the management issues related to merchandising businesses (pp. 189–191).

1. Accounting for **service businesses,** such as movers and dry cleaners, is relatively easy because this type of business does not have inventory (goods for resale) to manage.

2. A **merchandising business,** on the other hand, is a wholesaler or retailer that buys and sells goods in finished form. This kind of firm uses the same basic accounting methods as a service company. However, the merchandiser must also account for its inventory, requiring a more complicated process and producing a more sophisticated income statement.

3. The merchandiser engages in a series of operations known as the **operating cycle,** consisting of (a) the purchase of **merchandise inventory,** (b) the sale of the inventory, and (c) the collection of cash from merchandise sales.

4. Merchandisers must carefully manage cash flow, or liquidity. Such **cash flow management** is essential for the business to pay its bills when they fall due. **Profitability management** is also important for the merchandiser. It involves purchasing goods at favorable prices, selling those goods at a price that will cover costs and help turn a profit, and keeping operating expenses in check.

5. The merchandising company must choose a system to account for its inventory. The two basic systems are the **periodic inventory system** and the **perpetual inventory system.** These systems will be explained later in Objective 3.

6. A merchandising business typically handles a great deal of cash and inventory. Unfortunately, these assets are very susceptible to theft and embezzlement. Accordingly, an **internal control structure** must be established to help protect the company's assets. The specific procedures that are commonly adopted are discussed later in Objectives 5 through 7.

Objective 2: Compare the income statements for service and merchandising concerns and define the components of the merchandising income statement (pp. 191–196).

7. Service companies calculate net income by simply deducting expenses from revenues. However, the income of a merchandising firm is computed as follows:

   Net sales
   − Cost of goods sold
   = Gross Margin
   − Operating expenses
   = Income before income taxes
   − Income taxes
   = **Net income**

8. A merchandiser's amount of goods on hand at any one time is called merchandise inventory.

The accountant uses merchandise inventory figures to calculate cost of goods sold as follows:

Beginning inventory (at cost)
+ Net cost of purchases (see paragraph 9)
= Goods available for sale
− **Ending inventory** (at cost)
= Cost of goods sold

9. **Net cost of purchases** is calculated as follows:

    (Gross) purchases
    − Purchases returns and allowances
    − Purchases discounts
    = Net purchases
    + Freight in
    = Net cost of purchases

10. **Net sales** (or simply *sales*) consist of gross proceeds from the sale of merchandise (**gross sales**) less **sales returns and allowances** and sales discounts.

11. **Cost of goods sold** (also called *cost of sales*) is the amount that the merchandising company originally paid for the goods that it sold during a given period. If, for example, a merchandising firm sells for $100 a radio that cost the company $70, then revenues from sales are $100, cost of goods sold is $70, and **gross margin** (also called *gross profit*) is $30. This $30 gross margin helps pay for **operating expenses** (all expenses other than cost of goods sold and income taxes). What is left after subtracting operating expenses represents **income before income taxes** (also called *operating income* or *income from operations*). Preparing an income statement in this way provides useful information to management, which is continually trying to improve net income.

12. Operating expenses consist of selling expenses and general and administrative expenses. Selling expenses are advertising expenses, salespeople's salaries, sales office expenses, **freight out,** and all other expenses directly related to the sales effort. General and administrative expenses are all expenses not directly related to the manufacturing or sales effort. Examples are general office expenses and executive salaries.

Objective 3: Distinguish between the perpetual and the periodic inventory systems and explain the importance of taking a physical inventory (pp. 196–198).

13. There are two ways of determining inventory.
    a. The perpetual inventory system is used when it is necessary to keep a record of the cost of each inventory item when it is purchased and when it is sold.
    b. The periodic inventory system is used when it is unnecessary or impractical to keep track of the cost of each item. Under this method, the company instead waits until the end of the accounting period to take a **physical inventory.** This physical count figure is then multiplied by a derived cost-per-unit figure (explained in Chapter 8) to arrive at the cost of ending inventory.

14. The ending inventory of one period automatically becomes the beginning inventory of the next period. The beginning inventory is removed from the inventory account and the ending inventory is entered into the inventory account by means of closing entries.

15. Merchandise inventory appears as an asset in the balance sheet and includes all salable goods owned by the company, no matter where the goods are located. Goods in transit to which a company has acquired title are included in ending inventory. However, goods that the company has formally sold are not included, even if the company has not yet delivered them. To simplify inventory taking, which usually takes place on the last day of the fiscal year, many companies end their fiscal year during the slow season.

Objective 4: Contrast and record transactions related to sales and purchases under the periodic and the perpetual inventory systems (pp. 198–205).

16. Merchandising transactions are broadly categorized as sales transactions and purchases transactions. The way these transactions are recorded differs somewhat under the periodic and the perpetual inventory systems. These differences will be discussed in later paragraphs.

17. As a matter of convenience, manufacturers and wholesalers frequently quote prices of merchandise based on a discount from the list or catalogue price (called a **trade discount**).

18. When goods are sold on credit, terms will vary as to when payment must be made. For instance, n/30 means that full payment is due within 30 days after the invoice date, and n/10 eom means that full payment is due 10 days after the end of the month.

19. Often a customer is given a discount for early payment, and the merchandiser records a **sales discount.** Terms of 2/10, n/30, for example, mean that a 2 percent discount will be given if payment is made within 10 days of the invoice

date. Otherwise, the net amount is due within 30 days.

20. When a merchandising firm incurs transportation costs on goods purchased, it debits Freight In (or Transportation In) and credits Accounts Payable. A merchandiser in Chicago, for instance, must pay the freight in from Boston if the terms specify FOB Boston or **FOB shipping point.** However, the supplier in Boston pays if the terms are FOB Chicago or **FOB destination.** Freight out is a cost of selling (not buying) merchandise, and should not be confused with freight in.

21. Under the periodic inventory system, all purchases of merchandise are debited to the **Purchases** account and credited to Cash or Accounts Payable. The purpose of the Purchases account is to accumulate the cost of merchandise purchased for resale during the period. Under the perpetual inventory system, Merchandise Inventory is debited instead of Purchases.

22. Under the periodic inventory system, when goods are returned to a supplier, the merchandiser debits Cash or Accounts Payable and credits **Purchases Returns and Allowances.** Purchases Returns and Allowances is a contra account to Purchases in the income statement. Under the perpetual inventory system, Merchandise Inventory is credited instead of Purchases Returns and Allowances.

23. When a cash sale is made, Cash is debited and Sales is credited for the amount of the sale. When a credit sale is made, Accounts Receivable is debited and Sales is credited. Under the perpetual (but not the periodic) inventory system, a second entry is needed to record Cost of Goods Sold (a debit) and to update Merchandise Inventory (a credit). Generally, a sale is recorded when the goods are delivered and title passes to the customer, regardless of when payment is made.

24. When a cash customer returns goods for a refund, Sales Returns and Allowances is debited and Cash is credited. For a credit customer, Sales Returns and Allowances is debited and Accounts Receivable is credited. The Sales Returns and Allowances account is debited instead of the Sales account to provide management with data about dissatisfied customers. In the income statement it is a contra account to Gross Sales. Under the perpetual (but not the periodic) inventory system, a second entry is needed to reinstate Merchandise Inventory (a debit) and to reduce Cost of Goods Sold (a credit).

25. Inventory losses result from theft and spoilage, and are included in cost of goods sold. As one might imagine, these losses are easier to track under the perpetual system than under the periodic system.

Objective 5: Define *internal control* **and identify the three elements of the internal control structure, including seven examples of control procedures (pp. 205–207).**

26. A business establishes a system of **internal control** to (a) safeguard its assets, (b) check the accuracy and reliability of its accounting data, (c) promote operational efficiency, and (d) encourage adherence to prescribed managerial policies. To achieve these objectives, management must establish an internal control structure consisting of three elements: the control environment, the accounting system, and the control procedures.
    a. The **control environment** reflects such things as management's philosophy and operating style, the company's organizational structure, methods of assigning authority and responsibility, and personnel policies and practices.
    b. The **accounting system** consists of methods and records established by management to provide assurance that the objectives of internal control are achieved.
    c. Management must establish **control procedures** to ensure the safeguarding of assets and the reliability of the accounting records. Examples of control procedures are (1) required authorization for certain transactions, (2) recording of all transactions, (3) design and use of adequate documents, (4) limited access to assets, (5) periodic independent verification of records, (6) separation of duties, and (7) sound personnel procedures. **Bonding** an employee (an example of a good control procedure) means insuring the company against theft by that individual.

Objective 6: Describe the inherent limitations of internal control (p. 207).

27. To be effective, a system of internal control must rely on the people who perform the duties assigned. Thus, the effectiveness of internal control is limited by the people involved. For example, human error, collusion, and changing conditions can all contribute to the weakening of a system of internal control.

Accounting for Merchandising Operations

Objective 7: Apply control procedures to certain merchandising transactions (pp. 208–215).

28. Accounting controls over merchandising transactions help prevent losses from theft or fraud, and help assure accurate accounting records. Administrative controls over merchandising transactions should help to keep inventory levels balanced, to keep enough cash on hand to make timely payments for purchases discounts, and to avoid credit losses.

29. Several procedures should be followed to achieve effective internal control over sales and the exchange of cash.

30. Cash received by mail should be handled by two or more employees. Cash received from sales over the counter should be controlled through the use of cash registers and prenumbered sales tickets. At the end of each day, Cash is debited for cash receipts, and Sales is credited for the amount on the cash register tape. All cash should be deposited promptly.

31. All cash payments for purchases should be made by check. However, before employees pay cash, they should get authorization in the form of certain signed documents. The system of authorization and the documents used will differ among companies, but the most common documents are described below.
    a. A **purchase requisition** is completed by a department requesting that the company purchase something for the department.
    b. A **purchase order** is completed by the department responsible for the company's purchasing activities; it is sent to the vendor.
    c. An **invoice** is the bill sent to the buyer from the vendor.
    d. A **receiving report** is completed by the receiving department; it contains information about the quantity and condition of goods received.
    e. A **check authorization** is a document showing that the purchase order, purchase requisition, receiving report, and invoice are in agreement, and that payment is therefore approved.
    f. When payment is approved, a **check** is issued to the vendor for the amount of the invoice, less the appropriate discount. Remittance advice should be attached to the check, describing the articles being paid for.

Supplemental Objective 8: Apply sales and purchases discounts to merchandising transactions (pp. 215–216).

32. Often a merchandising company offers (and is offered) a discount if payment is received (or made) within a given number of days.
    a. Sales discounts are recorded when payment is received within the discount period. Cash and Sales Discounts are debited; Accounts Receivable is credited. Sales Discounts is a contra account to Gross Sales in the income statement.
    b. A purchase is initially recorded at the gross purchase price. If the company makes payment within the discount period, it debits Accounts Payable, credits Purchases Discounts, and credits Cash. **Purchases Discounts** is a contra account to Purchases in the Income Statement.

Summary of Journal Entries Introduced in Chapter 5

Periodic Inventory System

A. (L.O. 4) Purchases — XX (purchase price)
    Accounts Payable — XX (amount due)
        Purchased merchandise on credit

B. (L.O. 4) Freight In — XX (price charged)
    Accounts Payable — XX (amount due)
        Incurred transportation charges

C. (L.O. 4) Accounts Payable — XX (amount returned)
    Purchases Returns and Allowances — XX (amount returned)
        Returned goods to supplier, for credit

D. (L.O. 4) Accounts Payable — XX (amount paid)
    Cash — XX (amount paid)
        Made payment on account

E. (L.O. 4) Accounts Receivable — XX (amount to be received)
    Sales — XX (sales price)
        Sold merchandise on credit

F. (L.O. 4) Freight Out Expense — XX (amount incurred)
    Cash — XX (amount paid)
        Paid for goods shipped to customer

G. (L.O. 4) Sales Returns and Allowances — XX (price of goods returned)
    Accounts Receivable — XX (amount credited to account)
        Customer returned goods, account credited

H. (L.O. 4) Cash — XX (amount received)
    Accounts Receivable — XX (amount settled)
        Received payment on account

Perpetual Inventory System

I. (L.O. 4) Merchandise Inventory — XX (purchase price)
    Accounts Payable — XX (amount due)
        Purchased merchandise on credit

J. (L.). 4) Freight In — XX (price charged)
    Accounts Payable — XX (amount due)
        Incurred transportation charges

K. (L.O. 4) Accounts Payable — XX (amount returned)
    Merchandise Inventory — XX (amount returned)
        Returned goods to supplier, for credit

L. (L.O. 4) Accounts Payable — XX (amount paid)
    Cash — XX (amount paid)
        Made payment on account

Accounting for Merchandising Operations

M. (L.O. 4) Accounts Receivable   XX (amount to be received)
            Sales   XX (sales price)
                Sold merchandise on credit

            Cost of Goods Sold   XX (inventory cost)
                Merchandise Inventory   XX (Inventory cost)
                    Recorded cost of goods sold and updated the in-
                    ventory account for goods sold above

N. (L.O. 4) Freight Out Expense   XX (amount incurred)
                Cash   XX (amount paid)
                    Paid for goods shipped to customer

O. (L.O. 4) Sales Returns and Allowances   XX (price of goods returned)
                Accounts Receivable   XX (amount credited to account)
                    Customer returned goods, for credit

            Merchandise Inventory   XX (inventory cost)
                Cost of Goods Sold   XX (inventory cost)
                    Reinstated inventory and reduced cost of goods
                    sold for goods returned above

P. (L.O. 4) Cash   XX (amount received)
                Accounts Receivable   XX (amount settled)
                    Received payment on account

Q. (S.O. 8) Cash   XX (net amount received)
            Sales Discounts   XX (discount given)
                Accounts Receivable   XX (gross amount settled)
                    Customer paid within discount period

R. (S.O. 8) Accounts Payable   XX (gross amount settled)
                Purchases Discounts   XX (discount taken)
                Cash   XX (net amount paid)
                    Paid supplier within discount period

TESTING YOUR KNOWLEDGE

Matching

Match each term with its definition by writing the appropriate letter in the blank.

___ 1. Merchandiser
___ 2. Cost of goods sold
___ 3. Gross margin
___ 4. Operating expenses
___ 5. Sales returns and allowances
___ 6. Sales discounts
___ 7. Freight out
___ 8. Purchases
___ 9. Cost of goods available for sale
___ 10. Perpetual inventory system
___ 11. Periodic inventory system
___ 12. Freight in
___ 13. FOB (free on board)
___ 14. Purchases returns and allowances
___ 15. Purchases discounts
___ 16. Internal control
___ 17. Purchase requisition
___ 18. Purchase order
___ 19. Receiving report
___ 20. Check authorization

a. Transportation cost for goods purchased
b. A document that authorizes payment
c. A buyer and seller of goods that are in finished form
d. A system whereby continuous cost records are maintained for merchandise
e. All expenses except for cost of goods sold
f. The point after which the buyer must bear the transportation cost
g. Under the periodic inventory system, the account used to accumulate the cost of goods bought during the period
h. What a merchandising firm paid for the goods that it sold during the period
i. Beginning inventory plus net cost of purchases
j. Net sales minus cost of goods sold
k. The account used by the seller to record the discount when the buyer pays for goods within the discount period
l. The account used by the seller when the buyer returns goods
m. A system whereby continuous cost records are *not* maintained for merchandise
n. The account used by the buyer to record the discount when it pays for goods within the discount period.
o. An order for goods that is sent to the vendor
p. Under the periodic inventory system, the account used by the buyer when it returns goods
q. A description of goods received by a company
r. A system designed to safeguard assets, promote operational efficiency, encourage adherence to managerial policies, and help achieve accounting accuracy
s. Delivery charge for goods sold
t. A document requesting the purchasing department to order certain items

Accounting for Merchandising Operations

Short Answer

Use the lines provided to answer each item.

1. List the seven parts of a merchandiser's condensed income statement in their proper order. Use mathematical signs to indicate their relationship.

2. List the items in the condensed cost of goods sold section of an income statement. Use mathematical signs to indicate their relationship.

3. Using mathematical signs, write the sequence of items involved in computing net cost of purchases.

4. Using mathematical signs, write the sequence of items involved in computing net sales.

5. List and briefly describe the three elements of an internal control structure.

   a. _____

   b. _____

   c. _____

6. List seven control procedures that help make a system of internal control effective.

7. List any six procedures that may be employed to control and safeguard cash.

True-False

Circle T if the statement is true, F if it is false. Please provide explanations for the false answers, using the blank lines at the end of the section.

T F 1. Failure to include a warehouse's merchandise in ending inventory will result in an overstated net income.

T F 2. Terms of n/10 eom mean that payment must be made 10 days before the end of the month.

T F 3. An overstated beginning inventory will result in an overstate cost of goods sold.

T F 4. A low-volume car dealer is more likely to use the periodic inventory system than the perpetual inventory system.

T F 5. FOB destination means that the seller is bearing the transportation cost.

T F 6. Sales Discounts is a contra account to Net Sales.

T F 7. Ending inventory is needed for both the balance sheet and the income statement.

T F 8. Cost of goods available for sale minus cost of goods sold equals ending inventory.

T F 9. The perpetual inventory system requires more detailed record keeping than does the periodic system.

T F 10. The beginning inventory of a period is the same as the ending inventory of the previous period.

T F 11. Sales Returns and Allowances normally has a credit balance.

T F 12. Under the periodic inventory system, a cash purchase of office supplies that are meant to be used in the day-to-day operation of a business requires a debit to Purchases and a credit to Cash.

T F 13. Cost of goods sold will not appear in the income statement of a company that provides services only.

T F 14. If gross margin is not enough to cover operating expenses, then a net loss has been suffered.

T F 15. Under a periodic inventory system, as soon as a sale is made, the cost of the goods sold must be recorded and the inventory account must be decreased.

T F 16. One example of a trade discount is 2/10, n/30.

T F 17. When goods are shipped FOB shipping point, title passes when the goods are received by the buyer.

T F 18. A good system of internal control will guarantee that the accounting records are accurate.

T F 19. Collusion refers to a secret agreement between two or more persons to defraud a company.

T F 20. The mail should be opened in the accounting department so that transactions may be recorded immediately.

T F 21. A company orders goods by sending the supplier a purchase requisition.

T F 22. Rotating employees in job assignments is poor internal control because employees would continually be forced to learn a new job skill.

_____
_____
_____
_____
_____
_____
_____

_____
_____
_____
_____
_____
_____
_____

Accounting for Merchandising Operations

Multiple Choice

Circle the letter of the best answer.

1. Burns buys $600 of merchandise from Allen, with terms of 2/10, n/30. Burns immediately returns $100 of goods, and pays for the remainder eight days after purchase. Burns's entry on the date of payment would include a
   a. debit to Accounts Payable for $600.
   b. debit to Sales Discounts for $12.
   c. credit to Purchases Returns and Allowances for $100.
   d. credit to Purchases Discounts for $10.

2. Which of the following normally has a credit balance?
   a. Sales Discounts
   b. Merchandise Inventory
   c. Purchases Returns and Allowances
   d. Freight In

3. If an item of ending inventory is counted twice, then
   a. net income will be understated.
   b. beginning inventory for the next period will be understated.
   c. cost of goods available for sale will be overstated.
   d. cost of goods sold will be understated.

4. Which of the following is irrelevant in computing cost of goods sold?
   a. Freight In
   b. Freight Out
   c. Merchandise Inventory, beginning
   d. Merchandise Inventory, ending

5. Which of the following documents is prepared (by a buyer of goods) before all of the others?
   a. Purchase order
   b. Receiving report
   c. Check authorization (or voucher)
   d. Purchase requisition

6. Which of the following is an example of poor internal control?
   a. The receiving department comparing goods received with the related purchase order
   b. Forcing employees to take earned vacations
   c. Requiring someone other than the petty cash custodian to enter petty cash transactions into the accounting records
   d. Bonding employees

7. Which of the following accounts would appear as an operating expense in a merchandiser's income statement?
   a. Advertising Expense
   b. Sales Discounts
   c. Freight In
   d. Purchases

8. Which of the following accounts is *not* used in conjunction with a perpetual inventory system?
   a. Cost of Goods Sold
   b. Freight In
   c. Purchases
   d. Merchandise Inventory

9. The operating cycle does *not* include which of the following transactions?
   a. Sale of inventory
   b. Cash payment for inventory purchases
   c. Purchase of inventory
   d. Cash collection from inventory sales

APPLYING YOUR KNOWLEDGE

Exercises

1. Following are the May transactions of Apex Merchandising Corporation. For each transaction, prepare the journal entry in the journal provided on the next page. Assume that the periodic inventory system is used.

   May 1 Purchased merchandise for $500 on credit, terms 2/10, n/60.
           3 Sold merchandise for $500 on credit, terms 2/10, 1/20, n/30.
           4 Paid $42 for freight charges relating to a merchandise purchase of April.
           5 Purchased office supplies for $100, on credit.
           6 Returned $20 of the May 5 office supplies, for credit.
           7 Returned $50 of merchandise purchased on May 1, for credit.
           9 Sold merchandise for $225, on credit, terms 2/10, 1/15, n/30.
         10 Paid for the merchandise purchased on May 1, less the return and any discount.
         14 The customer of May 9 returned $25 of merchandise, for credit.
         22 The customer of May 9 paid for the merchandise, less the return and any discount.
         26 The customer of May 3 paid for the merchandise.

2. Using the information below, prepare a partial income statement showing just the computation of gross margin.

Advertising Expense	$ 5,000
Dividends	12,000
Freight In	2,000
Freight Out	4,000
Income Taxes Expense	4,780
Income Taxes Payable	4,780
Interest Income	150
Merchandise Inventory (Jan. 1)	10,000
Merchandise Inventory (Dec. 31)	8,000
Purchases	50,000
Purchases Discounts	500
Purchases Returns and Allowances	500
Rent Expense	3,000
Retained Earnings	15,000
Sales	100,000
Sales Discounts	300
Sales Returns and Allowances	200
Wages Expense	7,000

Jefferson Merchandising Company
Partial Income Statement
For the Year 19xx

Accounting for Merchandising Operations

Date	Description	Debit	Credit

Crossword Puzzle
for Chapters 4 and 5

ACROSS

5. Entry opposite of adjusting
6. Inventory-related expense (4 words)
8. Method of accounting for inventory
9. Inventory-acquisition account
10. Add horizontally
12. FOB _____

DOWN

1. Income statement subtotal (2 words)
2. Reward for paying early
3. Aids to financial statement preparation (2 words)
4. Account used when clearing the accounts (2 words)
7. Clearing (the accounts)
8. Method of accounting for inventory
11. Word before purchases, sales, or income

Accounting for Merchandising Operations

CHAPTER 6 FINANCIAL REPORTING AND ANALYSIS

REVIEWING THE CHAPTER

Objective 1: State the objectives of financial reporting (pp. 241–242).

1. Financial reporting should fulfill three objectives. It should (a) provide information that is useful in making investment and credit decisions; (b) provide information that is useful in assessing cash flow prospects; and (c) provide information about business resources, claims to those resources, and changes in them. General-purpose external financial statements are the main way of presenting financial information to interested parties. They consist of the balance sheet, income statement, statement of retained earnings, and statement of cash flows.

Objective 2: State the qualitative characteristics of accounting information and describe their interrelationships (pp. 242–244).

2. Accounting attempts to provide decision makers with information that displays certain **qualitative characteristics,** or standards:
   a. **Understandability,** carrying the intended meaning, is a key qualitative characteristic.
   b. Another very important standard is **usefulness.** For it to be useful, information must be relevant and reliable. **Relevance** means that the information is capable of influencing the decision. Relevant information provides feedback, helps in making predictions, and is timely. **Reliability** means that accounting information accurately reflects what it is meant to reflect, that it is credible, verifiable, and neutral.

Objective 3: Define and describe the use of the conventions of *comparability* **and** *consistency, materiality, conservatism, full disclosure,* **and** *cost-benefit* **(pp. 244–247).**

3. To help users interpret financial information, accountants depend on five **conventions,** or rules of thumbs: comparability and consistency, materiality, conservatism, full disclosure, and cost-benefit.
   a. **Comparability** means that the information allows the decision maker to compare the same company over two or more accounting periods, or different companies over the same accounting period. **Consistency** means that a particular accounting procedure, once adopted, should not be changed unless the company can justify the change and discloses the dollar effect on the statements.
   b. The **materiality** convention states that strict accounting practice need not be applied to items of insignificant dollar value.
   c. The **conservatism** convention states that an accountant who has a choice of acceptable accounting procedures should choose the one that is least likely to overstate assets and income. Applying the lower-of-cost-or-market rule to inventory valuation is an example of conservatism.
   d. The **full disclosure** convention states that financial statements and their footnotes should contain all information relevant to the user's understanding of the statements.
   e. The **cost-benefit** convention states that the cost of providing additional accounting in-

formation should not exceed the benefits to be gained from the information.

Objective 4: Explain management's responsibility for ethical financial reporting and define *fraudulent financial reporting* **(pp. 247–248).**

4. Users depend on management and its accountants to act ethically and with good judgment in the preparation of financial statements. This responsibility is often expressed in the report of management that accompanies financial statements.

5. The intentional preparation of misleading financial statements is called **fraudulent financial reporting.** It can result from the distortion of records, falsified transactions, or the misapplication of accounting principles.

Objective 5: Identify and describe the basic components of a classified balance sheet (pp. 248–253).

6. **Classified financial statements** divide assets, liabilities, owners' equity, revenues, and expenses into subcategories to offer the reader more useful information.

7. On a classified balance sheet, assets are usually divided into four categories: (a) current assets; (b) investments; (c) property, plant, and equipment; and (d) intangible assets. (Sometimes another category called other assets is added for miscellaneous items.)

8. These categories are usually listed in order of liquidity (the ease with which an asset can be turned into cash).

9. **Current assets** are cash and assets that are expected to be turned into cash or used up within the normal operating cycle of the company or one year, whichever is longer. (From here on we will call this time period the current period.)
   a. A company's normal operating cycle is the average time between the purchase of inventory and the collection of cash from the sale of that inventory.
   b. Cash, short-term investments, accounts receivable, notes receivable, prepaid expenses, supplies, and inventory are current assets.

10. Examples of **investments** are stock and bonds held for long-term investment, land held for future use, plant or equipment not used in the business, special funds, and a controlling interest in another company.

11. **Property, plant, and equipment** include things like land, buildings, delivery equipment, machinery, and office equipment. All except land are subject to depreciation.

12. **Intangible assets** have no physical substance. More importantly, they represent certain long-lived rights or privileges. Examples are patents, copyrights, goodwill, franchises, and trademarks.

13. **Other assets** is used as a category by some companies to group all assets other than current assets and property, plant, and equipment. In this case, other assets can include investments and intangible assets.

14. The liabilities of a classified balance sheet are usually divided into current and long-term liabilities.
    a. **Current liabilities** are obligations for which payment (or performance) is due in the current period. They are paid from current assets or by incurring new short-term liabilities. Examples are notes payable, accounts payable, taxes payable, and unearned revenues.
    b. **Long-term liabilities** are debts that are due after the current period or that will be paid from noncurrent assets. Examples are mortgages payable, long-term notes payable, bonds payable, employee pension obligations, and long-term leases.

15. The owners' equity section of a classified balance sheet is usually called owner's equity, partners' equity, or stockholders' equity. The exact name depends on whether the business is a sole proprietorship, a partnership, or a corporation.

16. In a corporation, the stockholders' equity section consists of contributed capital (also called *paid-in capital*) and retained earnings.

17. In a sole proprietorship or partnership, the owner's or partners' equity section shows the name of the owner or owners. Each is followed by the word *capital* and the dollar amount of investment as of the balance sheet date.

Objective 6: Prepare multistep and single-step classified income statements (pp. 253–255).

18. A **condensed financial statement,** which contains the statement's major categories with little or no detail, may be presented in either multistep or single-step form.
    a. The **multistep form** is the more detailed of the two, containing several subtractions and subtotals. It has separate sections for cost of

goods sold, operating expenses, and **other (nonoperating) revenues and expenses.** One important subtotal is **income from operations,** which equals gross margin from sales minus operating expenses.

b. In the **single-step form,** the revenues section lists all revenues, including other revenues, and the operating costs section lists all expenses, including other expenses. The difference is labeled net income or net loss.

19. A corporation's income statement should disclose provision for income taxes or **income taxes** separately from the other expenses. Sole proprietorships and partnerships are not taxable units.

20. **Earnings per share,** also called *net income per share,* equals net income divided by the number of shares of common stock. It usually appears below net income in the income statement and is a measure of the company's profitability.

Objective 7: Use classified financial statements for the simple evaluation of liquidity and profitability (pp. 255–262).

21. Classified financial statements help the reader evaluate liquidity and profitability.

22. **Liquidity** refers to a company's ability to pay its bills when they are due and to meet unexpected needs for cash. Two measures of liquidity are working capital and the current ratio.
    a. **Working capital** equals current assets minus current liabilities. It is the amount of current assets that would remain if all the current debts were paid.
    b. The **current ratio** equals current assets divided by current liabilities. A current ratio of 1:1, for example, shows that current assets are barely enough to pay current liabilities. A 2:1 current ratio would be considered more satisfactory.

23. **Profitability** means more than just a company's net income. And to draw conclusions, one must compare profitability measures with industry averages and past performance. Five common measures of profitability are profit margin, asset turnover, return on assets, debt to equity ratio, and return on equity.
    a. The **profit margin** equals net income divided by net sales. A 12.5 percent profit margin, for example, means that 12½¢ has been earned on each dollar of sales.

b. **Asset turnover** equals net sales divided by average total assets. This measures how efficiently assets are used to produce sales.
c. **Return on assets** equals net income divided by average total assets. This measure shows how efficiently the company is using its assets.
d. The **debt to equity** ratio measures the proportion of a business financed by creditors relative to the proportion financed by owners. It equals total liabilities divided by stockholders' equity. A debt to equity ratio of 1.0, for instance, indicates equal financing by creditors and owners.
e. **Return on equity** shows what percentage was earned on the owners' investment. It equals net income divided by average stockholders' equity.

Supplemental Objective 8: Identify the major components of a corporate annual report (pp. 262–268).

24. Financial statements of corporations are usually complicated and have a number of features not found in a sole proprietorship's or partnership's statements. Published statements appear in the company's **annual report,** a publication distributed to stockholders each year. The annual report usually also gives nonfinancial information.

25. **Consolidated financial statements** are the combined statements of a company and its controlled subsidiaries (Chapter 15 explains them in more detail). A company's financial statements may show data from consecutive periods side by side for comparison. Such statements are called **comparative financial statements.**

26. The consolidated statement of earnings should contain information regarding earnings per share. A measure of a company's profitability, it equals net income divided by the average number of shares of common stock outstanding.

27. A **statement of stockholders' equity** is usually presented in a corporate annual report in place of the statement of retained earnings. It explains the changes in each of the six components of stockholders' equity.

28. A section called **notes to the financial statements** accompanies, and is considered an integral part of, the financial statements. Its purpose is to help the reader interpret some of the more complex financial statement items.

29. A **summary of significant accounting policies** discloses the generally accepted accounting principles used in preparing the statements. It usually follows the last financial statement, perhaps as the first note to the financial statements.

30. Corporations are often required to issue **interim financial statements.** These statements give financial information covering less than a year (for example, quarterly data). Ordinarily they are reviewed, but not audited, by the independent CPA.

31. An annual report usually also includes a report of management's responsibilities and management's discussion and analysis of operating performance.

32. The **independent auditors' report** is issued by an independent auditor. It conveys to third parties that the financial statements were examined in accordance with generally accepted auditing standards (**scope section**), and expresses the auditor's opinion on how fairly the financial statements reflect the company's financial condition (**opinion section**). The language of the accountants' report has recently been reworded to emphasize management's responsibility for the financial statements and to clarify the nature and purpose of an audit.

TESTING YOUR KNOWLEDGE

Matching

Match each term with its definition by writing the appropriate letter in the blank.

_____ 1. Qualitative characteristics

_____ 2. Relevance

_____ 3. Reliability

_____ 4. Fraudulent financial reporting

_____ 5. Classified financial statements

_____ 6. Liquidity

_____ 7. Current assets

_____ 8. Property, plant, and equipment

_____ 9. Intangible assets

_____ 10. Current liabilities

_____ 11. Long-term liabilities

_____ 12. Other revenues and expenses

_____ 13. Consolidated financial statements

_____ 14. Interim financial statements

_____ 15. Independent auditors' report

_____ 16. Comparative financial statements

_____ 17. Earnings per share (*net income per share* or *net earnings per share*)

_____ 18. Summary of significant accounting policies

_____ 19. Notes to the financial statements

a. Statements that cover less than a year
b. Financial statements with data from consecutive periods placed side by side for analysis
c. The auditor's opinion concerning the financial statements
d. Long-lived tangible assets
e. The intentional preparation of misleading financial statements
f. A disclosure of the accounting principles used in preparing the financial statements
g. Guidelines for evaluating the quality of accounting reports
h. Short-term obligations
i. Financial reports broken down into subcategories
j. Combined financial statements of a parent company and its subsidiaries
k. Net income divided by average outstanding shares of common stock
l. The income statement section that contains non-operating items
m. The subcategory of assets that are expected to be turned into cash or used up within one year or the normal operating cycle, whichever is longer
n. The standard that accounting information should be related to the user's needs
o. Long-term assets that lack physical substance and that grant rights or privileges to their owner
p. A section that interprets or supplements financial statement information
q. Obligations due after the current period
r. The standard that accounting information should accurately reflect what it is meant to represent
s. The ability to pay bills when due and to meet unexpected needs for cash

Financial Reporting and Analysis

Short Answer

Use the lines provided to answer each item.

1. List the three forms of business organization, with each one's name for the owners' equity section in the balance sheet.

    Business Organization

    a. _____

    b. _____

    c. _____

    Name for Owners' Equity Section

    a. _____

    b. _____

    c. _____

2. What does each of the following ratios have to do with a company's profitability?

    Profit margin

    Asset turnover

    Return on assets

    Return on equity

    Debt to equity ratio

3. Define each of the following liquidity ratios.

    Working capital

    Current ratio

4. Explain the basic point of each of the following conventions:

    Consistency and comparability

    Materiality

    Cost-benefit

    Conservatism

    Full disclosure

66　　　　　　　　　　　　　　　　　　　　　　　　　　　　Chapter 6

True-False

Circle T if the statement is true, F if it is false. Please provide explanations for the false answers, using the blank lines at the end of the section.

T F 1. Receivables are not current assets if collection requires more than one year.

T F 2. Interim financial statements are normally reviewed but not audited.

T F 3. Gross margin from sales minus operating expenses equals income from operations.

T F 4. Operating expenses are made up of selling expenses and cost of goods sold.

T F 5. Accounting information is relevant if it could make a difference to the outcome of a decision.

T F 6. The net income figure is needed to compute the profit margin, the return on assets, and the return on equity.

T F 7. The investments section of a balance sheet would include both short- and long-term investments in stock.

T F 8. One meaning of the term *profitability* is the ease with which an asset can be converted into cash.

T F 9. A company's normal operating cycle cannot be less than one year.

T F 10. Net worth refers to the current value of a company's assets.

T F 11. Other revenues and expenses is a separate classification in a multistep income statement.

T F 12. The net income figures for a multistep and a single-step income statement will differ, given the same accounting period for the same company.

T F 13. The notes to the financial statements are divided into a scope section and an opinion section.

T F 14. Working capital equals current assets divided by current liabilities.

T F 15. The proportion of a company financed by the owners is shown by the debt to equity ratio.

T F 16. The qualitative characteristic of relevance means that accounting information can be confirmed or duplicated by independent parties.

T F 17. A corporate annual report usually includes much nonfinancial information, in addition to financial information.

T F 18. Condensed financial statements and consolidated financial statements are essentially the same thing.

Multiple Choice

Circle the letter of the best answer.

1. The basis for classifying assets as current or noncurrent is the period of time normally required by the business to turn cash invested in
   a. noncurrent assets back into current assets.
   b. receivables back into cash, or 12 months, whichever is shorter.
   c. inventories back into cash, or 12 months, whichever is longer.
   d. inventories back into cash, or 12 months, whichever is shorter.

2. Which of the following will not be found anywhere in a single-step income statement?
   a. Cost of goods sold
   b. Other expenses
   c. Gross margin
   d. Operating expenses

3. The current ratio would probably be of *most* interest to
   a. stockholders.
   b. creditors.
   c. management.
   d. customers.

4. Which item below will *not* appear in the stockholders' equity section of a corporation's balance sheet?
   a. Retained earnings
   b. Common stock
   c. Paid-in capital in excess of par value
   d. James Esmay, Capital

5. The independent auditors' report
   a. expresses an opinion as to the fairness of the financial statements audited.
   b. states whether or not a company is a sound investment.
   c. is prepared by a company's own internal auditors.
   d. should include forecasts to help the reader assess future profitability.

6. Net income divided by net sales equals
   a. the profit margin.
   b. return on assets.
   c. working capital.
   d. income from operations.

7. Operating expenses consist of
   a. other expenses and cost of goods sold.
   b. selling expenses and cost of goods sold.
   c. selling expenses and general and administrative expenses.
   d. selling expenses, general and administrative expenses, and other expenses.

8. Applying the lower-of-cost-or-market rule to inventory valuation and short-term investments follows the convention of
   a. consistency.
   b. materiality.
   c. conservatism.
   d. full disclosure.

9. Which of the following is *not* an objective of financial reporting, according to FASB *Statement of Financial Accounting Concepts No. 1?*
   a. To provide information about the timing of cash flows
   b. To provide information to investors, creditors, and others
   c. To provide information about business resources
   d. To provide information not found in the independent auditors' report

APPLYING YOUR KNOWLEDGE

Exercises

1. Assume that Springfield Company uses the following group headings on its classified balance sheet:
   a. Current assets
   b. Investments
   c. Property, plant, and equipment
   d. Intangible assets
   e. Current liabilities
   f. Long-term liabilities
   g. Owner's equity

   Indicate by letter where each of the following should be placed. Write an "X" next to items that do not belong on the balance sheet.

   ___ 1. Franchises
   ___ 2. Short-term advances from customers
   ___ 3. Accumulated depreciation
   ___ 4. Mark Mathews, Capital
   ___ 5. Prepaid rent
   ___ 6. Delivery truck
   ___ 7. Office supplies
   ___ 8. Fund for the purchase of land
   ___ 9. Notes payable due in ten years
   ___ 10. Bonds payable currently due (payable out of current assets)
   ___ 11. Goodwill
   ___ 12. Short-term investments
   ___ 13. Provision for income taxes
   ___ 14. Inventory
   ___ 15. Accounts payable

2. The following information relates to Spiffy Appliances, Inc., for 19xx.

Current assets	$ 60,000
Average total assets	200,000
Current liabilities	20,000
Long-term liabilities	30,000
Average stockholders' equity	150,000
Net sales	250,000
Net income	25,000

   In the spaces provided, indicate each measure of liquidity and profitability.
   a. Working capital = $_____
   b. Current ratio = _____ to _____
   c. Profit margin = _____%
   d. Return on assets = _____%
   e. Return on equity = _____%
   f. Asset turnover = _____ times

3. The following data relate to the Confrey Corporation for 19xx.

Cost of goods sold	$150,000
Interest revenues	2,000
Income tax expense	5,000
Net sales	200,000
Common stock outstanding	3,500 shares
Operating expenses	30,000

   a. In the space provided below, complete the condensed multistep income statement in good form. Include earnings per share information in the proper place.

Confrey Corporation
Income Statement (Multistep)
For the Year Ended December 31, 19xx

Financial Reporting and Analysis

b. In the space provided, complete the condensed single-step income statement in good form. Include earnings per share information in the proper place.

Confrey Corporation Income Statement (Single-Step) For the Year Ended December 31, 19xx		

CHAPTER 7 SHORT-TERM LIQUID ASSETS

REVIEWING THE CHAPTER

Objective 1: Identify and explain the management issues related to short-term liquid assets (pp. 293–298).

1. It is management's responsibility to use company assets to maximize income while maintaining liquidity. **Short-term liquid assets** (also known as *quick assets*) are financial assets that arise from cash transactions, the investment of cash, and the extension of credit. Examples are cash and cash equivalents, short-term investments, accounts receivable, and notes receivable.

2. A common measure of the adequacy of short-term liquid assets is the **quick ratio,** which equals quick assets divided by current liabilities. A quick ratio of 1.0 is generally considered desirable, but industry characteristics and company trends should also be carefully examined.

3. To maintain adequate liquidity, management must (a) manage cash needs during seasonal cycles, (b) set credit policies, and (c) consider the financing of receivables.
   a. During the course of a year, most businesses experience periods of both strong and weak sales, as well as variations in cash flow. For a business to remain liquid, management must carefully plan for cash inflows, cash outflows, borrowing, and investing.
   b. Companies sell on credit to be competitive and to increase sales. However, a business must carefully review the financial backgrounds of its potential credit customers before selling to them on credit. The effect of a company's credit policies is commonly measured by the **receivable turnover** (net sales divided by average net accounts receivable) and the **average days' sales uncollected** (365 divided by the receivable turnover).
   c. Occasionally, companies cannot afford to wait until their receivables are collected. They can use the receivables to obtain cash by borrowing funds and pledging the accounts receivable as collateral. Also, a business can sell its receivables to a **factor** (e.g., a bank or finance company) through a process called **factoring.** Receivables can be factored without recourse (as with major credit cards) or with recourse. The factoring fee is much greater when receivables are factored without recourse because of the greater risk involved. When receivables are sold with recourse, the seller of the receivable has a **contingent liability** in the event of nonpayment. Finally, a business can obtain financing through the **discounting** (selling) of its notes receivable.

Objective 2: Explain cash and cash equivalents and prepare a bank reconciliation (pp. 298–304).

4. **Cash** consists of coin and currency on hand, checks and money orders from customers, and deposits in checking accounts. A company's Cash account also can include a **compensating balance,** the minimum amount a bank requires a company to keep in its bank account.

5. **Cash equivalents** consist of investments, such as certificates of deposit and U.S. Treasury notes, that have a term of less than 90 days. Cash and

cash equivalents often are combined on the balance sheet.

6. Most companies need to keep some currency and coins on hand, for cash registers and for paying expenses that are impractical to pay by check. One way to control a cash fund or cash advances is through the use of an **imprest system.** A common form of this is the **petty cash fund,** which is established at a fixed amount. Each payment from the fund is documented by a receipt. The petty cash fund is replenished periodically to restore it to its original amount.

7. Making payment by check reduces the need for currency and provides a permanent record of the payment itself. However, the use of checks can be avoided through an **electronic funds transfer (EFT).**

8. Banks provide a variety of services to their customers, as well as convenient means for conducting their banking transactions. One of a bank's main services, the maintenance of checking accounts, is discussed below.

9. Once a month, the bank returns a company's canceled checks with a **bank statement.** The bank statement shows the bank balance at the beginning of the month, all additions and deductions during the month, and the balance at the end of the month.

10. The end-of-month balance in a bank statement rarely agrees with the balance in the company's books for that date. Thus, the accountant must prepare a **bank reconciliation** to account for the difference and to locate any errors made by the bank or the company. The bank reconciliation begins with the balance per books and balance per bank figures as of the bank statement date. Each figure is adjusted by additions and deductions, resulting in two adjusted cash balance figures, which should agree. The balance per books figure is adjusted by information that the bank knew on the bank statement date but the company did not. The balance per bank figure is adjusted by information that the company knew on the bank statement date but the bank did not. For example:
    a. Outstanding checks are a deduction from the balance per bank.
    b. Deposits in transit are an addition to the balance per bank.
    c. Service charges by the bank appear on the bank statement and are a deduction from the balance per books.
    d. A customer's non-sufficient funds (NSF) check is deducted from the balance per books.
    e. Interest earned on a checking account is added to the balance per books.
    f. Miscellaneous charges are deducted from the balance per books. Miscellaneous credits are added to the balance per books.

11. After the bank reconciliation has been prepared, adjusting entries must be made so that the accounting records reflect the new information supplied by the bank statement. Each adjustment includes either a debit or a credit to Cash.

Objective 3: Account for short-term investments (pp. 305–308).

12. Companies frequently have excess cash on hand for short periods of time. To put this idle cash to good use, most companies purchase **short-term investments,** or **marketable securities.** Short-term investments are categorized as held-to-maturity securities, trading securities, or available-for-sale securities.

13. **Held-to-maturity securities** are debt securities, such as U.S. Treasury bills, that are expected to be held until the maturity date and whose cash value is not needed until then. Upon purchase of these securities, Short-Term Investments is debited and Cash credited. At year end, accrued interest is recognized with a debit to Short-Term Investments and a credit to Interest Income; the investment would be valued on the balance sheet at its amortized cost. At maturity, Cash is debited for the maturity amount, and Short-Term Investments and Interest Income are credited.

14. **Trading securities** consist of both debt and equity securities that will be held for just a short period of time. These securities are valued on the balance sheet at their fair or market value, if available. Also, dollar increases or decreases in the total trading portfolio during the period are reflected in that period's income statement.
    a. Upon the purchase of trading securities, Short-Term Investments is debited and Cash is credited.
    b. At year end, the cost and market (fair) value of the securities are compared, and an adjustment is made. When a decline in value has been suffered, Unrealized Loss on Investments (an income statement account) is debited and Allowance to Adjust Short-Term Investments to Market (a contra-asset account) is credited. When, on the other hand,

an increase in value is experienced, Allowance to Adjust Short-Term Investments to Market is debited and Unrealized Gain on Investments is credited. In either case, the investments are reported on the balance sheet at market value.

c. When an investment is sold, Cash is debited for the proceeds, Short-Term Investments is credited for the original cost, and Realized Gain (or Realized Loss) on Investments is credited (or debited) for the difference.

15. **Available-for-sale securities** are equity and debt securities that do not qualify as either held-to-maturity or trading securities. These securities are recorded in the same way as trading securities, except that unrealized gains and losses are reported in the stockholders' equity section of the balance sheet rather than in the income statement.

Objective 4: Define *accounts receivable* **and apply the allowance method of accounting for uncollectible accounts, using both the percentage of net sales method and the accounts receivable aging method (pp. 308–317).**

16. **Accounts receivable** are short-term liquid assets that represent payment due from credit customers. This type of credit is called **trade credit.**

17. **Installment accounts receivable** are receivables that will be collected in a series of payments; they usually are classified on the balance sheet as current assets.

18. When loans and sales are made to the company's employees, officers, or stockholders, they should be shown separately on the balance sheet with a title such as Receivables from Employees and Officers.

19. When a customer overpays, his or her account shows a credit balance. When a balance sheet is prepared, Accounts Receivable should be the sum of all accounts with debit balances. The sum of all accounts with credit balances should be shown as current liabilities.

20. Most companies that sell to customers on credit keep an accounts receivable record for each customer. In this way, a company can determine how much a given customer owes at any time. All customer accounts are filed either alphabetically or numerically in the accounts receivable **subsidiary ledger.**

21. The general ledger contains an Accounts Receivable **controlling,** or **control, account.** The controlling account is updated at the end of each month and keeps a running total of all accounts receivable. Its balance should equal the sum of all the accounts in the accounts receivable subsidiary ledger.

22. Most companies also use an Accounts Payable controlling account and subsidiary ledger, which function much like the Accounts Receivable controlling account and subsidiary ledger.

23. Regardless of how thorough and efficient its control system is, a company will always have some customers who cannot or will not pay. **Uncollectible accounts** (also called *bad debts*), the accounting term for credit accounts that are not paid, are an expense of selling on credit. The company can afford such an expense because extending credit allows it to sell more, thereby increasing company earnings.

24. Some companies recognize the loss from an uncollectible account at the time it is determined to be uncollectible. This **direct charge-off method** is used by small companies and for tax purposes, but companies that follow GAAP do not use it on their financial statements because it does not match revenues and expenses.

25. The matching rule requires that uncollectible accounts expense appear on the same income statement as the corresponding sale, even if the customer defaults in a future period. Of course, at the time of a credit sale, the company does not know which customers are not going to pay. Therefore, an estimate of uncollectible accounts must be made at the end of the accounting period. Then an adjusting entry is made, debiting Uncollectible Accounts Expense and crediting Allowance for Uncollectible Accounts for the estimated amount. This method of accounting for uncollectible accounts is called the **allowance method.** Uncollectible Accounts Expense appears on the income statement and is closed out as are other expenses. **Allowance for Uncollectible Accounts** is a contra account to Accounts Receivable, reducing Accounts Receivable to the amount estimated to be collectible.

26. The two most common methods for estimating uncollectible accounts are the percentage of net sales method and the accounts receivable aging method.

27. Under the **percentage of net sales method,** the estimated percentage for uncollectible accounts is multiplied by net sales for the period. The product then is used in the adjusting entry for uncollectible accounts. Any previous balance in Allowance for Uncollectible Accounts represents estimates from previous years that have not yet been written off. It has no bearing on the adjusting entry under this method.

28. Under the **accounts receivable aging method,** customers' accounts are placed in a "not yet due" category or in one of several "past due" categories (called the **aging of accounts receivable**). The amounts in each category are totaled. Each total then is multiplied by a different percentage for estimated bad debts. The sum of these products represents estimated bad debts in ending Accounts Receivable. Again, the debit is to Uncollectible Accounts Expense, and the credit is to Allowance for Uncollectible Accounts. However, the entry is for the amount that will bring Allowance for Uncollectible Accounts to the figure arrived at in the aging calculation.

29. When it becomes clear that a specific account will not be collected, it should be written off by a debit to Allowance for Uncollectible Accounts and a credit to Accounts Receivable. The debit is not made to Uncollectible Accounts Expense. After a specific account is written off, Accounts Receivable and Allowance for Uncollectible Accounts decrease by the same amount, but the net figure for expected receivables stays the same.

30. When a customer whose account has been written off pays in full or in part, two entries must be made. First, the customer's receivable is reinstated by a debit to Accounts Receivable and a credit to Allowance for Uncollectible Accounts for the amount now thought to be collectible. Second, Cash is debited and Accounts Receivable is credited for each collection.

Objective 5: Define and describe a *promissory note*, and make calculations and journal entries involving promissory notes (pp. 318–321).

31. A **promissory note** is a written promise to pay a definite sum of money on demand or at a future date. The person who signs the note and thereby promises to pay is called the *maker* of the note. The person to whom money is owed is called the *payee*. The payee records long- or short-term **notes receivable,** and the maker records long- or short-term **notes payable.**

32. The **maturity date** and the **duration of note** must be stated on the promissory note, or it must be possible to figure them out from the information on the note.

33. To the borrower, **interest** is the cost of borrowing money. To the lender, it is the reward for lending money. Principal is the amount of money borrowed or loaned. The interest rate is the annual charge for borrowing money and is expressed as a percentage. A note can be either interest-bearing or non-interest-bearing.

34. Interest (not the interest rate) is a dollar figure, which is computed as follows:

    Interest = principal
    × interest rate
    × time (length of loan)

    For example, interest on $800 at 5 percent for 90 days is $10: $800 × 5/100 × 90/360. A 360-day year is used to simplify the computation. If the length of the note was expressed in months, then the third fraction would be the number of months divided by 12.

35. The **maturity value** of an interest-bearing note is the face value of the note (principal) plus interest. For a non-interest-bearing note, maturity value is equal to the face amount (which, however, includes implied interest).

36. There are four situations that result in journal entries for notes receivable: (a) receipt of a note, (b) collection on a note, (c) recording a dishonored note, and (d) recording adjusting entries.

37. When a promissory note is received—for example, in settlement of an existing account receivable—Notes Receivable is debited and Accounts Receivable is credited.

38. When collection is made on a note, Cash is debited for the maturity value, Notes Receivable is credited for the face value, and Interest Income is credited for the difference.

39. A **dishonored note** is one that is not paid at the maturity date. The payee debits Accounts Receivable for the principal plus interest, and credits Notes Receivable and Interest Income.

40. End-of-period adjustments must be made for notes that apply to both the current and future periods. In this way, interest can be divided correctly among the periods.

Supplemental Objective 6: Account for credit card transactions (pp. 321–322).

41. Companies that allow customers to use national credit cards (such as MasterCard) must follow special accounting procedures. The credit card company reimburses the company for the sale, less a service charge. The credit card company levies this service charge because it is responsible for establishing credit and collecting money from the customer. One of two procedures is used in accounting for credit card sales, depending on whether the merchant must wait for collection from the credit card company or can deposit the sales invoices into a checking account immediately. In either case, the *goal* is to record debits to Cash and Credit Card Discount Expense and a credit to Sales.

Summary of Journal Entries Introduced in Chapter 7

A. (L.O. 2) After a bank reconciliation is prepared, journal entries must be made to record the items on the bank statement that the company has not yet recorded (service charges, NSF checks, etc.). The sample entries presented in the textbook are not duplicated here, but please notice that all entries contain either a debit or a credit to Cash.

B. (L.O. 3) Short-Term Investments   XX (purchase price)
        Cash   XX (amount paid)
           Purchase of U.S. Treasury bills

C. (L.O. 3) Short-Term Investments   XX (accrued interest)
        Interest Income   XX (accrued amount)
           Year-end accrual of interest on T-bills

D. (L.O. 3) Cash   XX (maturity amount)
        Short-Term Investments   XX (debit balance)
        Interest Income   XX (accrued amount)
           Receipt of cash at maturity of T-bills and recognition of related income

E. (L.O. 3) Short-Term Investments   XX (purchase price)
        Cash   XX (amount paid)
           Purchase of stocks for trading

F. (L.O. 3) Unrealized Loss on Investments   XX (market decline)
        Allowance to Adjust Short-Term Investments to Market   XX (market decline)
           Year-end adjustment on trading portfolio, unrealized loss recognized

G. (L.O. 3) Cash   XX (proceeds on sale)
        Short-Term Investments   XX (purchase price)
        Realized Gain on Investments   XX (the difference)
           Sale of stock at a gain

H. (L.O. 3) Allowance to Adjust Short-Term Investments to Market   XX (market increase)
        Unrealized Gain on Investments   XX (market increase)
           Year-end adjustment on trading portfolio, unrealized gain recognized

I. (L.O. 4) Uncollectible Accounts Expense   XX (defaulted amount)
        Accounts Receivable   XX (defaulted amount)
           To write off receivable under the direct charge-off method

J. (L.O. 4) Uncollectible Accounts Expense   XX (amount estimated)
        Allowance for Uncollectible Accounts   XX (amount estimated)
           To record the estimated uncollectible accounts expense for the year

K. (L.O. 4) Allowance for Uncollectible Accounts   XX (defaulted amount)
        Accounts Receivable   XX (defaulted amount)
           To write off receivable of specific customer as uncollectible

L. (L.O. 4) Accounts Receivable   XX (amount reinstated)
        Allowance for Uncollectible Accounts   XX (amount reinstated)
           To reinstate the portion of a specific customer's
           account now considered collectible

M. (L.O. 4) Cash   XX (amount received)
        Accounts Receivable   XX (amount received)
           Collection from customer in L

N. (L.O. 5) Notes Receivable   XX (establishing amount)
        Accounts Receivable   XX (eliminating amount)
           Received note in payment of account

O. (L.O. 5) Cash   XX (maturity amount)
        Notes Receivable   XX (face amount)
        Interest income   XX (amount earned)
           Collected note

P. (L.O. 5) Accounts Receivable   XX (maturity amount)
        Notes Receivable   XX (face amount)
        Interest Income   XX (amount earned)
           To record dishonored note

Q. (L.). 5) Interest Receivable   XX (amount accrued)
        Interest Income   XX (amount earned)
           To accrue interest earned on a note receivable

R. (L.O. 5) Cash   XX (maturity amount)
        Notes Receivable   XX (face amount)
        Interest Receivable   XX (interest previously accrued)
        Interest Income   XX (interest this period)
           Receipt of note receivable plus interest (see Q)

S. (S.O. 6) Accounts Receivable   XX (net amount receivable)
        Credit Card Discount Expense   XX (fee charged)
           Sales   XX (gross amount sold)
             Sales made on credit card (vendor must wait
             for collection)

T. (S.O. 6) Cash   XX (amount received)
        Accounts Receivable   XX (amount received)
           Receipt of payment from credit card company
           (see S)

U. (S.O. 6) Cash   XX (amount net of fee)
        Credit Card Discount Expense   XX (fee charged)
           Sales   XX (gross amount sold)
             Sales on credit card (invoices deposited in special
             credit card bank account)

TESTING YOUR KNOWLEDGE

Matching

Match each term with its definition by writing the appropriate letter in the blank.

    1. Credit
    2. Factoring
    3. Uncollectible accounts expense
    4. Allowance for uncollectible accounts
    5. Installment accounts receivable
    6. Promissory note
    7. Maker
    8. Payee
    9. Maturity date
    10. Maturity value
    11. Interest rate
    12. Interest
    13. Principal
    14. Contingent liability
    15. Dishonored note
    16. Discounting
    17. Compensating balance
    18. Cash equivalents
    19. Bank reconciliation
    20. Petty cash fund

a. Short-term investments of less than 90 days
b. An accounting for the difference between book balance and bank balance at a particular date
c. The charge for borrowing money, expressed as a percentage
d. A note that is not paid at the maturity date
e. A written promise to pay
f. Estimated bad debts as shown on the income statement
g. Selling or transferring accounts receivable
h. A potential obligation
i. The time when payment is due on a note
j. Allowing customers to pay for merchandise over a period of time
k. A note's principal plus interest
l. The creditor named in a promissory note
m. Estimated bad debts as represented on the balance sheet
n. Selling a note prior to maturity
o. The charge for borrowing money, expressed in dollars
p. Receivables that will be collected in a series of payments
q. A minimum amount that a bank requires a company to keep in its account
r. The debtor named in a promissory note
s. Cash set aside to pay for items of small amounts
t. The amount of money borrowed or loaned

Short Answer

Use the lines provided to answer each item.

1. List three methods used in computing uncollectible accounts.

2. Explain the concept of contingent liability as it relates to discounted notes receivable.

3. Under what circumstance would there be a debit balance in Allowance for Uncollectible Accounts?

4. List the three categories of short-term investments.

5. List three items that would be deducted from the balance per books in a bank reconciliation.

6. List four examples of short-term liquid assets.

True-False

Circle T if the statement is true, F if it is false. Please provide explanations for the false answers, using the blank lines at the end of the section.

T F 1. Under the direct charge-off method, Allowance for Uncollectible Accounts does not exist.

T F 2. The percentage of net sales method violates the matching rule.

T F 3. Under the accounts receivable aging method, the balance in Allowance for Uncollectible Accounts is ignored in making the adjusting entry.

T F 4. Allowance for Uncollectible Accounts is a contra account to Accounts Receivable.

T F 5. Loans to officers of the company should not be included in Accounts Receivable on the balance sheet.

T F 6. When a customer overpays, his or her account on the company's books has a credit balance.

T F 7. Interest of 5 percent on $700 for 90 days would be computed as follows: 700 × .05 × 90.

T F 8. *Trade credit* refers to credit sales made to customers by wholesalers or retailers.

T F 9. When a note is discounted at the bank, the maker must make good on the note if the payee defaults.

T F 10. A note dated December 14 and due February 14 has a duration of 60 days.

T F 11. The figure for receivable turnover is built into the average days' sales uncollected calculation.

T F 12. Under the allowance method, the entry to write off a specific account as uncollectible decreases total assets.

Short-Term Liquid Assets

T F 13. The maturity value of an interest-bearing note equals principal plus interest.

T F 14. Under the allowance method, a specific account is written off with a debit to Uncollectible Accounts Expense and a credit to Accounts Receivable.

T F 15. When a note is dishonored, the payee nevertheless should record interest earned.

T F 16. Uncollectible accounts are an expense of selling on credit.

T F 17. Accounts receivable are an example of a cash equivalent.

T F 18. The use of a major credit card (e.g., MasterCard) is an example of factoring with recourse.

T F 19. The quick ratio equals current assets divided by current liabilities.

T F 20. A check that is outstanding for two consecutive months should be included in both months' bank reconciliations.

T F 21. A credit memorandum on a bank statement indicates an addition to the bank balance.

T F 22. After a bank reconciliation has been completed, the company must make journal entries to adjust for all outstanding checks.

T F 23. A bank reconciliation for the month of September should begin with the balance per books and the balance per bank on September 1.

T F 24. *Imprest system* refers to the mechanics of a petty cash fund.

T F 25. Held-to-maturity securities consist of debt securities, but not equity securities.

T F 26. Trading securities appear on the balance sheet at original cost.

T F 27. Individual customers' accounts receivable appear in the general ledger.

Multiple Choice

Circle the letter of the best answer.

1. A company has credit card sales for the day of $1,000. If the credit card company charges 5 percent, the company's entries to record sales and the eventual receipt of cash would include a
   a. credit to Sales for $950.
   b. debit to Accounts Receivable, Credit Card Companies for $1,050.
   c. credit to Credit Card Revenue for $50.
   d. debit to Cash for $950.

2. Which of the following does *not* equal the others?
   a. $600 for 60 days at 6 percent
   b. $1,200 for 120 days at 3 percent
   c. $300 for 120 days at 6 percent
   d. $600 for 30 days at 12 percent

3. A company estimates at the balance sheet date that $1,500 of net sales for the year will not be collected. A debit balance of $600 exists in Allowance for Uncollectible Accounts. Under the percentage of net sales method, Uncollectible Accounts Expense and Allowance for Uncollectible Accounts would be debited and credited for
   a. $600.
   b. $1,100.
   c. $1,500.
   d. $2,100.

4. A contingent liability exists when
   a. a note is discounted.
   b. a note is dishonored.
   c. interest accrues on a note.
   d. a note reaches maturity.

5. Based on the accounts receivable aging method, a company estimates that $850 of end-of-period accounts receivable will not be collected. A credit balance of $300 exists in Allowance for Uncollectible Accounts. Uncollectible Accounts Expense should be recorded for
   a. $300.
   b. $550.
   c. $850.
   d. $1,150.

6. Under the aging of accounts receivable method, a specific customer's account is written off by debiting
   a. Uncollectible Accounts Expense and crediting Allowance for Uncollectible Accounts.
   b. Accounts Receivable and crediting Allowance for Uncollectible Accounts.
   c. Allowance for Uncollectible Accounts and crediting Accounts Receivable.
   d. Uncollectible Accounts Expense and crediting Accounts Receivable.

7. Which of the following *cannot* be determined from the information on a note?
   a. Discount rate
   b. Interest rate
   c. Interest
   d. Maturity date

8. Which method for handling bad debts often violates the matching rule?
   a. Percentage of net sales method
   b. Direct charge-off method
   c. Accounts receivable aging method
   d. Both *a* and *c*

9. Which of the following is *not* considered a short-term liquid asset?
   a. Notes receivable
   b. Short-term investments
   c. Inventory
   d. Cash

10. The account Allowance to Adjust Short-Term Investments to Market
    a. is used for held-to-maturity securities.
    b. appears in the income statement.
    c. can be credited, but not debited.
    d. is a contra-asset account.

11. After the bank reconciliation has been completed, a company must make journal entries to adjust for all of the following *except*
    a. bank service charges.
    b. deposits in transit.
    c. a note collected by the bank.
    d. an error made by the bank.

Short-Term Liquid Assets

12. Interest earned on a checking account should be included in a bank reconciliation as a(n)
    a. addition to the balance per bank.
    b. deduction from the balance per bank.
    c. addition to the balance per books.
    d. deduction from the balance per books.

13. A company's bank statement erroneously shows a $1,000 deposit as $100, and the bank is notified. The $900 error appears in the bank reconciliation as a(n)
    a. addition to the balance per bank.
    b. deduction from the balance per bank.
    c. addition to the balance per books.
    d. deduction from the balance per books.

APPLYING YOUR KNOWLEDGE

Exercises

1. Calculate interest on the following amounts:
   a. $7,200 at 4% for 20 days = _____
   b. $52,000 at 7% for 3 months = _____
   c. $4,317 at 6% for 60 days = _____
   d. $18,000 at 8% for 1 day = _____

2. The facts that follow are needed to prepare a bank reconciliation for the Nelson Company as of March 31, 19xx. For each, write the correct letter (a, b, c, or d) to indicate where it should appear.

   a = Addition to the balance per bank

   b = Deduction from the balance per bank

   c = Addition to the balance per books

   d = Deduction from the balance per books

   ___ 1. The service charge by the bank was $8.
   ___ 2. A $1,700 note receivable was collected for the company by the bank. No collection fee was charged.
   ___ 3. There were two outstanding checks, totaling $3,200.
   ___ 4. A $355 NSF check drawn by a customer was deducted from the company's bank account and returned to the company.
   ___ 5. A deposit of $725 was made after banking hours on March 31.
   ___ 6. Check no. 185 was drawn for $342 but was recorded erroneously in the company's books as $324.

3. On November 17, 19x1, Ameci Corporation purchased 2,000 shares of Simpson Corporation stock for $30 per share. The purchase was made for trading purposes. At December 31, 19x1, the stock had a market value of $28 per share. On January 12, 19x2, Ameci sold all 2,000 shares for $66,000. In the journal provided below, prepare the entries for November 17, December 31, and January 12.

General Journal			
Date	Description	Debit	Credit

4. For the following set of facts, make the necessary entries for Green's Department Store in the journal provided on the next page.

Dec. 31 Interest of $75 has accrued on notes receivable.
31 Net sales for the year were $600,000. It is estimated that 4 percent will not be collected. Make the entry for uncollectible accounts.

Jan. 3 Anna Kohn purchased $10,000 worth of goods on credit in November. She now issues Green's her $10,000, 30-day, 6 percent note, thus extending her credit period.
8 Tom O'Brien goes bankrupt and notifies Green's that he cannot pay for the $1,000 worth of goods he had purchased last year on account.
14 The only credit card that Green's accepts is MasterCard. The store now records its credit card sales of $4,000 for the first two weeks in January. MasterCard will send payment to Green's on receipt of the invoices, and charges 5 percent for this service.
24 A check is received from MasterCard for the first two weeks' credit sales, less the service charge.
25 Tom O'Brien notifies Green's that he will be able to pay $600 of the $1,000 that he owes.
28 A check for $200 is received from Tom O'Brien.

Date	Description	Debit	Credit

Short-Term Liquid Assets

Crossword Puzzle
for Chapters 6 and 7

ACROSS

4. Interest deducted on a note
6. Section of auditors' report
8. Measure of profitability (3 words)
9. Promissory ____
10. ____, plant, and equipment
13. Allowance for ____ debts
15. Length of note
17. Asset not subject to depreciation
18. Income statement form (hyphenated)
19. Petty ____

DOWN

1. Source of information about a company (2 words)
2. Normal operating ____
3. Measure of liquidity (2 words)
4. ____ to equity ratio
5. See 11-Down
7. Combined, as financial statements
11. With 16-Down and 5-Down, income statement measure
12. Financial statements of less than a year
14. Method for estimating bad debts
16. See 11-Down

CHAPTER 8 INVENTORIES

REVIEWING THE CHAPTER

Objective 1: Identify and explain the management issues associated with accounting for inventories (pp. 345–350).

1. The **merchandise inventory** of a merchandising business consists of all goods owned and held for sale in the regular course of business. The inventory of a manufacturer, on the other hand, consists of raw materials, work in process, and finished goods. Inventory appears in the current asset section of the balance sheet.

2. To measure income properly and observe the matching rule, the following two questions must be answered for each nonfinancial asset:
   a. How much of the asset has been used up (expired) during the current period and should be transferred to expense?
   b. How much of the asset is unused (unexpired) and should remain on the balance sheet as an asset?

3. It is important for a merchandiser to maintain a sufficient level of inventory to satisfy customer demand. However, the higher the level maintained, the more costly it is for the business. Management can evaluate the level of inventory by calculating and analyzing the inventory turnover and average days' inventory on hand.
   a. **Inventory turnover** indicates the number of times a company's average inventory is sold during the period. It equals cost of goods sold divided by average inventory.
   b. **Average days' inventory on hand** indicates the average number of days required to sell the average inventory. It equals 365 divided by the inventory turnover.

4. Many companies, in an attempt to reduce their inventory, are changing to a **just-in-time operating environment.** They work closely with suppliers to coordinate and schedule shipments so that the goods arrive just in time to be used or sold.

Objective 2: Define *inventory cost* and relate it to goods flow and cost flow (pp. 350–351).

5. **Inventory cost** is the purchase price of the inventory less purchase discounts, plus freight or transportation in, including insurance in transit, and applicable taxes and tariffs.

6. Goods in transit should be included in inventory only if the company has title to the goods. When goods are sent FOB shipping point, title passes to the buyer when the goods reach the common carrier. When goods are shipped FOB destination, title passes when the goods reach the buyer. Goods that have been sold but are still on hand should not be included in the seller's inventory count.

7. When goods are held on **consignment,** the consignee (who earns a commission on making the sale) has possession of the goods, but the consignor retains title and, thus, includes the goods on its balance sheet.

8. When identical items of merchandise are purchased at different prices during the year, it is usually impractical to monitor the actual **goods flow** and record the corresponding costs. Instead, the accountant makes an assumption of the **cost flow** and uses one of the following methods: (a) specific identification, (b) average-cost, (c) first-

in, first-out (FIFO), or (d) last-in, first-out (LIFO). Ending inventory is computed by (a) counting the items on hand, (b) finding the cost of each item, and (c) multiplying the unit cost by the quantity to determine the total cost.

Objective 3a: Calculate the pricing of inventory, using the cost basis under the periodic inventory system according to the specific identification method (p. 352).

9. Under the **specific identification method,** the units of ending inventory can be identified as having come from specific purchases. The flow of costs reflects the actual flow of goods in this case. However, the specific identification method is not practical in most cases.

Objective 3b: Calculate the pricing of inventory, using the cost basis under the periodic inventory system according to the average-cost method (p. 352).

10. Under the **average-cost method,** the average cost per unit is figured for the goods available for sale during the period. That is, the cost of goods available for sale is divided by the units available for sale. Then, the average cost per unit is multiplied by the number of units in ending inventory to get the cost of ending inventory.

Objective 3c: Calculate the pricing of inventory, using the cost basis under the periodic inventory system according to the first-in, first-out (FIFO) method (pp. 352–353).

11. Under the **first-in, first-out (FIFO) method,** the cost of the first items purchased is assigned to the first items sold. Therefore, ending inventory cost is determined from the prices of the most recent purchases. During periods of rising prices, FIFO yields the highest net income of the four methods.

Objective 3d: Calculate the pricing of inventory, using the cost basis under the periodic inventory system according to the last-in, first-out (LIFO) method (pp. 353–354).

12. Under the **last-in, first-out (LIFO) method,** the last items purchased are assumed to be the first items sold. Therefore, the ending inventory cost is determined from the prices of the earliest purchases. During periods of rising prices, LIFO yields the lowest net income of the four methods. However, it best matches current merchandise costs with current sales prices.

Objective 4: Apply the perpetual inventory system to the pricing of inventories at cost (pp. 354–357).

13. When the periodic inventory system is used, a physical inventory is taken at the end of the period, and the cost of goods sold is derived by subtracting ending inventory from the cost of goods available for sale.

14. The perpetual inventory system is used by companies that want more control over their inventories. A continuous record is kept of the balance of each inventory item. As goods are sold, costs are transferred from the Inventory account to Cost of Goods Sold.

15. The perpetual inventory system lends itself to specific identification, average-cost, FIFO, and LIFO calculations. Under specific identification and FIFO, figures for inventory and cost of goods sold should match those under the periodic inventory system. The perpetual LIFO method, though time-consuming to apply manually, is facilitated by the use of computers.

Objective 5: State the effects of inventory methods and misstatements of inventory on income determination and income taxes (pp. 357–362).

16. During periods of rising prices, FIFO produces a higher net income than LIFO During periods of falling prices, the reverse is true. The average-cost method produces net income figures that are somewhere between those of FIFO and LIFO. Because the specific identification method depends on the particular items sold, no generalization can be made about the effect of changing prices. Even though LIFO best follows the matching rule, FIFO provides a more up-to-date ending inventory figure for balance sheet purposes.

17. There are several rules for the valuation of inventory for federal income tax purposes. For example, even though a business has a wide choice of methods, once a method has been chosen, it must be applied consistently. In addition, several regulations apply to LIFO, such as the requirement that LIFO also be used for the accounting records when it is being used for tax purposes.

18. A **LIFO liquidation** occurs when sales have reduced inventories below the levels established in earlier years. When prices have been rising steadily, a LIFO liquidation produces unusually high profits.

19. Beginning inventory plus purchases equals the cost of goods available for sale. The cost of goods sold is determined indirectly by deducting ending inventory from the cost of goods available for sale.

20. Because the cost of ending inventory is needed to compute the cost of goods sold, it affects net income dollar for dollar. It is important to match the cost of goods sold with sales so that net income is reasonably accurate.

21. This year's ending inventory automatically becomes next year's beginning inventory. Because beginning inventory also affects net income dollar for dollar, an error in this year's ending inventory results in misstated net income for both this year and next year.
    a. When ending inventory is understated, net income for the period is understated.
    b. When ending inventory is overstated, net income for the period is overstated.
    c. When beginning inventory is understated, net income for the period is overstated.
    d. When beginning inventory is overstated, net income for the period is understated.

Objective 6: Apply the lower-of-cost-or-market (LCM) rule to inventory valuation (pp. 363–364).

22. The **market** value of inventory (current replacement cost) can fall below its cost as a result of physical deterioration, obsolescence, or decline in price level. Accordingly, it should be valued at the **lower of cost or market (LCM).** The three basic methods of valuing inventory at the lower of cost or market are the **item-by-item method,** the **major category method,** and the **total inventory method.** The total inventory method is not acceptable for federal income tax purposes.

Supplemental Objective 7a: Estimate the cost of ending inventory using the retail inventory method (pp. 364–365).

23. The **retail method** of inventory estimation can be used when the difference between the cost and sale prices of goods is a constant percentage over a period of time. It can be used whether or not the business makes a physical count of goods. To apply the retail method, goods available for sale are figured both at cost and at retail. Next, a cost-to-retail ratio is computed. Sales for the period then are subtracted from goods available for sale at retail, to produce ending inventory at retail. Finally, ending inventory at retail is multiplied by the cost-to-retail ratio to produce an estimate of ending inventory at cost.

Supplemental Objective 7b: Estimate the cost of ending inventory using the gross profit method (pp. 365–366).

24. The **gross profit method** of inventory estimation assumes that the gross margin for a business remains relatively stable from year to year. This method is used when inventory records are lost or destroyed, and when records of beginning inventory and purchases are not kept at retail. To apply the gross profit method, the cost of goods available for sale is determined by adding purchases to beginning inventory. Then, the cost of goods sold is estimated as follows:

$$\text{Sales} \times (1 - \text{gross margin \%})$$

Finally, the estimated cost of goods sold is subtracted from the cost of goods available for sale to arrive at the estimated ending inventory.

TESTING YOUR KNOWLEDGE

Matching

Match each term with its definition by writing the appropriate letter in the blank.

_____ 1. LIFO liquidation

_____ 2. Merchandise inventory

_____ 3. Specific identification method

_____ 4. FIFO method

_____ 5. LIFO method

_____ 6. Average-cost method

_____ 7. Lower of cost or market

_____ 8. Retail method

_____ 9. Gross profit method

_____ 10. Periodic inventory system

_____ 11. Perpetual inventory system

_____ 12. Market

_____ 13. Consignment

a. The inventory method that utilizes an average-cost-per-unit figure
b. The current replacement cost of inventory
c. The inventory estimation method used when inventory is lost or destroyed
d. The inventory method in which the assumed flow of costs matches the actual flow of goods
e. The inventory system that maintains continuous records
f. The rule that governs how inventory should be valued on the financial statements
g. The inventory method that yields the highest ending inventory during periods of rising prices
h. Goods held for sale in the regular course of business
i. The inventory estimation method that uses a cost-to-retail ratio
j. The inventory method that best follows the matching principle
k. An arrangement whereby one company sells goods for another company, for a commission
l. The inventory system that does not maintain continuous records
m. An occurrence that produces unusually high profits under steadily rising prices

Short Answer

Use the lines provided to answer each item.

1. List the four basic cost-flow assumptions used to determine the cost of merchandise inventory.

   _____
   _____
   _____
   _____

2. List the three basic methods of valuing inventory at the lower of cost or market.

   _____
   _____
   _____

3. List two methods of estimating ending inventory.

   _____
   _____

4. Briefly distinguish between the periodic and perpetual inventory systems in terms of recordkeeping and inventory taking.

   _____
   _____
   _____
   _____

True-False

Circle T if the statement is true, F if it is false. Please provide explanations for the false answers, using the blank lines at the end of the section.

T F 1. The figure for inventory turnover is needed to calculate average days' inventory on hand.

T F 2. When beginning inventory is understated, the cost of goods sold for the period also is understated.

T F 3. When ending inventory is overstated, net income for the period also is overstated.

T F 4. An error in 19x1's ending inventory will cause net income to be misstated in both 19x1 and 19x2.

T F 5. Goods in transit belong in the buyer's ending inventory only if the buyer has paid for them.

T F 6. If prices never changed, all four methods of inventory valuation would result in identical net income figures.

T F 7. Under FIFO, goods are sold in exactly the same order as they are purchased.

T F 8. Of the four inventory methods, LIFO results in the lowest income during periods of falling prices.

T F 9. Under the retail method, each item sold must be recorded at both cost and retail.

T F 10. Under the gross profit method, the cost of goods sold is estimated by multiplying the gross profit percentage by sales.

T F 11. A perpetual inventory system does not close out beginning inventory at the end of the period.

T F 12. Under rising prices, the average-cost method results in a lower net income than LIFO does.

T F 13. If FIFO is being used for tax purposes, it must be used for reporting purposes as well.

T F 14. When goods are held on consignment, the consignee has both possession and title until the goods are sold.

Inventories

Multiple Choice

Circle the letter of the best answer.

1. Which of the following is least likely to be included in the cost of inventory?
   a. Freight in
   b. Cost to store goods
   c. Purchase cost of goods
   d. Excise tax on goods purchased

2. Under rising prices, which of the following inventory methods probably results in the highest net income?
   a. FIFO
   b. LIFO
   c. Specific identification
   d. Average-cost

3. Forgetting to inventory the merchandise in a warehouse results in
   a. overstated net income.
   b. overstated total assets.
   c. understated stockholders' equity.
   d. understated cost of goods sold.

4. Which inventory method is best suited for low-volume, high-priced goods?
   a. FIFO
   b. LIFO
   c. Specific identification
   d. Average-cost

5. Which of the following is *not* used or computed in applying the retail inventory method?
   a. Ending inventory at retail
   b. Freight at retail
   c. Beginning inventory at cost
   d. Sales during the period

6. The cost of inventory becomes an expense in the period in which the
   a. inventory is sold.
   b. merchandiser obtains title to the inventory.
   c. merchandiser pays for the inventory.
   d. merchandiser is paid for inventory that it has sold.

7. Goods in transit should be included in the inventory of
   a. neither the buyer nor the seller.
   b. the buyer when the goods have been shipped FOB destination.
   c. the seller when the goods have been shipped FOB shipping point.
   d. the company that has title to the goods.

8. When inventory is valued at the lower of cost or market, the term *market* is defined as
   a. the expected selling price.
   b. the original cost, adjusted for inflation.
   c. current liquidation value.
   d. current replacement cost.

9. Insurance companies often verify the extent of inventory lost or destroyed by applying the
   a. specific identification method.
   b. retail method.
   c. item-by-item method.
   d. gross profit method.

APPLYING YOUR KNOWLEDGE

Exercises

1. Cardoza Company had a beginning inventory of 100 units at $20. The firm made successive purchases as follows:

   Feb. 20 Purchased 200 units at $22
   May 8 Purchased 150 units at $20
   Oct. 17 Purchased 250 units at $24

   Calculate the cost that would be assigned to the ending inventory of 310 units and the cost of goods sold under the following methods (assume a periodic inventory system):

		Cost of Ending Inventory	Cost of Goods Sold
a.	LIFO	$ _____	$ _____
b.	FIFO	$ _____	$ _____
c.	Average-cost	$ _____	$ _____

2. The records of Melton Company show the following data for the month of May:

Sales	$156,000
Beginning inventory, at cost	70,000
Beginning inventory, at retail	125,000
Net purchases, at cost	48,000
Net purchases, at retail	75,000
Freight in	2,000

   Compute the estimated cost of ending inventory using the retail inventory method.

3. At the beginning of the accounting period, the cost of merchandise inventory was $150,000. Net sales during the period were $300,000; net purchases totaled $120,000; and the historical gross margin has been 20 percent. Compute the estimated cost of ending inventory using the gross profit method.

4. Westgate Enterprises uses the perpetual LIFO method for valuing its inventory. On May 1, its inventory consisted of 100 units that cost $10 each. Successive purchases and sales for May were as follows:

   May 4 Purchased 60 units at $12 each
   May 8 Sold 50 units
   May 17 Purchased 70 units at $11 each
   May 25 Sold 100 units

   In the space provided, calculate ending inventory and cost of goods sold.

Inventories

CHAPTER 9 LONG-TERM ASSETS

REVIEWING THE CHAPTER

Objective 1: Identify the types of long-term assets and explain the management issues related to accounting for them (pp. 388–392).

1. **Long-term assets** (also called *fixed assets*) are assets that (a) have a useful life of more than one year, (b) are acquired for use in the operation of the business, and (c) are not intended for resale to customers. Assets such as land and buildings that are not being used in the normal course of business should be classified as long-term investments. Property, plant, and equipment is the balance sheet classification for **tangible assets,** which have physical substance, such as land, buildings, equipment, and **natural resources.** **Intangible assets** is the balance sheet classification for assets that do not have physical substance, such as patents, trademarks, goodwill, copyrights, leaseholds, franchises, and organization costs.

2. The allocation of costs to different accounting periods is called **depreciation** in the case of plant and equipment (plant assets), **depletion** in the case of natural resources, and **amortization** in the case of intangible assets. Because land has an unlimited useful life, its cost never is converted into an expense. The unexpired portion of a plant asset's cost is called **carrying value,** or *book value.* It is calculated by deducting accumulated depreciation from original cost.

3. The decision to acquire long-term assets is called capital budgeting. One common capital budgeting technique compares the amount and timing of cash inflows and outflows over the life of the proposed asset. Information concerning long-term asset acquisitions may be found in the investing activities section of the statement of cash flows.

4. Long-term assets that cannot be purchased for cash must be financed. Common financing techniques include issuing stock, bonds, and long-term notes.

5. In dealing with long-term assets, the major accounting problem is to figure out how much of the asset has benefited the current period, and how much should be carried forward as an asset to benefit future periods. To resolve these issues, one must determine (a) the cost of the asset; (b) the method of matching the cost with revenues; (c) the treatment of subsequent expenditures such as repairs, maintenance, and additions; and (d) the treatment of asset disposal.

Objective 2: Distinguish between capital and revenue expenditures, and account for the cost of property, plant, and equipment (pp. 392–395).

6. Before recording an expenditure in connection with a long-term asset, one must determine whether it was a capital expenditure or a revenue expenditure. **Capital expenditures** are **expenditures** (payments or incurrence of liabilities) for the purchase or expansion of long-term assets. A capital expenditure is recorded as an asset because it will benefit several accounting periods. **Revenue expenditures** are expenditures for repairs, maintenance, fuel, and anything else necessary to maintain and operate the plant and equip-

ment. A **revenue expenditure** is charged as an expense in the period in which it is incurred, under the theory that it benefits only the current accounting period.

7. The cost of a long-term asset includes the purchase cost, freight charges, insurance while in transit, installation, and other costs involved in acquiring the asset and getting it ready for use. Interest incurred during the construction of a plant asset is included in the cost of the asset. However, interest incurred for the purchase of a plant asset is expensed when incurred.

8. When land is purchased, the Land account should be debited for the price paid for the land, real estate commissions, lawyers' fees, and such expenses as back taxes assumed; draining, clearing, and grading costs; assessments for local improvements; and the cost (less salvage value) of tearing down buildings on the property.

9. Land improvements, such as driveways, parking lots, and fences, are subject to depreciation and require a separate Land Improvements account.

10. When long-term assets are purchased for a lump sum, the cost should be divided among the assets acquired in proportion to their appraisal values.

Objective 3: Define *depreciation*, state the factors that affect its computation, and show how to record it (pp. 395–396).

11. *Depreciation,* as used in accounting, refers to the allocation of the cost (less the residual value) of a tangible asset to the periods benefited by the asset. It does not refer to the physical deterioration or the decrease in market value of the asset. That is, it is a process of allocation, not valuation.

12. A tangible asset should be depreciated over its estimated useful life in a systematic and rational manner. Tangible assets have limited useful lives because of **physical deterioration** (limitations resulting from use and exposure to the elements) and **obsolescence** (the process of becoming out of date).

13. Depreciation is computed after the asset's cost, residual value, depreciable cost, and estimated useful life are determined. **Residual value** is the estimated value at the disposal date and often is referred to as *salvage value* or *disposal value.* **Depreciable cost** equals the asset's cost less its residual value. **Estimated useful life** can be measured in time or in units, and requires careful consideration by the accountant.

Objective 4: Compute periodic depreciation under each of three methods (pp. 397–400).

14. The most common depreciation methods are (a) straight-line, (b) production, and (c) declining-balance. The last is described as an accelerated method.

Objective 4a: Compute periodic depreciation under the straight-line method (p. 397).

15. Under the **straight-line method,** the depreciable cost is spread evenly over the life of the asset. Depreciation for each year is computed as follows:

$$\frac{\text{cost} - \text{residual value}}{\text{estimated useful life (years)}}$$

Objective 4b: Compute periodic depreciation under the production method (pp. 397–398).

16. Under the **production method,** depreciation is based not on time but on use of the asset in units. Under this method, depreciation for each year is computed as follows:

$$\frac{\text{cost} - \text{residual value}}{\text{estimated units of useful life}} \times \text{actual units of output}$$

Objective 4c: Compute periodic depreciation under the declining-balance method (pp. 398–399).

17. The declining-balance method is called an **accelerated method** because depreciation is greatest in the first year and decreases each year thereafter. This method is justified by the matching rule (high depreciation charges in the most productive years) and by the smoothing effect that results when annual depreciation and repair expense are combined (that is, over the years, depreciation charges decrease and repair costs increase).

18. Under the **declining-balance method,** depreciation is computed by multiplying the existing carrying value (the unexpired part of the cost) of the asset by a fixed percentage. The **double-declining-balance method** is a form of the declining-balance method that uses a fixed percentage that is twice the straight-line percentage. Under the double-declining-balance method, depreciation for each year is computed as shown on p. 97.

$$2 \times \frac{100\%}{\text{useful life in years}} \times \text{existing carrying value}$$

Under the declining-balance or double-declining-balance method, an asset cannot be depreciated below its residual value.

Objective 5: Account for disposal of depreciable assets not involving exchanges (pp. 401–403).

19. When an asset is still in use after it has been fully depreciated, no more depreciation should be recorded. The asset should not be written off until its disposal. Disposal occurs when the asset is discarded, sold, or traded in.

20. When a business disposes of an asset, depreciation should be recorded for the period preceding disposal. This brings the asset's Accumulated Depreciation account up to the date of disposal.

21. When a machine, for example, is discarded (thrown out), Accumulated Depreciation, Machinery is debited and Machinery is credited for the present balance in the Accumulated Depreciation account. If the machine has not been fully depreciated, then Loss on Disposal of Machinery must be debited for the carrying value to balance the entry.

22. When a machine is sold for cash, Cash is debited, Accumulated Depreciation, Machinery is debited, and Machinery is credited. If the cash received is less than the carrying value of the machine, then Loss on Sale of Machinery also would be debited. On the other hand, if the cash received is greater than the carrying value, then Gain on Sale of Machinery would be credited to balance the entry.

Objective 6: Account for disposal of depreciable assets involving exchanges (pp. 403–406).

23. When an asset is traded in (exchanged) for a similar one, the gain or loss is computed first, as follows:

        Trade-in allowance
    − Carrying value of asset traded in
    = Gain (loss) on trade-in

    a. For financial reporting purposes, both gains and losses should be recognized (recorded) on the exchange of dissimilar assets, and losses should be recognized on the exchange of similar assets. However, gains are not recognized on the exchange of similar assets.

    b. For income tax purposes, neither gains nor losses should be recognized on the exchange of similar assets, but both should be recognized on the exchange of dissimilar assets.

    c. When a gain or loss is recognized, the asset acquired should be debited for its list price—cash paid plus trade-in allowance—using a realistic trade-in value. The old asset is removed from the books, as explained in paragraph 22.

    d. When a gain or loss is not recognized, the asset acquired should be debited for the carrying value of the asset traded in plus cash paid (this results in the nonrecognition of the gain or loss).

Objective 7: Identify natural resource accounting issues and compute depletion (pp. 406–408).

24. Natural resources, or *wasting assets,* are tangible assets in the form of valuable substances that can be cut, pumped, or mined and sold. They include standing timber, oil and gas fields, and mineral deposits.

25. *Depletion* refers both to the exhaustion of the resource and to the allocation of a natural resource's cost to accounting periods based on the amount extracted in each period. Depletion for each year is computed as follows:

$$\frac{\text{cost} - \text{residual value}}{\text{estimated units available}} \times \text{units extracted during period}$$

Units extracted but not sold in one year are recorded as inventory, to be charged as an expense in the year they are sold.

26. Assets that are acquired in conjunction with the natural resource, and that cannot be used after the natural resource is depleted, should be depreciated on the same basis as depletion is computed.

27. In accounting for the exploration and development of oil and gas resources, two methods have been used. Under **successful efforts accounting,** the cost of a dry well is written off immediately as a loss. The **full-costing** method, on the other hand, capitalizes and depletes the costs of both successful and dry wells. Both methods are in accordance with GAAP.

Objective 8: Apply the matching rule to intangible assets, including research and development costs and goodwill (pp. 408–413).

28. Intangible assets are long-term assets that have no physical substance. They represent certain rights and advantages to their owner. Examples of intangible assets are patents, copyrights, trademarks, goodwill, leaseholds, leasehold improvements, franchises, licenses, brand names, formulas, and processes. An intangible asset should be written off over its useful life (not to exceed 40 years) through amortization. This is to be accomplished by a direct reduction of the asset account and an increase in amortization expense.
    a. A **patent** is an exclusive right granted by the federal government for a period of 17 years to make a particular product or use a specific process.
    b. A **copyright** is an exclusive right granted by the federal government to the possessor to publish and sell literary, musical, and other artistic materials (includes computer programs) for a period of the author's life plus 50 years.
    c. A **leasehold** is a right to occupy land or buildings under a long-term rental contract.
    d. **Leasehold improvements** are improvements to leased property that become the property of the lessor at the end of the lease.
    e. A **trademark** is a registered symbol that gives the holder the right to use it to identify a product or service.
    f. A **brand name** is a registered name that gives the holder the right to use it to identify a product or service.
    g. A **franchise** is the right to an exclusive territory or market.
    h. A **license** is official or legal permission to do or own a specific thing.
    i. **Goodwill** is the excess of the cost of a group of assets (usually a business) over the fair market value of the assets individually.

29. Research and development involve developing new products, testing existing ones, and doing pure research. According to GAAP, the costs associated with these activities should be charged as expenses in the period incurred.

30. The cost to develop computer software should be treated as research and development up to the point that a product is deemed technologically feasible (i.e., when a detailed working program has been designed). At that point, software production costs should be capitalized and amortized over the useful life of the software, using the straight-line method.

31. *Goodwill,* as the term is used in accounting, refers to a company's ability to earn more than is normal for its particular industry. Goodwill should be recorded only when a company is purchased. It equals the excess of the purchase cost over the fair market value of the net assets if purchased separately. Once it is recorded, goodwill should be amortized over its estimated useful life, not to exceed 40 years.

Supplemental Objective 9: Apply depreciation methods to problems of partial years, revised rates, groups of similar items, special types of capital expenditures, and cost recovery (pp. 413–417).

32. When an asset is purchased after the beginning of the year or discarded before the end of the year, depreciation should be recorded for only part of the year. The accountant figures the year's depreciation and multiplies this figure by the fraction of the year that the asset was in use.

33. Often, the estimated useful life or residual value is found to be over- or understated after some depreciation has been taken. The accountant then must produce a revised figure for the remaining useful life or remaining depreciable cost. Future depreciation then is calculated by spreading the remaining depreciable cost over the remaining useful life, leaving previous depreciation unchanged.

34. When a company has several plant assets that are similar, it probably uses **group depreciation** rather than individual depreciation. Under group depreciation, the original costs of all similar assets are lumped together in one summary account. Then, depreciation is figured for the assets as a whole.

35. Businesses make capital expenditures for plant assets, natural resources, and intangible assets. Capital expenditures also include **additions** (such as a building wing) and **betterments** (such as the installation of an air-conditioning system).

36. **Ordinary repairs** are expenditures necessary to maintain an asset in good operating condition. They are charged as expenses in the period in which they are incurred. **Extraordinary repairs** are expenditures that either increase an asset's residual value or lengthen its useful life. They are recorded by debiting Accumulated Depreciation and crediting Cash or Accounts Payable.

37. Under the **Modified Accelerated Cost Recovery System (MACRS)** each depreciable asset is

placed in a category for tax purposes only and depreciated according to percentages and over a period of years established by Congress; estimated useful life and residual value are ignored. MACRS depreciation allows the rapid write-off of tangible assets to reduce current taxes but normally is not acceptable for financial reporting purposes. For example, most property other than real estate is depreciated by a 200 percent declining-balance method. Recovery of the cost of property placed in service after December 31, 1986, is calculated according to MACRS for tax purposes.

Summary of Journal Entries Introduced in Chapter 9

A. (L.O. 3) Depreciation Expense, Asset Name   XX (amount allocated)
        Accumulated Depreciation, Asset Name   XX (amount allocated)
           To record depreciation for the period (reminder of entry introduced in Chapter 3)

B. (L.O. 5) Depreciation Expense, Machinery   XX (amount allocated)
        Accumulated Depreciation, Machinery   XX (amount allocated)
           To record depreciation up to date of disposal

C. (L.O. 5) Accumulated Depreciation, Machinery   XX (existing balance)
        Loss on Disposal of Machinery   XX (carrying value)
           Machinery   XX (purchase price)
           Discarded machine no longer used in the business

D. (L.O. 5) Cash   XX (proceeds on sale)
        Accumulated Depreciation, Machinery   XX (existing balance)
           Machinery   XX (purchase price)
           Sale of machine for carrying value; no gain or loss

E. (L.O. 5) Cash   XX (proceeds on sale)
        Accumulated Depreciation, Machinery   XX (existing balance)
        Loss on Sale of Machinery   XX (CV minus cash)
           Machinery   XX (purchase price)
           Sale of machine at less than carrying value (CV); loss recorded

F. (L.O. 5) Cash   XX (proceeds on sale)
        Accumulated Depreciation, Machinery   XX (existing balance)
           Gain on Sale of Machinery   XX (cash minus CV)
           Machinery   XX (purchase price)
           Sale of machine at more than the carrying value (CV); gain recorded

G. (L.O. 6) Regarding the topic of exchanges of plant assets, the journal entries are all very similar (see entry H). The amounts, however, depend on a variety of factors, among them the similarity of assets exchanged and the purpose of the entry (financial accounting or income tax). In addition, gains and losses sometimes are recognized, sometimes not. Please see the textbook for a thorough explanation.

H. (L.O. 6)	Machinery (new)	XX (see text)
	Accumulated Depreciation, Machinery	XX (existing balance)
	Machinery (old)	XX (purchase price)
	Cash	XX (payment required)
	Exchange of machines—cost of old machine and its accumulated depreciation removed from the records, and new machine recorded at list price. (Note: If gain or loss must be recognized, it would be credited or debited, respectively.)	
I. (L.O. 7)	Depletion Expense, Coal Deposits	XX (amount allocated)
	Accumulated Depletion, Coal Deposits	XX (amount allocated)
	To record depletion of coal mine	
J. (L.O. 8)	Patent	XX (purchase price)
	Cash	XX (purchase price)
	Purchase of patent (Note: The debit could have been made to trademarks, copyrights, etc.)	
K. (L.O. 8)	Amortization Expense	XX (amount allocated)
	Patent	XX (amount allocated)
	Annual amortization of patent	
L. (L.O. 8)	Loss on patent	XX (carrying value)
	Patent	XX (carrying value)
	Loss resulting from patent's becoming worthless	
M. (S.O. 9)	Capital expenditures typically are debited to an asset account (such as Buildings or Equipment), and revenue expenditures typically are debited to an expense account (such as Repair Expense). An exception to these rules is for extraordinary repairs, as shown in N.	
N. (S.O. 9)	Accumulated Depreciation, Machinery	XX (amount of repair)
	Cash	XX (amount of repair)
	Extraordinary repair to machinery	

TESTING YOUR KNOWLEDGE

Matching

Match each term with its definition by writing the appropriate letter in the blank.

____ 1. Long-term assets (fixed assets)
____ 2. Depreciation
____ 3. Obsolescence
____ 4. Franchise
____ 5. Residual value (salvage or disposal value)
____ 6. Accelerated method
____ 7. Straight-line method
____ 8. Production method
____ 9. Full costing
____ 10. Double-declining-balance method
____ 11. Group depreciation
____ 12. Natural resources
____ 13. Depletion
____ 14. Amortization
____ 15. Modified Accelerated Cost Recovery System (MACRS)
____ 16. Capital expenditure
____ 17. Revenue expenditure
____ 18. Patent
____ 19. Copyright
____ 20. Leasehold
____ 21. Trademark
____ 22. Successful efforts accounting

a. The exclusive right to sell a particular product or use a specific process for 17 years
b. Using one depreciation rate for several similar items
c. The allocation of an intangible asset's cost to the periods benefited by the asset
d. Payment for the right to use property
e. Assets to be used in the business for more than one year
f. The allocation of the cost of a tangible asset to the periods benefited by the asset
g. An expenditure for services needed to maintain and operate plant assets (an expense)
h. The depreciation method under which cost allocation is based on units, not time
i. The exclusive right to publish literary, musical, or artistic materials or computer programs for the author's life plus 50 years
j. The accelerated depreciation method based on twice the straight-line rate
k. A depreciation method used for tax purposes only
l. The estimated value of an asset on the disposal date
m. An expenditure for the purchase or expansion of long-term assets (an asset)
n. One reason for an asset's limited useful life
o. Assets in the form of valuable substances that can be extracted and sold
p. An identifying symbol or name for a product or service that can be used only by its owner
q. The method of accounting for oil and gas that immediately writes off the cost of dry wells
r. The depreciation method that charges equal depreciation each year
s. The exclusive right to sell a product within a certain territory
t. The practice of charging the highest depreciation in the first year and decreasing depreciation each year thereafter
u. The allocation of a natural resource's cost to the periods over which the resource is consumed
v. The method of accounting for oil and gas that capitalizes the cost of dry wells

Short Answer

Use the lines provided to answer each item.

1. Distinguish between an addition and a betterment.

2. When a plant asset is sold for cash, under what unique circumstance would no gain or loss be recorded?

3. List four pieces of information necessary to compute the depletion expense of an oil well for a given year.

4. Distinguish between an ordinary and an extraordinary repair.

5. For each asset category, provide the accounting term for the allocation of its cost to the periods benefited.

Category	Term for Cost Allocation
Intangible assets	
Plant and equipment	
Natural resources	

6. Plant assets have limited useful lives for two reasons. What are they?

True-False

Circle T if the statement is true, F if it is false. Please provide explanations for the false answers, using the blank lines at the end of the section.

T F 1. Land is not subject to depreciation.

T F 2. The loss recorded on a discarded asset is equal to the carrying value of the asset at the time it is discarded.

T F 3. Land held for speculative reasons is not classified as property, plant, and equipment.

T F 4. Depreciation is a process of valuation, not allocation.

T F 5. Depreciation for a machine can be calculated by having an appraiser determine to what extent the machine has worn out.

T F 6. When land is purchased for use as a plant site, its cost should include the cost of clearing and draining the land.

T F 7. Each type of depreciable asset should have its own accumulated depreciation account.

T F 8. Estimated useful life in years is irrelevant when applying the production method of depreciation.

T F 9. Under the straight-line method, if depreciation expense is $1,000 in the first year, it will be $2,000 in the second year.

T F 10. When the estimated useful life of an asset is revised after some depreciation has been taken, the accountant should not go back to previous years to make corrections.

T F 11. For financial accounting purposes, both gains and losses on the exchange of dissimilar assets are recognized in the accounting records.

T F 12. In an asset's last year of depreciation, accelerated depreciation results in less net income than does straight-line depreciation.

T F 13. Depreciable cost equals cost minus accumulated depreciation.

T F 14. Under the double-declining-balance method, the carrying value of an asset equals zero at the end of its estimated useful life if no residual value has been assumed.

T F 15. Estimated useful life and residual value are ignored when applying MACRS depreciation.

T F 16. A copyright is a name or symbol that can be used only by its owner.

T F 17. If, by mistake, ordinary maintenance is capitalized instead of being charged as an expense, net income for the period would be overstated.

T F 18. A betterment is an example of a revenue expenditure.

T F 19. Recording an extraordinary repair leaves the carrying value of the asset unchanged.

T F 20. When a machine is sold for less than its carrying value, one of the debits is to Loss on Sale of Machinery and one of the credits is to Accumulated Depreciation, Machinery.

T F 21. *Capital expenditure* is another term for expense.

T F 22. For income tax purposes, neither gains nor losses are recognized on the exchange of similar plant assets.

T F 23. When a plant asset is sold during a year, depreciation expense need not be brought up to date and recorded.

T F 24. In determining the number of years over which to amortize intangible assets, useful life is far more important than legal life.

T F 25. As accumulated depreciation increases, carrying value decreases.

T F 26. Goodwill should not be recorded unless it has been purchased.

T F 27. Research and development costs should be capitalized when they can be associated with a specific new product.

T F 28. The full-costing method capitalizes the cost of both successful and dry wells.

Long-Term Assets

Multiple Choice

Circle the letter of the best answer.

1. A building and land are purchased for a lump-sum payment of $66,000. How much should be allocated to land if the land is appraised at $20,000 and the building at $60,000?
   a. $22,000
   b. $20,000
   c. $16,500
   d. $13,750

2. The expired cost of a plant asset is called its
   a. accumulated depreciation.
   b. carrying value.
   c. depreciable cost.
   d. residual value.

3. Which depreciation method, when applied to an asset in its first year of use, results in the greatest depreciation charge?
   a. Declining-balance
   b. Production
   c. Straight-line
   d. Impossible to determine without more information

4. When a certain machine was purchased, its estimated useful life was 20 years. However, after it had been depreciated for 5 years, the company decided that it originally had overestimated the machine's useful life by 3 years. What should be done?
   a. Go back and adjust depreciation for the first 5 years.
   b. Depreciate the remainder of the depreciable cost over the next 15 years.
   c. Depreciate the remainder of the depreciable cost over the next 12 years.
   d. Both *a* and *b*

5. According to GAAP, intangible assets should never be amortized over more than
   a. 5 years.
   b. 17 years.
   c. 40 years.
   d. 50 years.

6. Land improvements
   a. should be included in the cost of land.
   b. are subject to depreciation.
   c. should be deducted from the cost of land.
   d. should be charged as an expense in the year purchased.

7. A machine that cost $9,000 with a carrying value of $2,000 is sold for $1,700, and an entry is made. Which of the following is true about the entry?
   a. Accumulated Depreciation is debited for $2,000.
   b. Machinery is credited for $2,000.
   c. Loss on Sale of Machinery is credited for $300.
   d. Accumulated Depreciation is debited for $7,000.

8. Which of the following is *not* a revenue expenditure?
   a. Ordinary maintenance of a machine
   b. Replacing an old roof with a new one
   c. The installation of new light bulbs
   d. A tire repair on a company truck

9. Charging a depreciable item as an expense, instead of capitalizing it, results in
   a. overstated total assets.
   b. understated net income for the succeeding period.
   c. overstated depreciation expense for the succeeding period.
   d. understated net income for the period.

10. Overestimating the number of barrels that can be pumped from an oil well over its lifetime results in
    a. understating net income each year.
    b. understating depletion cost per unit each year.
    c. overstating depletion expense each year.
    d. understating total assets each year.

11. The cost of developing computer software should be
    a. expensed up to the point that the product is technologically feasible.
    b. capitalized in its entirety and amortized over 40 years.
    c. expensed once the product is deemed to be technologically feasible.
    d. expensed in its entirety when incurred.

12. Which of the following normally is charged as an expense in the period of expenditure?
    a. Goodwill
    b. Leaseholds
    c. Leasehold improvements
    d. Research and development costs

APPLYING YOUR KNOWLEDGE

Exercises

1. A machine that cost $26,000 had an estimated useful life of five years and a residual value of $2,000 when purchased on January 1, 19x1. Fill in the amount of depreciation expense for 19x2, as well as the accumulated depreciation and carrying value of the machine as of December 31, 19x2, under both of the listed methods.

	Depreciation Expense for 19x2	Accumulated Depreciation as of 12/31/x2	Carrying Value as of 12/31/x2
a. Straight-line	$ _____	$ _____	$ _____
b. Double-declining-balance	$ _____	$ _____	$ _____

2. A machine that was to produce a certain type of toy was purchased for $35,000 on April 30, 19xx. The machine was expected to produce 100,000 toys during the ten years that the company expected to keep the machine. The company estimated that it then could sell the machine for $5,000. Using the production method, calculate the depreciation expense in 19xx, when the machine produced 7,500 toys.

3. Classify each of the following expenditures as a capital or revenue expenditure by placing a C or an R next to each item.
   _____ a. Replacement of the roof on a building
   _____ b. Replacement of the battery in a company vehicle
   _____ c. The cost of painting the executive offices
   _____ d. Installation of aluminum siding on a building
   _____ e. Replacement of the motor in a machine
   _____ f. The cost to repair an air-conditioning unit
   _____ g. The cost to install a piece of machinery
   _____ h. The addition of a building wing
   _____ i. The tune-up of a company vehicle

4. On January 1, 19xx, Bristol Enterprises traded in, along with $15,500 in cash, a machine that cost $25,000 and had a carrying value of $8,000, for a new machine with a retail price of $23,000. The machines are similar in nature. Prepare the journal entry that Bristol would make to conform to GAAP, as well as the entry that would conform to income tax rulings. Use the journal provided.

	General Journal		
Date	Description	Debit	Credit

5. In 19xx, National Coal Company purchased a coal mine for $800,000. It is estimated that 2 million tons of coal can be extracted from the mine. In the space provided, prepare National's adjusting entry for December 31, 19xx, to reflect the extraction and sale of 100,000 tons during the year.

	General Journal		
Date	Description	Debit	Credit

Crossword Puzzle
for Chapters 8 and 9

ACROSS

2. Residual (value)
4. Allocate the cost of a natural resource
8. Improvement to plant assets
10. _____ -balance method
15. Trade in
16. _____ profit method
17. Just-in-_____ operating environment
18. Inventory estimation technique
19. Inventory method

DOWN

1. Tax depreciation method
3. Allocate the cost of an intangible asset
5. Intangible with a 17-year life
6. Possessing physical substance
7. Allocate the cost of plant assets
9. (Goods) sold by one for another
10. Sale, trade-in, or abandonment
11. Asset not subject to allocation process
12. _____ life
13. The "C" of MACRS
14. Inventory valuation rule (abbr.)

Long-Term Assets

CHAPTER 10 CURRENT LIABILITIES AND THE TIME VALUE OF MONEY

REVIEWING THE CHAPTER

Objective 1: Identify the management issues related to recognition, valuation, classification, and disclosure of current liabilities (pp. 439–442).

1. **Liabilities** are one of the three major parts of the balance sheet. They are present obligations for either the future payment of assets or the future performance of services. The primary reason for incurring current liabilities is to meet needs for cash during the operating cycle. Management must carefully manage the cash flows related to current liabilities; the appropriate level of liabilities is critical to business success. A liability generally should be recorded when an obligation arises, but it is also necessary to make end-of-period adjustments for accrued and estimated liabilities. On the other hand, contracts representing future obligations are not recorded as liabilities until they become current obligations.

2. Liabilities are valued at the actual or estimated amount due, or at the fair market value of goods or services that must be delivered.

3. **Current liabilities** are present obligations that are expected to be satisfied within one year or the normal operating cycle, whichever is longer. Payment is expected to be out of current assets or by taking on another current liability. **Long-term liabilities** are obligations that are not expected to be satisfied in the current period.

4. Supplemental disclosure of liabilities may be required in the notes to the financial statements. An explanation of special credit arrangements, for example, can be very helpful to the financial statement user.

Objective 2: Identify, compute, and record definitely determinable and estimated current liabilities (pp. 442–452).

5. Current liabilities consist of definitely determinable liabilities and estimated liabilities.

6. **Definitely determinable liabilities** are obligations that can be measured exactly. They include accounts payable, short-term notes payable, dividends payable, sales and excise taxes payable, current portions of long-term debt, accrued liabilities, payroll liabilities, and unearned or deferred revenues.
    a. Accounts payable, sometimes called trade accounts payable, are current obligations due to suppliers of goods and services.
    b. Companies often obtain a **line of credit** from a bank in order to finance operations. In addition, a company may borrow short-term funds by issuing **commercial paper** (unsecured loans sold to the public).
    c. Short-term notes payable are current obligations evidenced by promissory notes. Interest may be either stated separately or included in the face amount. In the latter case, the actual amount borrowed is less than the face amount.
    d. Accrued liabilities are actual or estimated liabilities that exist at the balance sheet date but are unrecorded. An end-of-period adjust-

ment is needed to record both the expenses and the accrued liabilities.
e. Dividends payable is an obligation to distribute the earnings of a corporation to its stockholders. It arises only when the board of directors declares a dividend.
f. Most states and many cities levy a sales tax on retail transactions. The federal government also charges an excise tax on some products. The merchant must collect the taxes at the time of the sale and would record both the receipt of cash and the proper tax liabilities.
g. If a portion of long-term debt is due within the next year and is to be paid from current assets, then this amount should be classified as a current liability; the remaining debt should be classified as a long-term liability.
h. Payroll liabilities consist of the employee-related obligations incurred by a business. Not only is the business responsible for paying **wages,** paid at an hourly rate, and **salaries,** paid at a monthly or yearly rate, earned by its employees, it is obligated for such items as social security taxes, Medicare, and unemployment taxes. It is also liable for amounts withheld from its employees' gross earnings that must be remitted to government and other agencies.
i. **Unearned revenues** represent obligations to deliver goods or services in return for advance payment. When delivery takes place, Unearned Revenue is debited and a revenue account is credited.

7. **Estimated liabilities** are definite obligations. However, the amount of the obligation must be estimated at the balance sheet date because the exact figure will not be known until a future date. Examples of estimated liabilities are income taxes, property taxes, product warranties, and vacation pay.
a. A corporation's income tax depends on its net income, a figure that often is not determined until well after the balance sheet date.
b. Property taxes are taxes levied on real and personal property. Very often a company's accounting period ends before property taxes have been assessed. Therefore, the company must make an estimate. The debit is to Property Taxes Expense, and the credit is to Estimated Property Taxes Payable.
c. When a company sells its products, many of the warranties will still be in effect during the next accounting period. However, the war-

ranty expense and liability must be recorded in the period of the sale no matter when the company makes good on the warranty. Therefore, at the end of each accounting period, the company should make an estimate of future warranty expense that will apply to the present period's sales.
d. In most companies, employees earn vacation pay for working a certain length of time. Therefore, the company must estimate the vacation pay that applies to each payroll period. The debit is to Vacation Pay Expense, and the credit is to Estimated Liability for Vacation Pay.

Objective 3: Define *contingent liability* **(pp. 452–453).**

8. A **contingent liability** is a potential liability that may or may not become an actual liability. The uncertainty about its outcome is settled when a future event does or does not occur. Contingent liabilities arise from things like pending lawsuits, tax disputes, discounted notes receivable, the guarantee of another company's debt, and failure to follow government regulations.

Objective 4: Define *interest* **and distinguish between simple and compound interest (pp. 453–455).**

9. The timing of the receipt and payment of cash (measured in interest) should be a consideration in making business decisions. **Interest** is the cost of using money for a specific period of time, and may be calculated on a simple or compounded basis.
a. When **simple interest** is computed for two or more periods, the amount on which interest is computed does not increase each period (that is, interest is not computed on accrued interest).
b. However, when **compound interest** is computed for two or more periods, the amount on which interest is computed *does* increase each period (that is, interest is computed on accrued interest).

Objective 5: Use compound interest tables to compute the future value of a single invested sum at compound interest and of an ordinary annuity (pp. 455–457).

10. **Future value** is the amount that an investment will be worth at a future date if invested at compound interest.

a. Future value may be computed on a single sum invested at compound interest. Table G-1 of your text facilitates this computation.
b. Future value may also be computed on an **ordinary annuity** (that is, a series of equal payments made at the end of equal intervals of time) at compound interest. Table G-2 of your text facilitates this computation.

Objective 6: Use compound interest tables to compute the present value of a single sum due in the future and of an ordinary annuity (pp. 457–463).

11. **Present value** is the amount that must be invested now at a given rate of interest to produce a given future value or values.
    a. Present value may be computed on a single sum due in the future. Table G-3 of your text facilitates this computation.
    b. Present value may also be computed on an ordinary annuity. Table G-4 of your text facilitates this computation.

12. All four tables may facilitate both annual compounding and compounding for less than a year. For example, when computing 12 percent annual interest that is compounded quarterly, one would refer to the 3 percent column for four periods per year.

Objective 7: Apply the concept of present value to simple accounting situations (pp. 463–467).

13. Present value may be used in accounting to (a) impute interest on non-interest-bearing notes, (b) determine the value of an asset being considered for purchase, (c) account for assets purchased on deferred payment plans, (d) assist in the investment of idle cash, (e) calculate amounts that will accumulate in a fund, and (f) determine numerous other accounting quantities, such as pension obligations and depreciation.

Summary of Journal Entries Introduced in Chapter 10

A. (L.O. 2) Cash . . . . XX (amount received)
       Notes Payable . . . . XX (face amount)
          To record promissory note with interest stated separately

B. (L.O. 2) Notes Payable . . . . XX (face amount)
       Interest Expense . . . . XX (amount incurred)
          Cash . . . . XX (maturity amount)
          Payment of note with interest stated separately

C. (L.O. 2) Interest Expense . . . . XX (amount accrued)
       Interest Payable . . . . XX (amount accrued)
          To record interest expense on note with interest stated separately

D. (L.O. 2) Cash . . . . XX (face amount minus interest)
       Discount on Notes Payable . . . . XX (interest in face amount)
          Notes Payable . . . . XX (face amount)
          To record promissory note with interest included in face amount

E. (L.O. 2) Notes Payable . . . . XX (face amount)
       Cash . . . . XX (face amount)
          Payment of note with interest included in face amount (see also F below)

F. (L.O. 2) Interest Expense . . . . XX (amount incurred)
       Discount on Notes Payable . . . . XX (amount incurred)
          Interest expense on matured note

G. (L.O. 2) Interest Expense . . . . XX (amount accrued)
       Discount on Notes Payable . . . . XX (amount accrued)
          To record interest expense on note with interest included in face amount

H. (L.O. 2) Cash . . . . XX (amount collected)
       Sales . . . . XX (price charged)
       Sales Tax Payable . . . . XX (amount to remit)
       Excise Tax Payable . . . . XX (amount to remit)
          Sale of merchandise and collection of sales and excise taxes

I. (L.O. 2) Wages Expense . . . . XX (gross amount)
       Employees' Federal Income Taxes Payable . . . . XX (amount withheld)
       Employees' State Income Taxes Payable . . . . XX (amount withheld)
       Social Security Taxes Payable . . . . XX (employees' share)
       Medicare Taxes Payable . . . . XX (employees' share)
       Medical Insurance Payable . . . . XX (employees' share)
       Pension Contributions Payable . . . . XX (employees' share)
       Wages Payable . . . . XX (take-home pay)
          To record payroll

J.	(L.O. 2) Payroll Expense	XX	(total employer payroll taxes)
	Social Security Taxes Payable	XX	(employer's share)
	Medicare Taxes Payable	XX	(employer's share)
	Medical Insurance Payable	XX	(employer's share)
	Pension Contributions Payable	XX	(employer's share)
	Federal Unemployment Taxes Payable	XX	(amount incurred)
	State Unemployment Taxes Payable	XX	(amount incurred)
	To record payroll taxes and other costs		
K.	(L.O. 2) Cash	XX	(amount prepaid)
	Unearned Subscriptions	XX	(amount to earn)
	Receipt of annual subscriptions in advance		
L.	(L.O. 2) Unearned Subscriptions	XX	(amount earned)
	Subscription Revenues	XX	(amount earned)
	Delivery of monthly magazine issues		
M.	(L.O. 2) Federal Income Tax Expense	XX	(amount incurred)
	Federal Income Tax Payable	XX	(amount to be paid)
	To record estimated federal income taxes		
N.	(L.O. 2) Property Taxes Expense	XX	(amount incurred)
	Estimated Property Taxes Payable	XX	(amount to be paid)
	To record estimated property taxes		
O.	(L.O. 2) Estimated Property Taxes Payable	XX	(amount incurred)
	Prepaid Property Taxes	XX	(amount to incur)
	Cash	XX	(amount paid)
	Payment of property taxes		
P.	(L.O. 2) Product Warranty Expense	XX	(estimated amount)
	Estimated Product Warranty Liability	XX	(estimated amount)
	To record estimated product warranty expense		
Q.	(L.O. 2) Cash	XX	(fee charged)
	Estimated Product Warranty Liability	XX	(cost of part)
	Service Revenue	XX	(fee charged)
	Merchandise Inventory	XX	(cost of part)
	Replacement of part under warranty		
R.	(L.O. 2) Vacation Pay Expense	XX	(amount earned)
	Estimated Liability for Vacation Pay	XX	(amount earned)
	Estimated vacation pay expense		
S.	(L.O. 2) Estimated Liability for Vacation Pay	XX	(amount taken)
	Cash (or Wages Payable)	XX	(amount paid or to pay)
	Wages of employees on vacation		
T.	(L.O. 7) Purchases	XX	(present value of note)
	Discount on Notes Payable	XX	(imputed interest)
	Notes Payable	XX	(face amount)
	Purchase of merchandise		

Current Liabilities and the Time Value of Money

U. (L.O. 7) Interest Expense   XX (amount accrued)
           Discount on Notes Payable   XX (amount accrued)
               Interest expense for one year (see T above)

V. (L.O. 7) Interest Expense   XX (interest for period)
           Notes Payable   XX (face amount)
               Discount on Notes Payable   XX (interest for period)
               Cash   XX (face amount)
               Payment of note (see T above)

W. (L.O. 7) Notes Receivable   XX (face amount)
           Discount on Notes Receivable   XX (imputed interest)
           Sales   XX (present value of note)
               Sale of merchandise

X. (L.O. 7) Discount on Notes Receivable   XX (amount accrued)
           Interest Income   XX (amount accrued)
               Interest income for one year (see W above)

Y. (L.O. 7) Discount on Notes Receivable   XX (interest for period)
           Cash   XX (face amount of note)
               Interest Income   XX (interest for period)
               Notes Receivable   XX (face amount)
               Payment of note (see W above)

Z. (L.O. 7) Tractor   XX (present value of payment)
           Accounts Payable   XX (present value of payment)
               Purchase of tractor

AA. (L.O. 7) Accounts Payable   XX (present value of payment)
            Interest Expense   XX (imputed amount)
                Cash   XX (amount paid)
                Payment on account including imputed interest
                expense (see Z above)

BB. (L.O. 7) Accounts Receivable   XX (present value of payment)
            Sales   XX (present value of payment)
                Sale of tractor

CC. (L.O. 7) Cash   XX (amount received)
            Accounts Receivable   XX (present value of payment)
            Interest Income   XX (imputed amount)
                Receipt on account including imputed interest
                earned (see BB above)

DD. (L.O. 7) Short-Term Investments   XX (amount invested)
            Cash   XX (amount invested)
                Investment of cash

EE. (L.O. 7) Short-Term Investments   XX (interest for month)
            Interest Income   XX (interest for month)
                Interest income for period

FF. (L.O. 7) Loan Repayment Fund   XX (amount contributed)
            Cash   XX (amount contributed)
                Annual contribution to loan repayment fund

TESTING YOUR KNOWLEDGE

Matching

Match each term with its definition by writing the appropriate letter in the blank.

___ 1. Current liabilities
___ 2. Long-term liabilities
___ 3. Definitely determinable liabilities
___ 4. Estimated liabilities
___ 5. Contingent liabilities
___ 6. Unearned revenues
___ 7. Vacation pay
___ 8. Interest
___ 9. Simple interest
___ 10. Compound interest
___ 11. Future value
___ 12. Present value
___ 13. Ordinary annuity
___ 14. Line of credit
___ 15. Commercial paper

a. The amount that must be invested now to produce a given future value
b. Unsecured loans sold to the public
c. The computation whereby interest is computed without considering accrued interest
d. Obligations that exist but cannot be precisely measured at the balance sheet date
e. A series of equal payments made at the end of each period
f. Obligations that can be precisely measured
g. The cost of using money for a specific period of time
h. The amount an investment will be worth at a future date
i. An arrangement with the bank that allows a company to borrow funds when needed
j. The computation whereby interest is computed on the original amount plus accrued interest
k. Obligations that are not expected to be satisfied in the current period
l. Potential liabilities that may or may not become actual liabilities
m. Obligations to deliver goods or services in return for advance payment
n. Obligations that are expected to be satisfied within one year or the normal operating cycle, whichever is longer
o. Compensation received during one's earned time off

Short Answer

Use the lines provided to answer each item.

1. Current liabilities fall into two principal categories. What are they?

2. Give three examples of contingent liabilities.

3. Give three examples of estimated liabilities.

4. Give three examples of definitely determinable liabilities.

5. List four withholdings from an employee's salary that are always or almost always required.

6. List the four components of payroll taxes expense.

True-False

Circle T if the statement is true, F if it is false. Please provide explanations for the false answers, using the blank lines at the end of the section.

T F 1. Unearned revenues can be found on the income statement.

T F 2. A contract to purchase goods in the future does not require the recording of a current liability.

T F 3. Failure to record an accrued liability will result in an overstatement of net income.

T F 4. The current portion of a long-term debt is a current liability (assume that it is to be satisfied with cash).

T F 5. Sales Tax Payable is an example of an estimated liability.

T F 6. Warranties fall into the category of definitely determinable liabilities.

T F 7. The multipliers incorporated into the "present value of a single sum to be received in the future" table are all less than 1.000.

T F 8. An ordinary annuity is a series of equal payments made at the beginning of equal intervals of time.

T F 9. The higher the interest rate applied, the higher the present value of an amount or annuity to be received in the future.

T F 10. Every contingent liability must eventually become an actual liability or no liability at all.

T F 11. The account Discount on Notes Payable is associated with notes whose interest is stated separately on the face of the note.

Current Liabilities and the Time Value of Money

T F 12. If a refrigerator is sold in year 1 and repairs are made in year 2, Product Warranty Expense should be recorded in year 2.

T F 13. When the payroll is recorded, Wages Payable is credited for gross earnings.

T F 14. Social security taxes are borne by both the employer and employee.

T F 15. Typically, unemployment taxes are a component of Payroll Taxes Expense.

Multiple Choice

Circle the letter of the best answer.

1. Which of the following is not a definitely determinable liability?
   a. Dividends payable
   b. Deferred revenues
   c. Property taxes payable
   d. Excise tax payable

2. Estimated liabilities would not apply to
   a. warranties.
   b. vacation pay.
   c. a corporation's income tax.
   d. pending lawsuits.

3. When an employee receives vacation pay, the company should
   a. debit Vacation Pay Expense and credit Cash.
   b. debit Vacation Pay Receivable and credit Cash.
   c. debit Estimated Liability for Vacation Pay and credit Cash.
   d. debit Vacation Pay Expense and credit Estimated Liability for Vacation Pay.

4. A company that uses a calendar year receives a property tax bill each March (for that particular calendar year), to be paid by April 10. If entries are made at the end of each month to record property tax expense, the April 10 entry to record payment would include a
   a. debit to Cash.
   b. credit to Estimated Property Taxes Payable.
   c. debit to Property Taxes Expense.
   d. debit to Prepaid Property Taxes.

5. Compound interest is computed semiannually on $100 in the bank for five years at 10 percent annual interest. The future value table is used by multiplying the $100 by which multiplier?
   a. 5 periods at 10 percent
   b. 10 periods at 5 percent
   c. 10 periods at 10 percent
   d. 5 periods at 5 percent

Use the following present value information to answer Questions 6 and 7.

Period	Present Value of $1 Discounted at 12% Per Period
1	0.893
2	0.797

6. What amount should be deposited in a bank today at 12 percent interest (compounded annually) to grow to $100 two years from today?
   a. $100/0.797
   b. $100 × 0.893 × 2
   c. ($100 × 0.893) + ($100 × 0.797)
   d. $100 × 0.797

7. If $200 were placed in the bank today at 12 percent interest (compounded annually), what amount would be available two years from today?
   a. $200 × 0.797
   b. $200 × 0.797 × 2
   c. $200/0.797
   d. ($200/0.893) × 2

8. Marina Pools, Inc., purchased some equipment by executing a $10,000 non-interest-bearing note due in three years. The equipment should be recorded by Marina at
   a. $10,000 minus the discounted interest on the note.
   b. $10,000 plus the discounted interest on the note.
   c. the amount of the discounted interest on the note.
   d. $10,000.

9. When accounting for a note whose interest is included in its face amount, the account Discount on Notes Payable is eventually converted into
   a. Interest Receivable.
   b. Interest Expense.
   c. Interest Payable.
   d. Interest Income.

Current Liabilities and the Time Value of Money

APPLYING YOUR KNOWLEDGE

Exercises

1. During 19x1, White's Appliance Store sold 300 washing machines, each with a one-year guarantee. It was estimated that 5 percent will eventually require some type of repair, with an average cost of $35. Prepare the adjusting entry that White's would make concerning the warranty. Also, prepare the entry that the store would make on April 9, 19x2, for one such repair that cost $48.

General Journal				
Date		Description	Debit	Credit

2. Use Appendix G of your text to answer the following questions.

   a. What amount received today is equivalent to $1,000 receivable at the end of five years, assuming a 6 percent annual interest rate compounded annually? $_____
   b. If payments of $1,000 are invested at 8 percent annual interest at the end of each quarter for one year, compute the amount that will accumulate by the time the last payment is made. $_____
   c. If $1,000 is invested on June 30, 19x1, at 6 percent annual interest compounded semiannually, how much will be in the account on June 30, 19x3? $_____
   d. Compute the equal annual deposits required to accumulate a fund of $100,000 at the end of twenty years, assuming a 10 percent interest rate compounded annually. $_____

3. The manager of Foxfield Lanes is considering replacing the existing automatic pinsetters with improved ones that cost $10,000 each. It is estimated that each new pinsetter will save $2,000 annually and will last for 10 years. Using an interest rate of 18 percent and Appendix G of your text, what is the present value of each new pinsetter to Foxfield Lanes? $_____
   Should the purchase be made? _____

4. On January 1, 19x1, McKenzie Corporation purchased equipment from Courtright Sales by signing a two-year, non-interest-bearing note for $10,000. McKenzie currently pays 10 percent interest on money borrowed. In the journal provided on page 121, prepare McKenzie's journal entries (a) to record the purchase and the note, (b) to adjust the accounts after one year, and (c) to record payment of the note after two years. Use Appendix G of your text for time value of money information. Omit explanations.

General Journal				
Date		Description	Debit	Credit

5. Oswald Nelson, an office worker who is paid $6.50 per hour, worked 40 hours during the week of May 7. Social security taxes are 6.20 percent; Medicare taxes are 1.45 percent; union dues are $5; state taxes withheld are $8; and federal income taxes withheld are $52. In addition, Nelson's employer must pay (on the basis of gross earnings) social security taxes of 6.20 percent, Medicare taxes of 1.45 percent, federal unemployment taxes of 0.8 percent, and state unemployment taxes of 5.4 percent. Prepare journal entries that summarize Nelson's earnings for the week and that record the employer's payroll taxes. Round off amounts to the nearest cent.

General Journal				
Date		Description	Debit	Credit

Current Liabilities and the Time Value of Money

CHAPTER 11 LONG-TERM LIABILITIES

REVIEWING THE CHAPTER

Objective 1: Explain the advantages and disadvantages of issuing long-term debt (pp. 485–487).

1. To finance long-term assets, research and development, and other activities of long-run benefit, corporations must obtain funds that can be used for many years. This may be accomplished by issuing stock or by issuing long-term debt in the form of bonds, notes, mortgages, and leases. There are both advantages and disadvantages to issuing long-term debt, as explained below.

2. One advantage of issuing long-term debt is that common stockholders retain their level of control, since bondholders and other creditors do not have voting rights. Another advantage is that interest on debt is tax-deductible to the issuing corporation, thus lowering the tax burden. A third advantage is the **financial leverage** or **trading on the equity** that results from issuing debt. That is, if earnings on the funds obtained exceed the interest incurred, then earnings (and earnings per share) that accrue to the common stockholders will increase.

3. There are some disadvantages to issuing long-term debt, however. First, the more debt that is issued, the more periodic interest that must be paid. Similarly, the principal amount *must* be paid at maturity. Default on either interest or principal could force the business into bankruptcy. Another disadvantage is that if the interest incurred on the funds obtained exceeds the related earnings, then the attempt at financial leverage has backfired.

4. During the 1980s, there was a tremendous increase in the amount of long-term debt issued by companies either to refinance their own operations or to finance takeovers of other companies. Much of this financing was accomplished through **junk bonds**, unsecured, high-risk long-term bonds that carry high rates of interest.

Objective 2: Identify and contrast the major characteristics of bonds (pp. 487–488).

5. Corporations frequently issue long-term **bonds** or notes to raise funds. The holders of these bonds or notes are creditors of the corporation. They are entitled to periodic interest, plus the principal of the debt on some specified date. As is true for all creditors, their claims for interest and principal take priority over stockholders' claims.

6. When bonds are issued, the corporation executes a contract with the bondholders called a **bond indenture**. In addition, the company issues **bond certificates** as evidence of its debt to the bondholders. A **bond issue** is made up of the total number of bonds available at the same time. Bonds are usually issued with a face value that is some multiple of $1,000, and carry a variety of features.

a. **Secured bonds** give the bondholders a claim to certain assets of the company upon default. **Unsecured bonds** (also called *debenture bonds*) do not.
b. When all the bonds of an issue mature on the same date, they are called **term bonds.** When the bonds mature over several maturity dates, they are called **serial bonds.**
c. When **registered bonds** are issued, the corporation maintains a record of all bondholders and pays interest by check to the bondholders of record. **Coupon bonds,** on the other hand, entitle the bearer to interest when the detachable coupons are presented at a bank for collection.

7. Bond prices are expressed as a percentage of face value. For example, when bonds with a face value of $100,000 are issued at 97, the company receives $97,000.

Objective 3: Record the issuance of bonds at face value and at a discount or premium (pp. 488–491).

8. Bonds payable due in the current period should be classified as a current liability only if they will be paid with current assets. In addition, the characteristics of all bonds should be disclosed in the notes to the financial statements.

9. When the **face interest rate** equals the **market interest rate** (also called the *effective interest rate*) for similar bonds on the issue date, the company will probably receive face value for the bonds.

10. Regardless of the issue price, bondholders are entitled to interest, which is based on the face amount. Interest for a period of time is computed by this formula:

    Interest = principal × rate × time

11. When the face interest rate is less than the market interest rate for similar bonds on the issue date, the bonds will probably sell at a **discount** (less than face value).

12. Unamortized Bond Discount is a contra account to Bonds Payable on the balance sheet. The difference between the two amounts is called the *carrying value* or *present value.* The carrying value increases as the discount is amortized and equals the face value of the bonds at maturity.

13. When the face interest rate is greater than the market interest rate for similar bonds on the issue date, the bonds usually sell at a **premium** (greater than face value). Unamortized Bond Premium is added to Bonds Payable in the balance sheet to produce the carrying value.

14. A separate account should be established for bond issue costs. These costs are amortized over the life of the bonds.

Objective 4: Determine the value of bonds using present values (pp. 491–493).

15. Theoretically, the value of a bond is equal to the sum of the present values of (a) the periodic interest payments and (b) the single payment of principal at maturity. The discount rate used is based on the current market rate of interest.

Objective 5a: Amortize bond discounts using the straight-line and effective interest methods (pp. 493–497).

16. When bonds are issued at a discount or premium, the interest payments do *not* equal the (true) total interest cost. Instead, total interest cost equals (a) interest payments over the life of the bond plus (b) the original discount amount, or minus (c) the original premium amount.

17. A **zero coupon bond** is a promise to pay a fixed amount at maturity, with no periodic interest payments. Investor earnings consist of the large discount upon issue, which in turn is amortized by the issuing corporation over the life of the bond.

18. A discount on bonds payable is considered an interest charge that must be amortized (spread out) over the life of the bond. Amortization is generally recorded on the interest payment dates, using either the straight-line method or the effective interest method.

19. Under the **straight-line method** of amortization, the amount to be amortized each interest period equals the bond discount divided by the number of interest payments during the life of the bond.

20. The effective interest method of amortization is more difficult to apply than the straight-line method but should be used instead when the results differ significantly.

21. To apply the **effective interest method** when a discount is involved, the market rate or effective rate of interest for similar securities when the bonds were issued must first be determined. This interest rate (halved for semiannual interest) is multiplied by the existing carrying value of the bonds for each interest period to obtain the bond interest expense to be recorded. The actual interest paid is then subtracted from the bond interest

expense recorded to obtain the discount amortization for the period. Because the unamortized discount is now less, the carrying value is now greater. This new carrying value is applied to the next period, and the same amortization procedure is applied.

Objective 5b: Amortize bond premiums using the straight-line and effective interest methods (pp. 497–501).

22. Amortization of a premium acts as an offset against interest paid in determining the interest expense to be recorded. Under the straight-line method, the premium to be amortized in each period equals the bond premium divided by the number of interest payments during the life of the bond.

23. The effective interest method is applied to bond premiums in the same way that it is applied to bond discounts. The only difference is that the amortization for the period is computed by subtracting the bond interest expense recorded from actual interest paid (the reverse is done for amortizing a discount).

Objective 6: Account for bonds issued between interest dates and make year-end adjustments (pp. 501–504).

24. When bonds are issued between interest dates, the interest that has accrued since the last interest date is collected from the investor upon issue. It is then returned to the investor (along with the interest earned) on the next interest date.

25. When the accounting period ends between interest dates, the accrued interest and the proportionate discount or premium amortization must be recorded.

Objective 7: Account for the retirement of bonds and the conversion of bonds into stock (pp. 504–506).

26. **Callable bonds** are bonds that may be retired by the corporation before the maturity date. The action of retiring a bond issue before its maturity date is called **early extinguishment of debt**. When the market rate for bond interest drops, a company may want to call its bonds and substitute debt with a lower interest rate. When bonds are called (for whatever reason), an entry is needed to eliminate Bonds Payable and any unamortized premium or discount, and to record the payment of cash at the **call price**. In addition, an extraordinary gain or loss on the retirement of the bonds would be recorded. (Extraordinary items are explained fully in Chapter 13.)

27. **Convertible bonds** are bonds that can be exchanged for other securities (usually common stock) at the option of the bondholder. When a bondholder converts his or her bonds into common stock, the common stock is recorded by the company at the carrying value of the bonds. Specifically, the entry eliminates Bonds Payable and any unamortized discount or premium, and records common stock and paid-in capital in excess of par value. No gain or loss is recorded.

Objective 8: Explain the basic features of mortgages payable, installment notes payable, long-term leases, and pensions and other postretirement benefits as long-term liabilities (pp. 507–514).

28. A **mortgage** is a long-term debt secured by real property, usually payable in equal monthly installments. Upon payment of an installment, both Mortgage Payable and Mortgage Interest Expense are debited, and Cash is credited. Each month, the interest portion of the payment decreases, while the principal portion of the payment increases.

29. The principal and interest on long-term notes are either payable on one maturity date or due in periodic payments. The latter notes are known as **installment notes payable** and are commonly used by businesses to finance equipment. The installment payments can be structured to include either (a) accrued interest plus equal amounts of principal or (b) accrued interest plus increasing amounts of principal. The former method results in decreasing payments, whereas the latter method produces equal payments. The effective interest calculation would be applied in either case.

30. A lease is a contract that allows a business or individual to use an asset for a specific length of time in return for periodic payments. A **capital lease** is so much like a sale (as determined by certain criteria) that it should be recorded by the lessee as an asset (to be depreciated) and a related liability. An **operating lease** is a lease that does not meet the criteria for capital leases; it should be recorded to Rent Expense for each period that the asset is leased.

31. A **pension plan** is a program whereby a company agrees to pay benefits to its employees after they retire. Benefits to retirees are usually paid

out of a **pension fund.** Pension plans are classified as defined contribution plans or defined benefit plans. **Other postretirement benefits,** such as health care, should be estimated and accrued while the employee is still working (in accordance with the matching rule).

Summary of Journal Entries Introduced in Chapter 11

A. (L.O. 3) Cash   XX (amount received)
     Bonds Payable   XX (face value)
      Sold bonds at face value

B. (L.O. 3) Bond Interest Expense   XX (amount incurred)
     Cash   XX (amount paid)
      Paid interest to bondholders

C. (L.O. 3) Cash   XX (amount received)
     Unamortized Bond Discount   XX (amount of discount)
     Bonds Payable   XX (face value)
      Sold bonds at a discount

D. (L.O. 3) Cash   XX (amount received)
     Unamortized Bond Premium   XX (amount of premium)
     Bonds Payable   XX (face value)
      Sold bonds at a premium

E. (L.O. 5a) Bond Interest Expense   XX (amount incurred)
     Unamortized Bond Discount   XX (amount amortized)
     Cash   XX (amount paid)
      Paid interest to bondholders and amortized the discount

F. (L.O. 5b) Bond Interest Expense   XX (amount incurred)
     Unamortized Bond Premium   XX (amount amortized)
     Cash   XX (amount paid)
      Paid interest to bondholders and amortized the premium

G. (L.O. 6) Cash   XX (amount received)
     Bond Interest Expense   XX (accrued amount)
     Bonds Payable   XX (face value)
      Sold bonds at face value plus accrued interest (see entry H)

H. (L.O. 6) Bond Interest Expense   XX (six months' amount)
     Cash   XX (amount paid)
      Paid semiannual interest on bonds issued in G

I. (L.O. 6) The year-end accrual for bond interest expense is identical to entry E for discounts and entry F for premiums, except that in both cases Interest Payable is credited instead of Cash.

J. (L.O. 7)   Bonds Payable   XX (face value)
          Unamortized Bond Premium   XX (current credit balance)
          Loss on Retirement of Bonds   XX (see explanation)
             Cash   XX (amount paid)
               Retired bonds at a loss; the loss equals the excess of
               the call price over the carrying value (Note: If
               appropriate, an unamortized bond discount or a gain on
               retirement would have been credited in the entry.)

K. (L.O. 7)   The early extinguishment of debt is journalized as in J.
           However, any gain or loss would be treated as extraordinary.

L. (L.O. 7)   Bonds Payable   XX (face value)
          Unamortized Bond Premium   XX (current credit balance)
             Common Stock   XX (par value)
             Paid-in Capital in Excess of Par Value, Common   XX (excess of par)
               Converted bonds payable into common stock (Note: No
               gain or loss recorded; also, an unamortized bond
               discount would have been credited in the entry, if
               appropriate.)

M. (L.O. 8)   Mortgage Payable   XX (principal)
          Mortgage Interest Expense   XX (interest)
             Cash   XX (monthly payment)
               Made monthly mortgage payment

N. (L.O. 8)   Cash   XX (amount borrowed)
             Notes Payable   XX (amount borrowed)
               Borrowed on a long-term installment note

O. (L.O. 8)   Notes Payable   XX (principal)
          Interest Expense   XX (interest)
             Cash   XX (installment payment)
               Installment payment on note

P. (L.O. 8)   Equipment Under Capital Lease   XX (present value)
             Obligations Under Capital Lease   XX (present value)
               Capital lease contract recorded

Q. (L.O. 8)   Depreciation Expense   XX (amount allocated)
             Accumulated Depreciation, Leased Equipment Under   XX (amount allocated)
               Capital Lease
               Recorded depreciation under capital lease

R. (L.O. 8)   Interest Expense   XX (amount incurred)
          Obligations Under Capital Lease   XX (amount reduced)
             Cash   XX (amount paid)
               To record lease payment under capital lease

Long-Term Liabilities

TESTING YOUR KNOWLEDGE

Matching

Match each term with its definition by writing the appropriate letter in the blank.

_____ 1. Bonds
_____ 2. Bond indenture
_____ 3. Secured bonds
_____ 4. Debentures
_____ 5. Term bonds
_____ 6. Serial bonds
_____ 7. Registered bonds
_____ 8. Coupon bonds
_____ 9. Callable bonds
_____ 10. Bond discount
_____ 11. Bond premium
_____ 12. Effective interest method
_____ 13. Capital lease
_____ 14. Operating lease
_____ 15. Convertible bonds
_____ 16. Pension plan
_____ 17. Pension fund
_____ 18. Bond certificate
_____ 19. Early extinguishment of debt
_____ 20. Zero coupon bonds
_____ 21. Financial leverage (trading on the equity)

a. Unsecured bonds
b. A lease that amounts to a sale
c. Bonds that may be retired by the company before maturity
d. Borrowing for the financial benefit of stockholders
e. The difference between face value and a lower amount paid for bonds
f. Bonds with detachable forms that are redeemed for interest
g. A true lease, recorded with debits to Rent Expense
h. Proof of a company's debt to a bondholder
i. Long-term debt instruments
j. Bonds whose owners receive interest by check directly from the company
k. The retirement of bonds prior to maturity
l. The amortization method based on carrying value
m. The difference between face value and a greater amount paid for bonds
n. A program whereby a company agrees to pay benefits to its employees when they retire
o. Bonds that mature on one specific date
p. The source of benefits that are paid to retirees
q. Bonds that are backed by certain assets
r. Bonds that may be exchanged for common stock
s. Bonds that mature in installments
t. Bonds whose holders receive no periodic interest, but that are issued at a large discount
u. The contract between the bondholder and the corporation

Short Answer

Use the lines provided to answer each item.

1. Distinguish between the terms *debenture* and *indenture*.

2. Under what circumstances would a premium probably be received on a bond issue?

3. What is the formula for computing interest for a period of time?

4. When valuing a bond, what two components are added together to determine the present value of the bond?

5. State three advantages of issuing long-term debt.

True-False

Circle T if the statement is true, F if it is false. Please provide explanations for the false answers, using the blank lines at the end of the section.

T F 1. Bondholders are owners of a corporation.

T F 2. A term bond matures on one particular date.

T F 3. Bond interest can be paid only when declared by the board of directors.

T F 4. Bonds with a lower interest rate than the market rate (for similar bonds) will probably sell at a discount.

T F 5. When a bond premium is amortized, the bond interest expense recorded is greater than the cash paid.

T F 6. When the effective interest method is used to amortize a bond discount, the amount amortized increases each year.

T F 7. When bonds are issued between interest dates, Bond Interest Expense is debited for accrued interest since the last interest date.

T F 8. As a bond premium is amortized, the carrying value of bonds payable decreases.

T F 9. When bonds are issued at a discount, the total interest cost to the issuing corporation equals the interest payments minus the bond discount.

T F 10. When bonds are retired, all of the premium or discount associated with the bonds must be canceled.

T F 11. When the effective interest method is used to amortize a premium on bonds payable, the premium amortized decreases each year.

T F 12. When bonds are issued at a premium, the total interest cost to the issuing corporation equals the interest payments minus the bond premium.

T F 13. Under operating leases, assets should be recorded at the present value of future lease payments.

T F 14. Pension expense is usually difficult to measure because it is based on many estimates, such as employee life expectancy and employee turnover.

T F 15. When bonds are converted into stock, a gain or loss should be recorded.

T F 16. Bond issue costs should be amortized over the life of the bonds.

T F 17. Postretirement health care benefits should be expensed while the employee is still working.

T F 18. A disadvantage of issuing long-term debt is the increased risk of default.

Long-Term Liabilities 129

Multiple Choice

Circle the letter of the best answer.

1. Assume that $900,000 of 5 percent bonds are issued (at face value) two months before the next semiannual interest date. Which of the following statements correctly describes the journal entry?
   a. Cash is debited for $800,000.
   b. Cash is debited for $807,500.
   c. Bond Interest Expense is credited for $7,500.
   d. Bond Interest Expense is credited for $15,000.

2. As a mortgage is paid off, the
   a. principal portion of the fixed payment increases.
   b. interest portion of the fixed payment increases.
   c. principal and interest portions do not change each interest period.
   d. monthly payments increase.

3. Unamortized Bond Premium is presented on the balance sheet as a(n)
   a. long-term asset.
   b. stockholders' equity account.
   c. deduction from Bonds Payable.
   d. addition to Bonds Payable.

4. When the interest dates on a bond issue are May 1 and November 1, the adjusting entry to record bond interest expense on December 31 might include a
   a. debit to Interest Payable.
   b. credit to Cash.
   c. credit to Unamortized Bond Discount.
   d. credit to Bond Interest Expense.

5. Under the effective interest method, as a discount is amortized each period, the
   a. amount amortized decreases.
   b. interest expense recorded increases.
   c. interest paid to bondholders increases.
   d. bonds' carrying value decreases.

6. Which of the following would probably be considered an operating lease?
   a. A 6-year lease on equipment with an option to renew for another 6 years
   b. A 5-year lease on machinery, cancelable at the end of the lease period by the lessor
   c. A 40-year lease on a building, equal to its useful life
   d. A 7-year lease on a company vehicle with an option to buy the vehicle for $1 at the end of the lease period

7. A $200,000 bond issue with a carrying value of $195,000 is called at 102 and retired. Which of the following statements about the journal entry prepared is true?
   a. An extraordinary gain of $5,000 is recorded.
   b. An extraordinary loss of $4,000 is recorded.
   c. An extraordinary loss of $9,000 is recorded.
   d. No gain or loss is recorded.

8. A company has $600,000 in bonds payable with an unamortized premium of $12,000. If one-third of the bonds are converted to common stock, the carrying value of the bonds payable will decrease by
   a. $196,000.
   b. $200,000.
   c. $204,000.
   d. $208,000.

APPLYING YOUR KNOWLEDGE

Exercises

1. A corporation issues $600,000 of 7 percent, 10-year bonds at 98½ on one of its semiannual interest dates. Assuming straight-line amortization, answer each of the following questions.
   a. What is the amount of the bond discount? $_____
   b. How much interest is paid on the next interest date? $_____
   c. How much bond interest expense is recorded on the next interest date? $_____
   d. After 3 years, what is the carrying value of the bonds? $_____

2. A corporation issues $500,000 of 7 percent, 20-year bonds at 110. Interest is paid semiannually, and the effective interest method is used for amortization. Assume that the market rate for similar investments is 6 percent and that the bonds are issued on an interest date.
   a. What amount was received for the bonds? $_____
   b. How much interest is paid each interest period? $_____
   c. How much bond interest expense is recorded on the first interest date? $_____
   d. How much of the premium is amortized on the first interest date? $_____
   e. What is the carrying value of the bonds after the first interest date? $_____

3. A corporation issued $600,000 of 8 percent, 10-year bonds at 106. In the space provided, calculate the total interest cost.

Long-Term Liabilities

4. On December 31, 19x1, Oakdale Company borrows $50,000 on a 10 percent installment note, to be paid annually over 5 years. In the journal provided, prepare the entry to record the note, as well as the December 31, 19x2, and December 31, 19x3, entries to record the first two annual payments. Assume that the principal is paid in equal installments and that the interest on the unpaid balance accrues annually.

	General Journal		
Date	Description	Debit	Credit

5. Assume the same facts and requirements as in Exercise 4 above, except that payments are made in equal installments of $13,190.

	General Journal		
Date	Description	Debit	Credit

Crossword Puzzle
for Chapters 10 and 11

ACROSS

1. Arrangement for retirement income (2 words)
5. Principal amount
9. Fund to retire bonds
10. Bond contract
13. Bonds with one maturity date
17. Remaining after deductions
18. Liability type
19. Buy back, as bonds
20. With 7-Down, time value of money amount
21. _____ coupon bonds

DOWN

1. Opposite of bond discount
2. Uses another's property for a fee
3. Bonds that mature in installments
4. Bond whose owner is recorded by the company
6. Potential liability
7. See 20-Across
8. Payable
11. _____ determinable liability
12. _____ tax liability
14. Debt secured by property
15. Series of equal payments
16. _____ value tables

Long-Term Liabilities

CHAPTER 12 CONTRIBUTED CAPITAL

REVIEWING THE CHAPTER

Objective 1: Define *corporation* **and state the advantages and disadvantages of the corporate form of business (pp. 533–536).**

1. A **corporation** is a business organization authorized by the state to conduct business and is a separate legal entity from its owners. It is the dominant form of American business because it makes it possible to gather together large amounts of capital.

2. The corporate form of business has several advantages over the sole proprietorship and partnership. It is a separate legal entity and offers limited liability to the owners. It also offers ease of capital generation and ease of transfer of ownership. Other advantages are the lack of mutual agency in a corporation and its continuous existence. In addition, a corporate form of business allows centralized authority and responsibility and professional management.

3. The corporate form of business also has several disadvantages when compared with the sole proprietorship and partnership. It is subject to greater government regulation and **double taxation** (the corporation's income is subject to income taxes and its stockholders are taxed on any dividends). The limited liability of the owners can limit the amount a small corporation can borrow. In addition, separation of ownership and control may allow management to make harmful decisions.

Objective 2: Account for organization costs (pp. 536–537).

4. The costs of forming a corporation (such as attorneys' fees and incorporation fees) are debited to an intangible asset or other asset account called **Organization Costs.** These costs typically are amortized over the early period of the corporation's life, usually 5 years (although up to 40 years is allowed).

Objective 3: Identify the components of stockholders' equity (pp. 537–539).

5. In a corporation's balance sheet, the owners' claims to the business are called stockholders' equity. The stockholders' equity section is divided into two parts: contributed capital (the stockholders' investment) and retained earnings (earnings that have remained in the business).

6. Ownership in a corporation is evidenced by a document called a **stock certificate.** A stockholder sells stock by endorsing the stock certificate and sending it to the corporation's secretary or its transfer agent. The secretary or transfer agent is responsible for transferring the corporation's stock, maintaining stockholders' records, and preparing a list of stockholders for stockholders' meetings and for the payment of dividends. In addition, corporations often hire an **underwriter,** an intermediary between the corporation and the investing public, to help in the initial issue of stock.

7. The articles of incorporation indicate the number of shares of stock that a corporation is **authorized** to issue. Stock that has been **issued** to stockholders and has not been bought back by the corporation is called **outstanding stock.** *Treasury stock* is shares bought back and held. **Par value** is the legal value of a share of stock. **Legal capital** equals the number of shares issued times the par value; it is the minimum amount that can be reported as contributed capital.

8. When only one type of stock is issued, it is called **common stock.** A second type of stock, called preferred stock, also can be issued. Because common stockholders' claim to assets on liquidation ranks behind that of creditors and preferred stockholders, common stock is considered the **residual equity** of a company.

Objective 4: Account for cash dividends (pp. 539–540).

9. A **dividend** is a distribution of assets by a corporation to its stockholders, normally in cash. Dividends usually are stated as a specified dollar amount per share of stock and are declared by the board of directors. The date of declaration is the date the board of directors formally declares a dividend, specifying that the owners of the stock on the date of record will receive the dividends on the date of payment. After the date of record, stock is said to be **ex-dividend** (without dividend rights). A **liquidating dividend** is the return of contributed capital to the stockholders. It normally is paid when a company is going out of business or is reducing its operations.

10. When cash dividends are declared, Cash Dividends Declared is debited and Cash Dividends Payable is credited; when they are paid, Cash Dividends Payable is debited and Cash is credited. The Cash Dividends Declared account is closed to Retained Earnings at the end of the year. No journal entry is made on the date of record.

Objective 5: Identify the characteristics of preferred stock, including the effect on division of dividends (pp. 540–544).

11. Holders of **preferred stock** are given preference over common shareholders on dividend declaration and liquidation. Each share of preferred stock entitles its owner to a dollar amount or percentage of par value each year before common stockholders receive anything. Once the preferred stockholders have received the annual dividends to which they are entitled, however, the common stockholders generally receive the remainder.

12. In addition, preferred stock can be (a) cumulative or noncumulative, (b) convertible or nonconvertible, and (c) callable. It usually has no voting rights.
   a. If the stock is **cumulative preferred stock** and the preferred stockholders do not receive the full amount of their annual dividend, the unpaid amount is carried over to the next year. Unpaid back dividends are called **dividends in arrears** and should be disclosed either in the balance sheet or as a footnote. When the stock is **noncumulative preferred stock,** unpaid dividends are not carried over to the next period.
   b. An owner of **convertible preferred stock** has the option to exchange each share of preferred stock for a set number of shares of common stock.
   c. Most preferred stocks are **callable preferred stocks,** which means that the corporation has the right to buy the stock back at a specified call or redemption price. Convertible preferred stock can be converted to common stock instead, if its holder wants.

Objective 6: Account for the issuance of stock for cash and other assets (pp. 544–548).

13. Capital stock may or may not have a par value, depending on the specifications in the charter. When par-value stock is issued, the Capital Stock account is credited for the legal capital (par value), and any excess is recorded as Paid-in Capital in Excess of Par Value. In the stockholders' equity section of the balance sheet, the entire amount is labeled Total Contributed Capital. On rare occasions, stock is issued at a discount (less than par value), requiring a debit to Discount on Capital Stock.

14. **No-par stock** is stock for which a par value has not been established. It can be issued with or without a stated value. **Stated value,** which is established by the board of directors, is the legal capital for a share of no-par stock. The total stated value is recorded in the Capital Stock account. Any amount received in excess of stated value is recorded in Paid-in Capital in Excess of Stated Value. If no stated value is set, the entire amount received is legal capital and is credited to Capital Stock.

15. Sometimes stock is issued in exchange for assets or for services rendered. This kind of transaction should be recorded at the fair market value of the stock. If the stock's fair market value cannot be determined, the fair market value of the assets or services should be used.

16. **Initial public offerings (IPOs),** popular with investors, are common stock issues of companies that are selling their stock to the public for the first time. The company is said to be "going public."

Objective 7: Account for treasury stock (pp. 548–551).

17. **Treasury stock** is common or preferred stock that has been issued and reacquired by the issuing company. That is, it is issued but no longer outstanding. Treasury stock is purchased (a) to distribute to employees through stock option plans, (b) to maintain a favorable market for the company's stock, (c) to increase earnings per share, (d) to use in purchasing other companies, and (e) to prevent a hostile takeover of the company.

18. Treasury stock can be held indefinitely, reissued, or canceled, and has no rights until it is reissued. Treasury stock, the last item in the stockholders' equity section of the balance sheet, appears as a deduction.

19. When treasury stock is purchased, its account is debited for the purchase cost. It may be reissued at cost, above cost, or below cost. When cash received from a reissue exceeds the cost, the difference is credited to Paid-in Capital, Treasury Stock. When cash received is less than cost, the difference is debited to Paid-in Capital, Treasury Stock (and Retained Earnings if needed). In no case should a gain or loss be recorded.

20. When treasury stock is retired, all the contributed capital associated with the retired shares must be removed from the accounts. When less is paid than was contributed originally, the difference is credited to Paid-in Capital, Retirement of Stock. When more is paid, the difference is debited to Retained Earnings.

Objective 8: Account for the exercise of stock options (pp. 551–552).

21. A **stock option plan** is an agreement whereby corporate employees can purchase a certain quantity of the company's stock at a certain price for a certain period of time. If the plan allows virtually all employees to purchase stock at the existing market price, then the journal entry on issue resembles the entry made when stock is sold to outsiders. However, if only certain employees (usually management) are allowed to purchase the corporation's stock in the future at a fixed price, the plan is said to be compensatory. The amount of compensation per share equals the market price on the date the option is granted minus the option price. Journal entries are made to record compensation expense (covered in a more advanced course) and the issuance of the stock on exercise of the option.

Summary of Journal Entries Introduced in Chapter 12

A. (L.O. 2) Organization Costs   XX (amount incurred)
        Cash   XX (amount paid)
            Fee for services rendered in corporate organization

B. (L.O. 2) Amortization Expense, Organization Costs   XX (amount allocated)
        Organization Costs   XX (amount allocated)
            To amortize organization costs for one year

C. (L.O. 4) Cash Dividends Declared   XX (amount declared)
        Cash Dividends Payable   XX (amount declared)
            Declaration of a cash dividend to common stockholders

D. (L.O. 4) Cash Dividends Payable   XX (amount paid)
        Cash   XX (amount paid)
            Payment of cash dividends declared in C above

E. (L.O. 6) Cash   XX (amount invested)
        Common Stock   XX (legal capital amount)
            Issued par value common stock for par value

F. (L.O. 6) Cash   XX (amount invested)
        Common Stock   XX (legal capital amount)
        Paid-in Capital in Excess of Par Value, Common   XX (excess of par)
            Issued par value common stock for amount in excess of
            par value

G. (L.O. 6) Cash   XX (amount invested)
        Common Stock   XX (legal capital amount)
            Issued no-par common stock (no stated value established)

H. (L.O. 6) Cash   XX (amount invested)
        Common Stock   XX (legal capital amount)
        Paid-in Capital in Excess of Stated Value, Common   XX (excess of stated value)
            Issued no-par common stock with stated value for amount
            in excess of stated value

I. (L.O. 6) Organization Costs   XX (fair market value)
        Common Stock   XX (par value)
        Paid-in Capital in Excess of Par Value, Common   XX (excess of par)
            Issued par value common stock for incorporation services

J. (L.O. 6) Land   XX (fair market value)
        Common Stock   XX (par value)
        Paid-in Capital in Excess of Par Value, Common   XX (excess of par)
            Issued par value common stock with a market value in
            excess of par value for a piece of land

K. (L.O. 7) Treasury Stock, Common   XX (cost)
        Cash   XX (cost)
            Acquired shares of the company's common stock

L. (L.O. 7) Cash   XX (amount received)
          Treasury Stock, Common   XX (cost)
              Reissued shares of treasury stock at cost

M. (L.O. 7) Cash   XX (amount received)
          Treasury Stock, Common   XX (cost)
          Paid-in Capital, Treasury Stock   XX ("gain")
              Sale of shares of treasury stock at amount above cost

N. (L.O. 7) Cash   XX (amount received)
          Paid-in Capital, Treasury Stock   XX ("loss")
          Retained Earnings (only if needed)   XX ("loss")
              Treasury Stock, Common   XX (cost)
                  Sale of shares of treasury stock at amount below cost

O. (L.O. 7) Common Stock   XX (par value)
          Paid-in Capital in Excess of Par Value, Common   XX (excess of par)
          Retained Earnings (only if needed)   XX (premium paid)
              Treasury Stock, Common   XX (cost)
                  Retirement of treasury stock; cost exceeded original
                  investment amount

P. (L.O. 7) If the treasury stock in O had been retired for an amount less
          than the original investment amount, then instead of Retained
          Earnings being debited for the excess paid, Paid-in Capital,
          Retirement of Treasury Stock would be credited for the
          difference.

Q. (L.O. 8) Cash   XX (amount invested)
          Common Stock   XX (par value)
          Paid-in Capital in Excess of Par Value, Common   XX (excess of par)
              Issued par value common stock under employee stock
              option plan

Contributed Capital

TESTING YOUR KNOWLEDGE

Matching

Match each term with its definition by writing the appropriate letter in the blank.

____ 1. Corporation
____ 2. Organization costs
____ 3. Issued stock
____ 4. Authorized stock
____ 5. Outstanding stock
____ 6. Common stock
____ 7. Preferred stock
____ 8. Dividends in arrears
____ 9. Par value
____ 10. No-par stock
____ 11. Stated value
____ 12. Treasury stock
____ 13. Ex-dividend
____ 14. Liquidating dividend
____ 15. Convertible preferred stock
____ 16. Callable preferred stock
____ 17. Cumulative preferred stock
____ 18. Stock option plan
____ 19. Stock certificate
____ 20. Residual equity

a. Unpaid back dividends
b. Descriptive of common stockholders' ownership in a corporation
c. Without dividend rights
d. The amount of legal capital of a share of no-par stock
e. Stock that is presently held by stockholders
f. The dominant form of business in the United States
g. The type of stock whose holders have prior claim over common stockholders to dividends
h. Issued stock that has been reacquired by the corporation
i. Stock whose unpaid dividends "carry over" to future years until paid
j. Proof of ownership in a corporation
k. Expenditures necessary to form a corporation
l. The maximum amount of stock that a corporation may issue
m. The name of the stock when only one type of stock has been issued
n. Stock that may or may not have a stated value
o. The legal value for stock that is stated in the charter
p. Stock that has been sold to stockholders, and may or may not have been bought back by the corporation
q. Stock that may be bought back at the option of the issuing corporation
r. An agreement whereby certain employees may purchase stock at a fixed price
s. The return of contributed capital to a corporation's stockholders
t. Preferred stock that an investor may exchange for common stock

Short Answer

Use the lines provided to answer each item.

1. List eight advantages of the corporate form of business.

2. List four disadvantages of the corporate form of business.

3. Name the two major portions of the stockholders' equity section of a balance sheet.

4. Preferred shareholders are given preference over common shareholders under what two circumstances?

5. Under what circumstance would a corporation have more shares of stock issued than outstanding?

6. What is the difference between treasury stock and unissued stock?

Contributed Capital

True-False

Circle T if the statement is true, F if it is false. Please provide explanations for the false answers, using the blank lines at the end of the section.

T F 1. Corporate income is taxed twice, at the corporate level and at the individual level (when it is distributed as dividends).

T F 2. The concept of legal capital was established to protect the corporation's creditors.

T F 3. Ordinarily, creditors cannot attach the personal assets of the corporation's stockholders.

T F 4. Organization costs must be charged as expenses in the year the corporation is formed.

T F 5. Contributed capital consists of capital stock plus paid-in capital in excess of par (stated) value.

T F 6. A transfer agent keeps records of stock transactions.

T F 7. Preferred stock cannot be both convertible and cumulative.

T F 8. Dividends in arrears do not exist when preferred stock is noncumulative.

T F 9. The worth of a share of stock can be measured by its par value.

T F 10. The purchase of treasury stock reduces total assets and total stockholders' equity.

T F 11. Preferred stockholders are guaranteed annual dividends; common stockholders are not.

T F 12. Preferred stock is considered the residual equity of a corporation.

T F 13. The amount of compensation in connection with a stock option plan is measured on the date the option is exercised.

T F 14. On the date a dividend is paid, total assets and total stockholders' equity decrease.

T F 15. Dividends in arrears should appear as a liability on the balance sheet.

T F 16. Treasury Stock is listed in the balance sheet as an asset.

T F 17. When a corporation sells stock to the investing public, it often engages the services of an underwriter.

T F 18. When treasury stock is sold at more than its cost, Gain on Sale of Treasury Stock is credited.

Multiple Choice

Circle the letter of the best answer.

1. When treasury stock is reissued below cost, all of the following may be true *except*
   a. Retained Earnings is debited.
   b. Treasury Stock is credited.
   c. Contributed Capital, Treasury Stock Transactions is debited.
   d. Loss on Reissue of Treasury Stock is debited.

2. The purchase of treasury stock does *not* affect
   a. the amount of stock outstanding.
   b. the amount of stock issued.
   c. total assets.
   d. total stockholders' equity.

3. Which of the following statements is true?
   a. Outstanding shares plus issued shares equal authorized shares.
   b. Unissued shares plus outstanding shares equal authorized shares.
   c. Authorized shares minus unissued shares equal issued shares.
   d. Unissued shares minus issued shares equal outstanding shares.

4. Novak Corporation has outstanding 1,000 shares of $100 par value, 7 percent noncumulative preferred stock, and 20,000 shares of $10 par value common stock. Last year, the company paid no dividends; this year, it distributed $40,000 in dividends. What portion of this $40,000 should common stockholders receive?
   a. $0
   b. $2,800
   c. $26,000
   d. $33,000

5. Which of the following is *not* a characteristic of corporations in general?
   a. Separation of ownership and management
   b. Ease of transfer of ownership
   c. Double taxation
   d. Unlimited liability of stockholders

6. On which of the following dates is a journal entry made?
   a. Date of record
   b. Date of payment
   c. Date of declaration
   d. Both *b* and *c*

7. Stock is said to be "ex-dividend" after
   a. it has been sold to another party.
   b. the date of record.
   c. the date of payment.
   d. the date of declaration.

8. When callable preferred stock is called and surrendered, the stockholder is *not* entitled to
   a. a call premium.
   b. the par value of the stock.
   c. any dividends in arrears.
   d. the market value of the stock.

Contributed Capital

APPLYING YOUR KNOWLEDGE

Exercises

1. In the journal provided, prepare the entries for the following transactions.

Jan. 1 Paid $8,000 in legal and incorporation fees to form Simi Corporation.

Feb. 9 Issued 5,000 shares of $100 par value common stock at $115 per share.

Apr. 12 Exchanged 20,000 shares of no-par preferred stock, which had a stated value of $10 per share, for a building with a market value of $240,000. The market value of the stock cannot be determined.

June 23 Declared a $4 per share dividend on the common stock, to be paid on July 8. The date of record is July 1.

July 8 Paid the dividend declared on June 23.

Dec. 20 The corporation's president exercised her option to purchase 200 shares of $100 par value common stock at $110 per share. The market price on that date was $130 per share.

Dec. 31 Amortized 20 percent of the incorporation fees.

Date	Description	Debit	Credit

2. Hilldale Corporation began operation on August 10, 19x1, by issuing 50,000 shares of $10 par value common stock at $50 per share. As of January 1, 19x3, its capital structure was the same. For each of the following sets of facts for January 19x3, prepare the proper entry in the journal provided. In all cases, assume sufficient cash and retained earnings.

Jan. 12 The corporation purchases 5,000 shares of stock from the stockholders at $60 per share.
    20 The corporation reissues 2,000 shares of treasury stock at $65 per share.
    27 The corporation reissues another 2,000 shares of treasury stock at $58 per share.
    31 The corporation retires the remaining 1,000 treasury shares.

Date	Description	Debit	Credit

General Journal

3. Knapp Corporation paid no dividends in its first two years of operations. In its third year, it paid $51,000 in dividends. For all three years, there have been 1,000 shares of 6 percent, $100 par value cumulative preferred stock, and 5,000 shares of $10 par value common stock outstanding. How much of the $51,000 in dividends goes to

a. preferred stockholders? $_____

b. common stockholders? $ _____

Contributed Capital

CHAPTER 13 RETAINED EARNINGS AND CORPORATE INCOME STATEMENTS

REVIEWING THE CHAPTER

Objective 1: Define *retained earnings* and prepare a statement of retained earnings (p. 574).

1. The stockholders' equity section of a corporation's balance sheet is composed of contributed capital and retained earnings. Contributed capital represents the owners' capital investment. **Retained earnings** are the profits that a corporation has earned since its beginning, minus any losses, dividends declared, or other transfers out of retained earnings.

2. The statement of retained earnings is a labeled summary of the changes in retained earnings over the accounting period.

3. Ordinarily, Retained Earnings has a credit balance. When a debit balance exists, the corporation is said to have a **deficit**.

4. **Prior period adjustments** are entries made in the current period for certain transactions that relate to, but were not determinable in, earlier accounting periods. A prior period adjustment can be made only for one of two reasons: (a) to correct an error in the financial statements of a prior period or (b) to record a tax gain from carrying forward a preacquisition operating loss of a purchased subsidiary. Prior period adjustments appear on the current period's statement of retained earnings as an adjustment to the beginning balance; they do not appear on the income statement. All other items of income and loss during the period that do not qualify as prior period adjustments must be listed on the income statement. Prior period adjustments are rare.

Objective 2: Account for stock dividends and stock splits (pp. 574–579).

5. A **stock dividend** is a proportional distribution of shares of stock to a corporation's stockholders. Stock dividends are declared to (a) give evidence of the company's success without paying a cash dividend, (b) reduce a stock's market price, (c) allow a nontaxable distribution, and (d) communicate an increase in permanent capital. The result of a stock dividend is the transfer of a part of retained earnings to contributed capital. For a small stock dividend (less than 20 to 25 percent), the market value of the shares distributed is transferred from retained earnings. For a large stock dividend (greater than 20 to 25 percent), the par or stated value is transferred. A stock dividend does not change total stockholders' equity or any individual's proportionate equity in the company.

6. A **stock split** is an increase in the number of shares of stock outstanding, with a corresponding decrease in the par or stated value of the stock. For example, a 3 for 1 split on 40,000 shares of $30 par value would result in the distribution of 80,000 additional shares. (That is, someone who owned one share now would own three shares.) The par value would be reduced to $10. A stock split does not increase the number of

shares authorized; nor does it affect the balances in stockholders' equity.

7. The purpose of a stock split is to improve the stock's marketability by pushing its market price down. In the example above, if the stock was selling for $180 per share, a 3 for 1 split probably would cause the market price to fall to about $60 per share. A memorandum entry should be made for a stock split, disclosing the decrease in par or stated value as well as the increase in the number of shares of stock outstanding.

Objective 3: Describe the disclosure of restrictions on retained earnings (pp. 579–580).

8. Retained earnings can be unrestricted or restricted. Unrestricted retained earnings dictate the asset amount (if available) that can be distributed to stockholders as dividends. A **restriction on retained earnings** dictates the asset amount that must be retained in the business for other purposes. Retained earnings are restricted for contractual, legal, or voluntary reasons—by the board of directors only. Retained Earnings is not a cash account; it is simply a guide to asset distribution. Restrictions on retained earnings are disclosed in the stockholders' equity section of the balance sheet or as notes to the financial statements.

Objective 4: Prepare a statement of stockholders' equity (pp. 580–582).

9. The **statement of stockholders' equity** can be used in place of the statement of retained earnings. It is a labeled computation of the changes in the stockholders' equity accounts during the accounting period. It contains all the components of the statement of retained earnings, as well as a summary of the period's stock transactions.

Objective 5: Calculate book value per share and distinguish it from market value (pp. 582–584).

10. The **book value** of a share of stock equals the net assets represented by one share of a company's stock. If the company has common stock only, the book value per share is arrived at by dividing stockholders' equity by the number of outstanding and distributable shares. When the company also has preferred stock, the liquidating value of the preferred stock plus any dividends in arrears are deducted from stockholders' equity in computing the book value per share of common stock.

11. **Market value** is the price that investors are willing to pay for a share of stock on the open market.

Objective 6: Prepare a corporate income statement (p. 584).

12. Corporate income statements should present **comprehensive income**—all revenues, expenses, gains, and losses, except for prior period adjustments. This approach to the measurement of income has resulted in several items being added to the income statement—discontinued operations, extraordinary items, and accounting changes. In addition, earnings per share figures must be disclosed.

Objective 7: Show the relationships among income taxes expense, deferred income taxes, and net of taxes (pp. 584–590).

13. Corporate taxable income is determined by subtracting allowable business deductions from includable gross income. Tax rates currently range from a 15 percent to a 39 percent marginal rate.

14. Computing income taxes for financial reporting differs from computing income taxes due the government for the same accounting period. This difference is caused by the fact that financial reporting income is governed by generally accepted accounting principles, whereas taxable income is governed by the Internal Revenue Code. When income for financial reporting differs materially from taxable income, the **income tax allocation** technique should be used. Under this method, the difference between the current tax liability and income tax expense is debited or credited to an account called **Deferred Income Taxes**. Adjustments to this amount must be made in light of legislated changes in income tax laws and regulations in the current year.

15. Certain income statement items must be reported **net of taxes** to avoid distorting net operating income. These items are discontinued operations, extraordinary gains and losses, and accounting changes.

Objective 8: Describe the disclosure on the income statement of discontinued operations, extraordinary items, and accounting changes (pp. 590–592).

16. The results of operations for the period and any gains or losses from the **discontinued operations** of a segment of a business should be disclosed (net of taxes) after income from continu-

ing operations. A **segment** is defined as a separate major line of business or class of customer.

17. An **extraordinary item** is an event that is unusual and occurs infrequently. Extraordinary items should be disclosed separately in the income statement (net of taxes) after discontinued operations.

18. A company can change from one accounting principle to another (e.g., from FIFO to LIFO) only if it can justify the new method as better accounting practice. The **cumulative effect of an accounting change** on prior years (net of taxes) should appear on the income statement after extraordinary items.

Objective 9: Compute earnings per share (pp. 592–594).

19. Readers of financial statements use the earnings per share figure to judge a company's performance, to estimate its future earnings and to compare it with other companies. Earnings per share figures should be disclosed for (a) income from continuing operations, (b) income before extraordinary items and the cumulative effect of accounting changes, (c) the cumulative effect of accounting changes, and (d) net income. These figures should appear on the face of the income statement.

20. A company that has issued no securities that are convertible into common stock has a **simple capital structure.** In this case, earnings per share is computed by dividing net income applicable to common stock by the weighted-average shares outstanding.

21. A company that has issued securities that can be converted into common stock has a **complex capital structure.** For example, **common stock equivalents** such as stock options and certain convertible securities might exist, producing **potentially dilutive securities** that have the potential to decrease earnings per share. In this case, a dual presentation of **primary** and **fully diluted earnings per share** is required.

Summary of Journal Entries Introduced in Chapter 13

A. (L.O. 2) Stock Dividends Declared   XX (amount transferred)
      Common Stock Distributable   XX (par value amount)
      Paid-in Capital in Excess of Par Value, Common   XX (excess of par)
          Declared a stock dividend on common stock

B. (L.O. 2) Common Stock Distributable   XX (par value amount)
      Common Stock   XX (par value amount)
          Distributed a stock dividend

C. (L.O. 7) Income Taxes Expense   XX (amount per GAAP)
      Income Taxes Payable   XX (currently payable)
      Deferred Income Taxes   XX (eventually payable)
          To record estimated current and deferred income taxes

TESTING YOUR KNOWLEDGE

Matching

Match each term with its definition by writing the appropriate letter in the blank.

_____ 1. Retained earnings
_____ 2. Deficit
_____ 3. Prior period adjustment
_____ 4. Income tax allocation
_____ 5. Simple capital structure
_____ 6. Complex capital structure
_____ 7. Discontinued operations
_____ 8. Comprehensive income
_____ 9. Stock dividend
_____ 10. Stock split
_____ 11. Restricted retained earnings
_____ 12. Segments
_____ 13. Statement of retained earnings
_____ 14. Extraordinary item
_____ 15. Earnings per share
_____ 16. Accounting change
_____ 17. Book value per share
_____ 18. Market value
_____ 19. Statement of stockholders' equity
_____ 20. Potentially dilutive securities

a. An unusual and infrequent gain or loss
b. The makeup of a corporation that has issued convertible securities
c. A negative figure for retained earnings
d. Distinct parts of business operations
e. A summary of the changes in stockholders' equity accounts during the period
f. The net assets represented by one share of a company's stock
g. All revenues, expenses, gains, and losses, except for prior period adjustments
h. Use of a different but more appropriate accounting method
i. A proportional distribution of stock to a corporation's stockholders
j. The profits that a corporation has earned since its inception, minus any losses, dividends declared, or transfers to contributed capital
k. A measure of net income earned for each share of stock
l. A corporate stock maneuver in which par or stated value is changed
m. The makeup of a corporation that has not issued convertible securities
n. The income statement section immediately before extraordinary gains or losses
o. A summary of the changes in retained earnings during the period
p. The quantity of assets that are not available for dividends
q. The price that investors are willing to pay for a share of stock
r. An entry made in the current period that relates to an earlier period
s. The technique to reconcile accounting income and taxable income
t. Options and convertible preferred stocks that could lower the earnings per share figure

Short Answer

Use the lines provided to answer each item.

1. List five ways in which the Retained Earnings account can be reduced.

   _____

   _____

   _____

   _____

   _____

2. What are the two major distinctions between a stock dividend and a stock split?

   _____

   _____

   _____

3. What two conditions must be met for an item to qualify as extraordinary?

   _____

   _____

4. Number the following items to indicate their order of appearance in an income statement:

   _____ Cumulative Effect of Accounting Change

   _____ Revenues

   _____ Extraordinary Gains and Losses

   _____ Net Income

   _____ Discontinued Operations

   _____ Income from Continuing Operations

True-False

Circle T if the statement is true, F if it is false. Please provide explanations for the false answers, using the blank lines at the end of the section.

T F   1. If an extraordinary gain of $20,000 has occurred, it should be reported net of taxes at more than $20,000.

T F   2. A restriction on retained earnings represents cash set aside for a special purpose.

T F   3. The book value of a share of common stock decreases when dividends are declared.

T F   4. After a stock dividend is distributed, each stockholder owns a greater percentage of the corporation.

T F   5. The market value of a stock on the date a stock dividend is declared has no bearing on the journal entry.

T F   6. The main purpose of a stock split is to reduce the stock's par value.

T F   7. A gain on the sale of a plant asset qualifies as an extraordinary item.

T F   8. Extraordinary items should appear on the statement of retained earnings.

T F   9. The effect of a change from straight-line depreciation to accelerated depreciation should be reported in the income statement immediately after extraordinary items.

T F 10. Common Stock Distributable is a current liability in the balance sheet.

Retained Earnings and Corporate Income Statements

T F 11. Both primary and fully diluted earnings per share data should be provided for a corporation with a complex capital structure.

T F 12. If taxable income always equaled accounting income, there would be no need for income tax allocation.

T F 13. A prior period adjustment never should appear in the current period's income statement.

T F 14. Common stock equivalents never are included in the earnings per share calculation.

T F 15. Stock Dividends Declared is closed to Retained Earnings at the end of the accounting period.

Multiple Choice

Circle the letter of the best answer.

1. Which of the following has no effect on retained earnings?
   a. Stock split
   b. Stock dividend
   c. Cash dividend
   d. Prior period adjustment

2. A company with 10,000 shares of common stock outstanding distributed a 10 percent stock dividend and then split its stock 4 for 1. How many shares are now outstanding?
   a. 2,750
   b. 41,000
   c. 44,000
   d. 55,000

3. When retained earnings are restricted, which of the following statements is true?
   a. Total retained earnings increase.
   b. The company is no longer limited in the amount of dividends it can pay.
   c. Total retained earnings are reduced.
   d. Total stockholders' equity remains the same.

4. On the date that a stock dividend is distributed,
   a. Common Stock Distributable is credited.
   b. Cash is credited.
   c. Retained Earnings remains the same.
   d. no entry is made.

5. An extraordinary item should appear
   a. on the income statement.
   b. on the balance sheet.
   c. on the statement of retained earnings.
   d. in a footnote.

6. Mahoney Corporation had 60,000 shares of common stock outstanding from January 1 to October 1, and 40,000 shares outstanding from October 1 to December 31. What is the weighted-average number of shares used to calculate earnings per share?
   a. 45,000 shares
   b. 50,000 shares
   c. 55,000 shares
   d. 100,000 shares

7. If retained earnings were $70,000 on January 1, 19xx, and $100,000 on December 31, 19xx, and if cash dividends of $15,000 were declared and paid during the year, net income for the year must have been
   a. $30,000.
   b. $45,000.
   c. $55,000.
   d. $85,000.

8. Which of the following would *not* appear in a statement of stockholders' equity?
   a. Conversion of preferred stock into common stock
   b. Dividends declared
   c. Extraordinary gains and losses
   d. Purchase of treasury stock

9. A corporation has issued only one type of stock and wants to compute book value per share. It needs all the information below *except*
   a. retained earnings.
   b. the current year's dividends.
   c. total contributed capital.
   d. total shares outstanding and distributable.

10. Retained earnings
    a. are the same as cash.
    b. are the amount invested by stockholders in a corporation.
    c. equal cumulative profits, less losses and dividends declared.
    d. are not affected by revenues and expenses.

Retained Earnings and Corporate Income Statements

APPLYING YOUR KNOWLEDGE

Exercises

1. For each of the following sets of facts, prepare the proper entry in the journal provided.

   Sept. 1 Allred Corporation began operations by issuing 10,000 shares of $100 par value common stock at $120 per share.

   Mar. 7 A 5 percent stock dividend is declared. The market price of the stock is $130 per share on March 7.

   30 This is the date of record for the stock dividend.

   Apr. 13 The stock dividend is distributed.

General Journal			
Date	Description	Debit	Credit

2. A company has $100,000 in operating income before taxes. It also had an extraordinary loss of $30,000 when lightning struck one of its warehouses. The company must pay a 40 percent tax on all items. Complete the partial income statement in good form.

Operating Income Before Taxes	$100,000

3. Conejo Corporation had taxable income of $40,000, $40,000, and $80,000 in 19x1, 19x2, and 19x3, respectively. Its income for accounting purposes was $60,000, $30,000, and $70,000 for 19x1, 19x2, and 19x3, respectively. The difference between tax and accounting income was due to $30,000 in expenses that were deductible in full for tax purposes in 19x1 but were expensed one-third per year for accounting purposes. Make the correct journal entry to record income taxes in each of the three years. Assume a 40 percent tax rate.

Date	Description	Debit	Credit

Retained Earnings and Corporate Income Statements

4. Clinton Corporation's balance sheet as of December 31, 19xx, includes the following information regarding stockholders' equity:

Contributed Capital	
Preferred Stock, $50 par value, 7% cumulative, 4,000 shares authorized, issued, and outstanding	$200,000
Common Stock, no-par, 30,000 shares authorized, issued, and outstanding	360,000
Paid-in Capital in Excess of Par Value, Preferred	40,000
Total Contributed Capital	$600,000
Retained Earnings	80,000
Total Stockholders' Equity	$680,000

Dividends in arrears total $28,000.

In the space that follows, compute the book value per share of both preferred stock and common stock.

Crossword Puzzle
for Chapters 12 and 13

ACROSS

5. _____ income
7. Dividends in _____
8. Opposite of 13-Across
9. Corporate stock maneuver
10. Unusual and infrequent gain or loss
13. Legal capital amount
14. Fully _____ earnings per share
16. Common stock equity
17. Stock value for 8-Across
18. Callable
19. Net of _____

DOWN

1. Stock quantity
2. Financial statement reader
3. Negative retained earnings
4. Mutual _____
5. Capital structure type
6. _____ period adjustment
7. Restricted, as retained earnings
11. True stock value
12. Common dividend form
15. Sold to stockholders

Retained Earnings and Corporate Income Statements

CHAPTER 14 THE STATEMENT OF CASH FLOWS

REVIEWING THE CHAPTER

Objective 1: Describe the statement of cash flows, and define *cash* and *cash equivalents* (p. 620).

1. The **statement of cash flows** is considered a major financial statement, as are the income statement, balance sheet, and statement of stockholders' equity. The statement of cash flows, however, provides much information and answers certain questions that the other three statements do not. Its presentation is required by the FASB.

2. The statement of cash flows shows the effect on **cash** and cash equivalents of the operating, inventing, and financing activities of a company for an accounting period. **Cash equivalents** are short-term, highly liquid investments such as money market accounts, commercial paper (short-term notes), and U.S. Treasury bills. Short-term investments (marketable securities) are *not* considered cash equivalents.

Objective 2: State the principal purposes and uses of the statement of cash flows (pp. 620–621).

3. The principal purpose of the statement of cash flows is to provide information about a company's cash receipts and cash payments during an accounting period. This goal is in accordance with the FASB's "Statement of Financial Accounting Concepts No. 1," which states that financial statements should provide investors and creditors with information regarding the business's cash flows. The statement of cash flows' secondary purpose is to provide information about a company's operating, investing, and financing activities during the period.

4. Investors and creditors can use the statement of cash flows to assess such things as the company's ability to generate positive future cash flows, ability to pay its liabilities, ability to pay dividends, and need for additional financing. In addition, management can use the statement of cash flows (among other things) to assess the debt-paying ability of the business, determine dividend policy, and plan for investing and financing needs.

Objective 3: Identify the principal components of the classifications of cash flows, and state the significance of noncash investing and financing transactions (pp. 621–625).

5. The statement of cash flows categorizes cash receipts and cash payments as operating, investing, and financing activities.
   a. **Operating activities** include receiving cash from customers from the sale of goods and services, receiving interest and dividends on loans and investments, and making cash payments for wages, goods and services, interest, taxes, and purchases of trading securities.
   b. **Investing activities** include purchasing and selling long-term assets and marketable securities (other than trading securities or cash

equivalents) as well as making and collecting on loans to other entities.

c. **Financing activities** include issuing and buying back capital stock as well as borrowing and repaying loans on a short- or long-term basis (i.e., issuing bonds and notes). Dividends paid would also be included in this category, but repayment of accounts payable or accrued liabilities would not.

6. The statement of cash flows should include an accompanying schedule of **noncash investing and financing transactions,** involving only long-term assets, long-term liabilities, or stockholders' equity. Transactions such as the issuance of a mortgage for land or the conversion of bonds into stock represent simultaneous investing and financing activities that do not, however, result in an inflow or outflow of cash.

7. In the formal statement of cash flows, individual cash inflows from operating, investing, and financing activities are shown separately in their respective categories. To prepare the statement, one needs the assistance of a comparative balance sheet, the current income statement, and additional information about transactions affecting noncurrent accounts during the period. The four steps in statement preparation are (1) determining cash flows from operating activities, (2) determining cash flows from investing activities, (3) determining cash flows from financing activities, and (4) presenting the information obtained in the first three steps in the form of a statement of cash flows.

Objective 4a: Determine cash flows from operating activities using the direct method (pp. 624–632).

8. Cash flows from operating activities result from converting accrual-basis net income to a cash basis and may be determined using either the direct method or the indirect method. Under the **direct method,** the net cash flows from operating activities is determined by taking cash receipts from sales, adding interest and dividends received, and deducting cash payments for purchases, operating expenses, interest, and income taxes. (See the table at the bottom of the page.)

Objective 4b: Determine cash flows from operating activities using the indirect method (pp. 626–632).

9. Under the **indirect method,** the net cash flows from operating activities is determined by taking

$$\text{Cash Receipts from Sales} = \text{Sales} \begin{cases} + \text{Decrease in Accounts Receivable} \\ \quad \text{or} \\ - \text{Increase in Accounts Receivable} \end{cases}$$

$$\text{Cash Payments for Purchases} = \text{Cost of Goods Sold} \begin{cases} + \text{Increase in Inventory} \\ \quad \text{or} \\ - \text{Decrease in Inventory} \end{cases} \begin{cases} + \text{Decrease in Accounts Payable} \\ \quad \text{or} \\ - \text{Increase in Accounts Payable} \end{cases}$$

$$\begin{matrix} \text{Cash Payments for} \\ \text{Operating Expenses} \end{matrix} = \begin{matrix} \text{Operating} \\ \text{Expenses} \end{matrix} \begin{cases} + \text{Increase in} \\ \quad \text{Prepaid Expenses} \\ \quad \text{or} \\ - \text{Decrease in} \\ \quad \text{Prepaid Expenses} \end{cases} \begin{cases} + \text{Decrease in} \\ \quad \text{Accrued Liabilities} \\ \quad \text{or} \\ - \text{Increase in} \\ \quad \text{Accrued Liabilities} \end{cases} \begin{cases} - \text{Depreciation and} \\ \quad \text{Other Noncash Expenses} \end{cases}$$

$$\text{Cash Payments for Income Taxes} = \text{Income Taxes} \begin{cases} + \text{Decrease in Income Taxes Payable} \\ \quad \text{or} \\ - \text{Increase in Income Taxes Payable} \end{cases}$$

net income and adding or deducting items that do not affect cash flow from operations. Items to add include depreciation expense, amortization expense, depletion expense, losses, decreases in certain current assets (accounts receivable, inventory, and prepaid expenses), and increase in certain current liabilities (accounts payable, accrued liabilities, and income taxes payable). Items to deduct include gains, increases in certain current assets (see above), and decreases in certain current liabilities (see above). The direct and indirect methods produce the same results and are both considered GAAP. The FASB, however, recommends use of the direct method accompanied by a separate schedule (the indirect method) reconciling net income to net cash flows.

Objective 5a: Determine cash flows from investing activities (pp. 632–636).

10. When determining cash flows from investing and financing activities, the objective is to explain the change in the appropriate account balances from one year to the next. As previously stated, investing activities focus on the purchase and sale of long-term assets and short-term investments.
    a. Under the indirect approach, gains and losses from the sale of the above assets should be deducted from and added back to, respectively, net income to arrive at net cash flows from operating activities.
    b. Under the direct approach, gains and losses are simply ignored in determining net cash flows from operating activities.
    c. Under both approaches, the full cash proceeds are entered into the Cash Flows from Investing Activities section of the statement of cash flows.

Objective 5b: Determine cash flows from financing activities (pp. 636–637).

11. Financing activities focus on certain liability and stockholders' equity accounts and include short- and long-term borrowing (notes and bonds) and repayment, issuance and repurchase of capital stock, and payment of dividends. Changes in the Retained Earnings account are explained in the statement of cash flows, for the most part, through analyses of net income and dividends declared.

Objective 6: Prepare a statement of cash flows using the (a) direct and (b) indirect methods (pp. 638–640).

12. The only difference between the direct and indirect methods of preparing a statement of cash flows is in the structure of the Cash Flows from Operating Activities section. Exhibit 14-6 of your textbook presents a completed statement of cash flows that has incorporated the direct method. When the direct method is used, a schedule explaining the difference between reported net income and cash flows from operating activities must be provided.

13. Exhibit 14-7 of your textbook presents a completed statement of cash flows using the indirect method. As already explained, the essence of the indirect approach is the conversion of net income into net cash flows from operating activities.

Objective 7: Analyze the statement of cash flows (pp. 640–643).

14. The statement of cash flows can be analyzed by examining certain relationships. Two such cash-flow relationships, or measures, are cash-generating efficiency and free cash flow.

15. **Cash-generating efficiency,** which focuses on net cash flows from operating activities, is the ability of a company to generate cash from its current or continuing operations. It may be expressed as cash flow yield, cash flows to sales, or cash flows to assets.
    a. **Cash flow yield** equals net cash flows from operating activities divided by net income (or income from continuing operations). A cash flow yield of 2.0 times, for example, means that operating activities have generated twice as much cash flow as net income.
    b. **Cash flows to sales** equals net cash flows from operating activities divided by net sales. A ratio of 5.7 percent, for example, means that operating cash flows of 5.7 cents have been generated for every dollar of net sales.
    c. **Cash flows to assets** equals net cash flows from operating activities divided by average total assets. A ratio of 4.8 percent, for example, means that operating cash flows of 4.8 cents have been generated for every dollar of average total assets.

16. **Free cash flow** is a measure of cash remaining from operating activities after providing for certain commitments. It equals net cash flows from operating activities minus dividends minus net capital expenditures (purchases minus sales of plant assets). A *positive* free cash flow means that the company has met its cash commitments

and has cash remaining to reduce debt or expand further. A *negative* free cash flow means that the company will have to sell investments, borrow money, or issue stock to continue at its planned levels.

17. As is true with all financial statement ratios, the trends in the cash-generating efficiency and free cash flow over several years should be examined to analyze a company's cash flows.

Supplemental Objective 8: Prepare a work sheet for the statement of cash flows (pp. 643–648).

18. A work sheet for preparing the statement of cash flows is especially useful in complex situations. Using the indirect approach, it essentially allows for the systematic analysis of all changes in the balance sheet accounts.

19. Exhibit 14-8 of your textbook presents the format of a completed work sheet. In preparing the work sheet, five steps should be followed.
    a. Enter all balance sheet accounts into the Description column, listing all debit accounts before credit accounts.
    b. Enter all end-of-prior-period amounts and end-of-current-period amounts in the appropriate columns, and foot. The total debits should equal the total credits in each column.
    c. In the bottom portion of the work sheet, write the captions Cash Flows from Operating Activities, Cash Flows from Investing Activities, and Cash Flows from Financing Activities, leaving sufficient space between sections to enter data.
    d. Analyze the change in each balance sheet account, using the income statement and information on other transactions that affect noncurrent accounts during the period. Then enter the resulting debits and credits in the Analysis of Transactions columns, labeling each entry with a key letter corresponding to a reference list of changes.
    e. Foot the top and bottom portions of the Analysis of Transactions columns. The top portion should balance immediately, but the bottom portion should balance only when the net increase or decrease in cash is entered (credited for an increase or debited for a decrease). The changes in cash entered into the top and bottom of the work sheet should equal each other and should be labeled with the same key letter.

TESTING YOUR KNOWLEDGE

Matching

Match each term with its definition by writing the appropriate letter in the blank.

_____ 1. Statement of cash flows
_____ 2. Cash equivalents
_____ 3. Operating activities
_____ 4. Investing activities
_____ 5. Financing activities
_____ 6. Noncash investing and financing transactions
_____ 7. Direct method
_____ 8. Indirect method
_____ 9. Cash-generating efficiency
_____ 10. Free cash flow

a. The items placed at the bottom of the statement of cash flows in a separate schedule
b. Net cash flows from operating activities minus dividends minus net capital expenditures
c. In determining cash flows from operations, the procedure that starts with the figure for net income
d. A measure expressed as cash flow yield, cash flows to sales, or cash flows to assets
e. The statement of cash flows section that deals mainly with stockholders' equity accounts and borrowing
f. The financial report that explains the change in cash during the period
g. The statement of cash flows section that deals with long-term assets and marketable securities
h. In determining cash flows from operations, the procedure that adjusts each income statement item from an accrual basis to a cash basis
i. The statement of cash flows section that most closely relates to net income (loss)
j. Short-term, highly liquid investments

Short Answer

Use the lines provided to answer each item.

1. Give two examples of noncash investing and financing transactions.

2. When the statement of cash flows is prepared under the indirect method, why are depreciation, amortization, and depletion expense added back to net income to determine cash flows from operating activities?

3. Which sections of the statement of cash flows are prepared identically under the direct and indirect methods?

4. List three examples of cash equivalents.

The Statement of Cash Flows

True-False

Circle T if the statement is true, F if it is false. Please provide explanations for the false answers, using the blank lines at the end of the section.

T F 1. The statement of cash flows is a major financial statement required by the FASB.

T F 2. Payment on an account payable is considered a financing activity.

T F 3. The proceeds from the sale of investments would be considered an investing activity, whether the investments are classified as short-term or long-term.

T F 4. To calculate cash payments for purchases, the cost of goods sold must be known, along with the changes in inventory and accounts payable during the period.

T F 5. Under the indirect method, a decrease in prepaid expenses would be added to net income in determining net cash flows from operating activities.

T F 6. The schedule of noncash investing and financing transactions might include line items for depreciation, depletion, and amortization recorded during the period.

T F 7. In the Analysis of Transactions columns of the bottom portion of a statement of cash flows work sheet, Retained Earnings is credited and Dividends Paid debited for dividends paid during the period.

T F 8. In the Cash Flows from Operating Activities section of a statement of cash flows work sheet, the items that are credited in the Analysis of Transactions columns must be deducted from net income in the statement of cash flows.

T F 9. A net positive figure for cash flows from investing activities implies that the business is generally expanding.

T F 10. The issuance of common stock for cash would be disclosed in the financing activities section of the statement of cash flows.

T F 11. Under the indirect method, a loss on the sale of buildings would be deducted from net income in the operating activities section of the statement of cash flows.

T F 12. To calculate cash payments for operating expenses, operating expenses must be modified by (among other items) depreciation, which is treated as an add-back.

T F 13. Cash obtained by borrowing is considered a financing activity, whether the debt is classified as short-term or long-term.

T F 14. The purchase of land in exchange for the issuance of common stock in effect represents simultaneous investing and financing activities.

T F 15. It is possible for the direct and indirect methods to produce different net-change-in-cash figures on a statement of cash flows.

T F 16. Free cash flow does not include a deduction for dividends because dividend payment is never required.

Multiple Choice

Circle the letter of the best answer.

1. How would interest and dividends received be included in a statement of cash flows that employs the indirect method?
   a. Included as components of net income in the operating activities section
   b. Deducted from net income in the operating activities section
   c. Included in the investing activities section
   d. Included in the financing activities section
   e. Included in the schedule of noncash investing and financing transactions

2. How would a gain on the sale of investments be disclosed in a statement of cash flows that employs the indirect method?
   a. Added to net income in the operating activities section
   b. Deducted from net income in the operating activities section
   c. Included in the investing activities section
   d. Included in the financing activities section
   e. Included in the schedule of noncash investing and financing transactions

3. How would an increase in accounts payable be disclosed in a statement of cash flows that employs the indirect method?
   a. Added to net income in the operating activities section
   b. Deducted from net income in the operating activities section
   c. Included in the investing activities section
   d. Included in the financing activities section
   e. Included in the schedule of noncash investing and financing transactions

4. How would the purchase of a building by incurring a mortgage payable be disclosed in a statement of cash flows that employs the indirect method?
   a. Added to net income in the operating activities section
   b. Deducted from net income in the operating activities section
   c. Included in the investing activities section
   d. Included in the financing activities section
   e. Included in the schedule of noncash investing and financing transactions

5. How would dividends paid be disclosed in a statement of cash flows that employs the indirect method?
   a. Added to net income in the operating activities section
   b. Deducted from net income in the operating activities section
   c. Included in the investing activities section
   d. Included in the financing activities section
   e. Included in the schedule of noncash investing and financing transactions

6. How would interest paid be included in a statement of cash flows that employs the indirect method?
   a. Included as a component of net income in the operating activities section
   b. Deducted from net income in the operating activities section
   c. Included in the investing activities section
   d. Included in the financing activities section
   e. Included in the schedule of noncash investing and financing transactions

7. How would an increase in inventory be disclosed in a statement of cash flows that employs the indirect method?
   a. Added to net income in the operating activities section
   b. Deducted from net income in the operating activities section
   c. Included in the investing activities section
   d. Included in the financing activities section
   e. Included in the schedule of noncash investing and financing transactions

8. All of the following represent cash flows from operating activities *except* cash
   a. payments for income taxes.
   b. receipts from sales.
   c. receipts from the issuance of stock.
   d. payments for purchases.

9. When net income is recorded (debited) in the Analysis of Transactions columns of a statement of cash flows work sheet, which item is credited?
   a. Cash
   b. Income summary
   c. Net increase in cash
   d. Retained earnings

The Statement of Cash Flows

10. Barrett Corporation had cash sales of $30,000 and credit sales of $70,000 during the year, and the Accounts Receivable account increased by $14,000. Cash receipts from sales totaled
   a. $70,000.
   b. $86,000.
   c. $100,000.
   d. $114,000.

11. The calculations of cash flow yield, cash flows to sales, and cash flows to assets are all based upon
   a. net cash flows from financing activities.
   b. net increase or decrease in cash.
   c. net cash flows from operating activities.
   d. net cash flows from investing activities.

APPLYING YOUR KNOWLEDGE

Exercises

1. Use the following information to calculate the items below.

Accounts Payable, Jan. 1, 19xx	$ 47,000
Accounts Payable, Dec. 31, 19xx	54,000
Accounts Receivable, Jan. 1, 19xx	32,000
Accounts Receivable, Dec. 31, 19xx	22,000
Accrued Liabilities, Jan. 1, 19xx	17,000
Accrued Liabilities, Dec. 31, 19xx	11,000
Cost of Goods Sold for 19xx	240,000
Depreciation Expense for 19xx	20,000
Income Taxes Expense for 19xx	33,000
Income Taxes Payable, Jan. 1, 19xx	4,000
Income Taxes Payable, Dec. 31, 19xx	6,000
Inventory, Jan. 1, 19xx	86,000
Inventory, Dec. 31, 19xx	74,000
Operating Expenses for 19xx	70,000
Prepaid Expenses, Jan. 1, 19xx	2,000
Prepaid Expenses, Dec. 31, 19xx	3,000
Sales for 19xx	350,000

    a. Cash payments for operating expenses =

    $ _____

    b. Cash receipts from sales =

    $ _____

    c. Cash payments for income taxes =

    $ _____

    d. Cash payments for purchases =

    $ _____

    e. Net cash flows from operating activities =

    $ _____

2. For 19x7, Baker Corporation had average total assets of $800,000, net sales of $900,000, net income of $60,000, net cash flows from operating activities of $120,000, dividend payments of $30,000, purchases of plant assets of $75,000, and sales of plant assets of $40,000. Using this information, compute the following cash flow measures.

    a. Cash flow yield = _____ times

    b. Cash flows to sales = _____ %

    c. Cash flows to assets = _____ %

    d. Free cash flow = $_____

3. Use the following information to complete Webb Corporation's statement of cash flows work sheet on the next page for the year ended December 31, 19x9. Make sure to use the key letters in the Analysis of Transactions columns to refer to the following explanation list:

    a. Net income for 19x9 was $22,000.

    b–d. These key letters record changes in current assets and current liabilities.

    e. Sold plant assets that cost $30,000 with accumulated depreciation of $10,000, for $24,000.

    f. Purchased plant assets for $62,000.

    g. Recorded depreciation expense of $26,000 for 19x9.

    h. Converted bonds payable with a $10,000 face amount into common stock.

    i. Declared and paid dividends of $12,000.

    x. This key letter codes the change in cash.

Webb Corporation
Work Sheet for Statement of Cash Flows
For the Year Ended December 31, 19x9

Description	Account Balances 12/31/x8	Analysis of Transactions for 19x9 Debit	Analysis of Transactions for 19x9 Credit	Account Balances 12/31/x9
Debits				
Cash	35,000			29,000
Accounts Receivable	18,000			21,000
Inventory	83,000			72,000
Plant Assets	200,000			232,000
Total Debits	336,000			354,000
Credits				
Accumulated Depreciation	40,000			56,000
Accounts Payable	27,000			19,000
Bonds Payable	100,000			90,000
Common Stock	150,000			160,000
Retained Earnings	19,000			29,000
Total Credits	336,000			354,000

Cash Flows from Operating Activities

Cash Flows from Investing Activities

Cash Flows from Financing Activities

Net Decrease in Cash

CHAPTER 15 FINANCIAL STATEMENT ANALYSIS

REVIEWING THE CHAPTER

Objective 1: Describe and discuss the objectives of financial statement analysis (pp. 680–681).

1. Decision makers get specific information from general-purpose financial statements by means of **financial statement analysis.**

2. The users of financial statements are classified as either internal or external. The main internal user is management. The main external users are creditors and investors. Both creditors and investors will probably acquire a **portfolio,** or group of loans or investments, which allows the creditors and investors to average both the return and the risk.

3. Creditors and investors use financial statement analysis (a) to assess past performance and current position and (b) to assess future potential and the risk connected with that potential. Information about the past and present is very helpful in making projections about the future. Moreover, the easier it is to predict future performance, the less risk is involved. The lower risk means that the investor or creditor will require a lower expected return.

Objective 2: Describe and discuss the standards for financial statement analysis (pp. 681–683).

4. Decision makers assess performance by means of (a) rule-of-thumb measures, (b) analysis of past performance of the company, and (c) comparison with industry norms.

   a. Rule-of-thumb measures for key financial ratios are helpful but should not be the only basis for making a decision. For example, a company may report high earnings per share but may lack sufficient current assets to pay current debts.
   b. The past performance of a company can help show trends. The skill lies in the analyst's ability to predict whether a trend will continue or will reverse itself.
   c. Comparing a company's performance with the performance of other companies in the same industry is helpful, but there are three limitations to using industry norms as standards. First, no two companies are exactly the same. Second, many companies, called **diversified companies,** or *conglomerates,* operate in many unrelated industries, so that comparison is hard. (However, the FASB requirement to report financial information by segments has been somewhat helpful.) Third, different companies often use different accounting procedures for recording similar items.

Objective 3: State the sources of information for financial statement analysis (pp. 683–687).

5. The chief sources of information about publicly held corporations are reports published by the company, SEC reports, business periodicals, and credit and investment advisory services.

a. A company's annual report provides useful financial information, and includes the following sections: (1) management's analysis of the past year's operations, (2) the financial statements, (3) footnotes, including the company's principal accounting procedures, (4) the auditors' report, and (5) a five- or ten-year summary of operations.
b. **Interim financial statements** may indicate significant changes in a company's earnings trend. They consist of limited financial information for less than a year (usually quarterly).
c. Publicly held corporations are required to file with the SEC an annual report (Form 10-K), a quarterly report (Form 10-Q), and a current report of significant events (Form 8-K). These reports are available to the public and are sources of valuable financial information.
d. Financial analysts obtain information from such sources as the *Wall Street Journal, Forbes, Barron's, Fortune,* the *Commercial and Financial Chronicle,* Moody's, Standard & Poor's, and Dun & Bradstreet.

Objective 4: Identify the issues related to evaluating the quality of a company's earnings (pp. 687–690).

6. The most commonly used predictors of a company's performance are expected changes in earnings per share and in return on equity. Because net income is a component of both these ratios, the quality of earnings must be good if the measure is to be valid. The quality of earnings is affected by (a) the accounting methods and estimates the company's management chooses and (b) the nature of nonoperating items in the income statement. A different net income figure results, for example, when different estimates and procedures for dealing with uncollectible accounts, inventory, depreciation, depletion, and amortization are chosen. In general, the method that produces a lower, or more conservative, figure also produces a better quality of earnings. In addition, nonoperating and nonrecurring items, such as discontinued operations, extraordinary gains and losses, and the effects of accounting changes, can impair comparability if the financial analyst refers only to the bottom-line figure.

7. In most cases, management is honest and open in its financial reporting. However, when a company has committed financial wrongdoings, its employees occasionally disclose the nature of the misdeeds publicly. These individuals, protected by law, are called **whistle-blowers.**

Objective 5: Apply horizontal analysis, trend analysis, and vertical analysis to financial statements (pp. 690–696).

8. The most common tools and techniques of financial analysis are horizontal analysis, trend analysis, vertical analysis, and ratio analysis.
   a. Comparative financial statement show the current and prior year's statements side by side to aid in financial statement analysis. In **horizontal analysis,** absolute and percentage changes in specific items from one year to the next are shown. The first of the two years being considered is called the **base year,** and the percentage change is computed by dividing the amount of the change by the base-year amount.
   b. **Trend analysis** is the same as horizontal analysis, except that percentage changes are calculated for several consecutive years. For percentage changes to be shown over several years, **index numbers** must be used.
   c. In **vertical analysis,** the percentage relationship of individual items on the statement to a total within the statement (e.g., cost of goods sold as a percentage of net sales) is presented. The result is a **common-size statement.** On a common-size balance sheet, total assets and total liabilities and stockholders' equity would each be labeled 100 percent. On a common-size income statement, sales would be labeled 100 percent. Common-size statements may be presented in comparative form to show information both within the period and between periods.

Objective 6: Apply ratio analysis to financial statements in a comprehensive analysis of a company's financial situation (pp. 696–703).

9. In **ratio analysis,** certain relationships (ratios) between financial statement items are determined and then compared with those of prior years or other companies. Ratios provide information about a company's liquidity, profitability, long-term solvency, cash flow adequacy, and market strength. The most common ratios are shown in the table on the next page.

Ratio	Components	Use or Meaning
Liquidity Ratios		
Current ratio	$\dfrac{\text{Current assets}}{\text{Current liabilities}}$	Measure of short-term debt-paying ability
Quick ratio	$\dfrac{\text{Cash + marketable securities + receivables}}{\text{Current liabilities}}$	Measure of short-term debt-paying ability
Receivable turnover	$\dfrac{\text{Net sales}}{\text{Average accounts receivable}}$	Measure of relative size of accounts receivable balance and effectiveness of credit policies
Average days' sales uncollected	$\dfrac{\text{Days in year}}{\text{Receivable turnover}}$	Measure of average time taken to collect receivables
Inventory turnover	$\dfrac{\text{Cost of goods sold}}{\text{Average inventory}}$	Measure of relative size of inventory
Average days' inventory on hand	$\dfrac{\text{Days in year}}{\text{Inventory turnover}}$	Measure of average days taken to sell inventory

(**Note:** The term **operating cycle** means the time it takes to sell and collect for products sold. It equals average days' inventory on hand plus average days' sales uncollected.)

Ratio	Components	Use or Meaning
Profitability Ratios		
Profit margin	$\dfrac{\text{Net income}}{\text{Net sales}}$	Measure of net income produced by each dollar of sales
Asset turnover	$\dfrac{\text{Net sales}}{\text{Average total assets}}$	Measure of how efficiently assets are used to produce sales
Return on assets	$\dfrac{\text{Net income}}{\text{Average total assets}}$	Measure of overall earning power or profitability
Return on equity	$\dfrac{\text{Net income}}{\text{Average stockholders' equity}}$	Measure of profitability of stockholders' investments
Long-Term Solvency Ratios		
Debt to equity ratio	$\dfrac{\text{Total liabilities}}{\text{Stockholders' equity}}$	Measure of capital structure and leverage
Interest coverage ratio	$\dfrac{\text{Net income before taxes + interest expense}}{\text{Interest expense}}$	Measure of creditors' protection from default on interest payments
Cash Flow Adequacy Ratios		
Cash flow yield	$\dfrac{\text{Net cash flows from operating activities}}{\text{Net income}}$	Measure of ability to generate operating cash flows in relation to net income
Cash flows to sales	$\dfrac{\text{Net cash flows from operating activities}}{\text{Net sales}}$	Measure of ability of sales to generate operating cash flows
Cash flows to assets	$\dfrac{\text{Net cash flows from operating activities}}{\text{Average total assets}}$	Measure of ability of assets to generate operating cash flows
Free cash flow	Net cash flows from operating activities − dividends − net capital expenditures	Measure of cash generated or cash deficiency after providing for commitments
Market Strength Ratios		
Price/earnings (P/E) ratio	$\dfrac{\text{Market price per share}}{\text{Earnings per share}}$	Measure of investor confidence in a company
Dividends yield	$\dfrac{\text{Dividends per share}}{\text{Market price per share}}$	Measure of current return to an investor in a stock

Financial Statement Analysis

TESTING YOUR KNOWLEDGE

Matching

Match each term with its definition by writing the appropriate letter in the blank.

_____ 1. Financial statement analysis
_____ 2. Portfolio
_____ 3. Diversified companies (conglomerates)
_____ 4. Interim financial statements
_____ 5. Horizontal analysis
_____ 6. Base year
_____ 7. Trend analysis
_____ 8. Index number
_____ 9. Vertical analysis
_____ 10. Common-size statement
_____ 11. Ratio analysis
_____ 12. Operating cycle
_____ 13. Whistle-blowers

a. The time it takes to sell and collect for products sold
b. A group of investments or loans
c. Employees who publicly disclose company wrongdoings
d. A financial statement expressed in terms of percentages, the result of vertical analysis
e. Limited financial information for less than a year (usually quarterly)
f. The first year being considered when horizontal analysis is used
g. Getting specific information from general-purpose financial statements
h. A presentation of the percentage change in specific items over several years
i. A number used in trend analysis to show change in related items from one year to another
j. A presentation of absolute and percentage changes in specific items from one year to the next
k. A presentation of the percentage relationships of individual items on a statement to a total within the statement
l. Companies that operate in many unrelated industries
m. The determination of certain relationships between financial statement items

Short Answer

Use the lines provided to answer each item.

1. List four ratios that measure profitability.

2. Briefly distinguish between horizontal and vertical analysis.

3. List the three methods by which decision makers assess performance.

4. Why is it wiser to acquire a portfolio of small investments rather than one large investment?

5. List four measures of cash flow adequacy.

True-False

Circle T if the statement is true, F if it is false. Please provide explanations for the false answers, using the blank lines at the end of the section.

T F 1. Horizontal analysis is possible for both an income statement and a balance sheet.

T F 2. Common-size financial statement show dollar changes in specific items from one year to the next.

T F 3. A company with a 2.0 current ratio will experience a decline in the current ratio when a short-term liability is paid.

T F 4. The figure for inventory is not used in computing the quick ratio.

T F 5. Inventory turnover equals average inventory divided by cost of goods sold.

T F 6. The price/earnings ratio must be computed before earnings per share can be determined.

T F 7. When computing the return on equity, interest expense must be added back to net income.

T F 8. When a company has no debt, its return on assets equals its return on equity.

T F 9. The lower the debt to equity ratio, the riskier the situation.

T F 10. Receivable turnover measures the time it takes to collect an average receivable.

T F 11. A low interest coverage would be cause for concern for a company's bondholders.

T F 12. Average days' inventory on hand is a liquidity ratio.

T F 13. Dividends yield is a profitability ratio.

T F 14. On a common-size income statement, net income is given a label of 100 percent.

T F 15. Interim financial statement may serve as an early signal of significant changes in a company's earning trend.

T F 16. Probably the best source of financial news is the *Wall Street Journal.*

T F 17. Return on assets equals the profit margin times asset turnover.

T F 18. The quality of earnings is affected by the existence of an extraordinary item in the income statement.

Financial Statement Analysis

Multiple Choice

Circle the letter of the best answer.

1. Which of the following is a measure of long-term solvency?
   a. Current ratio
   b. Interest coverage
   c. Asset turnover
   d. Profit margin

2. Short-term creditors would probably be *most* interested in which of the following ratios?
   a. Current ratio
   b. Average days' inventory on hand
   c. Debt to equity ratio
   d. Quick ratio

3. Net income is irrelevant in computing which of the following ratios?
   a. Cash flow yield
   b. Return on assets
   c. Asset turnover
   d. Return on equity

4. A high price/earnings ratio indicates
   a. investor confidence in high future earnings.
   b. that the stock is probably overvalued.
   c. that the stock is probably undervalued.
   d. little investor confidence in high future earnings.

5. Index numbers are used in
   a. trend analysis.
   b. ratio analysis.
   c. vertical analysis.
   d. common-size statements.

6. The main internal user of financial statements is
   a. the SEC.
   b. management.
   c. investors.
   d. creditors.

7. Comparing performance with industry norms is complicated by
   a. the existence of diversified companies.
   b. the use of different accounting procedures by different companies.
   c. the fact that companies in the same industry usually differ in some respect.
   d. all of the above.

8. A low receivable turnover indicates that
   a. few customers are defaulting on their debts.
   b. the company's inventory is moving very slowly.
   c. the company is making collections from its customers very slowly.
   d. a small proportion of the company's sales are credit sales.

9. In a common-size income statement, net income is labeled
   a. 0 percent.
   b. the percentage that net income is in relation to sales.
   c. the percentage that net income is in relation to operating expenses.
   d. 100 percent.

10. Which of the following measures equals cash generated or cash deficiency after providing for commitments?
    a. Cash flows to assets
    b. Cash flow yield
    c. Free cash flow
    d. Cash flows to sales

APPLYING YOUR KNOWLEDGE

Exercises

1. Complete the horizontal analysis for the comparative income statements shown here. Round percentages to the nearest tenth of a percent.

	19x1	19x2	Increase (Decrease) Amount	Percentage
Sales	$200,000	$250,000		
Cost of goods sold	120,000	144,000		
Gross margin	$ 80,000	$106,000		
Operating expenses	50,000	62,000		
Income before income taxes	$ 30,000	$ 44,000		
Income taxes	8,000	16,000		
Net income	$ 22,000	$ 28,000		

2. The following is financial information for Ellis Corporation for 19xx. Current assets consist of cash, accounts receivable, marketable securities, and inventory.

Average accounts receivable	$100,000
Average (and ending) inventory	180,000
Cost of goods sold	350,000
Current assets, Dec. 31	500,000
Current liabilities, Dec. 31	250,000
Market price, Dec. 31, on 21,200 shares	40/share
Net income	106,000
Net sales	600,000
Average stockholders' equity	480,000
Average total assets	880,000
Net cash flows from operating activities	75,000

Compute the following ratios as of December 31. Round off to the nearest tenth of a whole number for **a–l**, to the nearest hundredth of a whole number in **m** and **n**.

a. The current ratio = _____

b. The quick ratio = _____

c. Inventory turnover = _____

d. Average days' inventory on hand = _____

e. Return on assets = _____

f. Return on equity = _____

g. Receivable turnover = _____

h. Average days' sales uncollected = _____

Financial Statement Analysis 175

i. The profit margin = _____

j. The cash flow yield = _____

k. Cash flows to sales = _____

l. Cash flows to assets = _____

m. Asset turnover = _____

n. The price/earnings ratio = _____

CHAPTER 16 INTERNATIONAL ACCOUNTING AND INTERCOMPANY INVESTMENTS

REVIEWING THE CHAPTER

Objective 1: Define *exchange rate* and record transactions that are affected by changes in foreign exchange rates (pp. 734–738).

1. When businesses expand internationally (called **multinational** or **transnational corporations**), two accounting problems arise. (a) The financial statements of foreign subsidiaries involve different currencies. These must be translated into domestic currency by means of an **exchange rate**. (b) The foreign financial statements are not necessarily prepared in accordance with domestic generally accepted accounting principles.

2. Purchases and sales with foreign countries pose no accounting problem for the domestic company when the domestic currency is being used. However, when the transaction involves foreign currency, the domestic company should record an **exchange gain or loss**. This exchange gain or loss reflects the change in the exchange rate from the transaction date to the date of payment.

3. When financial statements are prepared between the transaction date and the date of payment, an unrealized gain or loss should be recorded if the exchange rate has changed.

Objective 2: Describe the restatement of a foreign subsidiary's financial statements in U.S. dollars (pp. 738–739).

4. A foreign subsidiary that a parent company controls should be included in the parent company's consolidated financial statements. The subsidiary's financial statements must therefore be restated into the parent's **reporting currency**. The method of **restatement** depends on the foreign subsidiary's **functional currency**—that is, the currency with which it transacts most of its business.

5. Type I subsidiaries are self-contained within a foreign country. Their financial statements must be restated from the functional currency (local currency in this case) to the reporting currency. Type II subsidiaries are simply an extension of the parent's operations. Their financial statements must be restated from the local currency to the functional currency (which in this case is the same as the reporting currency).

6. When a Type I subsidiary operates in a country where there is hyperinflation (more than 100 percent cumulative inflation over three years), it should be treated as a Type II subsidiary, with the functional currency being the U.S. dollar.

Objective 3: Describe progress toward international accounting standards (pp. 739–742).

7. **Insider trading** is the practice of buying or selling shares of a publicly held company based on information not yet known by the public. Though not illegal in all countries, insider trading is considered a crime in the United States. Suspected offenders are investigated by the SEC.

8. At present, there are *some* recognized worldwide standards of accounting. To their credit, the In-

ternational Accounting Standards Committee (IASC) and the International Federation of Accountants (IFAC) *have* made much progress in setting up these international accounting standards. Despite the efforts of these bodies, however, there are still serious inconsistencies in financial statements among countries, and comparison remains a difficult task. More and more countries, however, are recognizing the importance of uniform international accounting standards in conducting international trade.

Objective 4: Apply the cost adjusted to market method and the equity method to the appropriate situations in accounting for long-term investments (pp. 742–748).

9. Corporations frequently invest in the securities of other corporations on a long-term basis. Some reasons for doing this are to obtain control over a desirable investee, to save time and money by investing in an existing company, to realize tax advantages, and to simply earn a return on the investment.

10. All long-term investments in the stock of other companies are recorded at cost. After purchase, the accounting treatment depends on the extent of influence exercised by the investing company. If the investing company can affect the operating and financing policies of the investee, even though it owns less than 50 percent of the investee's voting stock, it has **significant influence.** If the investing company can decide the operating and financing policies of the investee because it owns more than 50 percent of the investee's voting stock, it has **control.**

11. The extent of influence exercised over another company is often difficult to measure accurately. However, unless there is evidence to the contrary, long-term investments in stock are classified as (a) noninfluential and noncontrolling (generally less than 20 percent ownership), (b) influential but noncontrolling (generally 20 to 50 percent ownership), and (c) controlling (over 50 percent ownership).

12. The cost adjusted to market method should be used in accounting for noninfluential and noncontrolling investments. The equity method should be used in accounting for all other (that is, influential or controlling) investments. In addition, consolidated financial statements should usually be prepared when a controlling relationship exists.

   a. Under the **cost adjusted to market method,** the investor records investment income as dividends are received. In addition, the securities are recorded on the balance sheet at market. Unrealized Loss on Long-Term Investments is debited and Allowance to Adjust Long-Term Investments to Market is credited for the excess of total cost over total market. For available-for-sale equity securities, the debit appears in the stockholders' equity section of the balance sheet as a negative amount, and the credit appears in the asset section as a contra account to Long-Term Investments. An adjusting entry opposite to the one described above would be made when market value relative to cost has increased.

   b. Under the **equity method,** the investor records investment income as a debit to the Investment account and a credit to an Investment Income account. The amount recorded is the investee's periodic net income times the investor's ownership percentage. When the investor receives a cash dividend, the Cash account is debited and the Investment account is credited.

   c. When a company has a controlling interest in another company, the investor is called the **parent company** and the investee is called the **subsidiary.** Companies in such a relationship must prepare **consolidated financial statements** (combined statements of the parent and its subsidiaries). The purchase method (described below) or the pooling of interests method (the subject of a more advanced accounting course) is used.

Objective 5: Explain when to prepare consolidated financial statements, and describe their uses (pp. 748–750).

13. Consolidated financial statements should be prepared when an investing company has legal and effective control over another company (usually more than 50 percent ownership). In the past, there were a handful of circumstances that precluded the preparation of consolidated financial statements even though control existed. However, a relatively recent FASB pronouncement states that, with few exceptions, the financial statements of all majority-owned subsidiaries must now be consolidated with the parent company's financial statements for external reporting purposes. Consolidated financial statements are

useful because they present a financial picture of the entire economic entity.

14. The **purchase method** of consolidation must be used when two conditions apply: The parent company owns more than 50 percent of the subsidiary's voting stock, and the acquisition was not through an exchange of stock.

15. When consolidated financial statements are prepared, **eliminations** must be made on the consolidating work sheet for intercompany items. Among those items that must be eliminated are intercompany receivables, payables, sales, purchases, interest income, and interest expense, as well as the investment in the subsidiary company. In addition, under the purchase method, the entire stockholders' equity section of the subsidiary is eliminated.

Objective 6a: Prepare consolidated balance sheets at acquisition date for purchase at book value (pp. 750–752).

16. Under the purchase method, the parent records the investment at the purchase cost.
    a. When the book value of the net assets purchased equals their cost, the assets and liabilities acquired should appear at cost on the consolidated balance sheet. No goodwill should be recorded.
    b. The stockholders' equity section of the subsidiary at acquisition is not included in the consolidated balance sheet.
    c. When less than 100 percent of the subsidiary has been purchased, the **minority interest** (outside ownership) must be disclosed on the consolidated balance sheet.

Objective 6b: Prepare consolidated balance sheets at acquisition date for purchase at other than book value (pp. 752–754).

17. If the cost exceeds the book value of the net assets purchased, the extra amount should be allocated to the assets and liabilities acquired when consolidated financial statements are being prepared. The allocation should be based on fair market values at the date of acquisition. Any unassigned excess should be recorded as **goodwill** (or **goodwill from consolidation**) in the consolidated financial statements.

18. When the book value of the net assets purchased exceeds their cost, the book value of the assets should be reduced proportionately until the extra amount is eliminated.

Objective 7: Prepare consolidated income statements for intercompany transactions (pp. 754–755).

19. Intercompany items must be eliminated when preparing a consolidated income statement. They are (a) intercompany purchases and sales, (b) intercompany income and expenses on loans, receivables, or bond indebtedness, and (c) other intercompany income and expenses.

Summary of Journal Entries Introduced in Chapter 16

A. (L.O. 1)   Accounts Receivable, foreign company   XX (amount billed)
         Sales   XX (amount billed)
           Credit sale made, fixed amount billed in foreign currency

B. (L.O. 1)   Cash   XX (amount received)
         Exchange Gain or Loss   XX (the difference)
           Accounts Receivable, foreign company   XX (amount billed)
           Received payment in foreign currency, exchange loss arose from weakening of foreign currency in relation to U.S. dollar

C. (L.O. 1)   Purchases   XX (amount billed)
         Accounts Payable, foreign company   XX (amount billed)
           Credit purchase made, fixed amount billed in foreign currency

D. (L.O. 1)   Accounts Payable, foreign company   XX (amount billed)
         Exchange Gain or Loss   XX (the difference)
           Cash   XX (amount paid)
           Made payment in foreign currency, exchange gain arose from weakening of foreign currency in relation to U.S. dollar

E. (L.O. 1)   Note: When a U.S. company transacts business entirely in U.S. dollars, no exchange gain or loss will occur. Those simple journal entries illustrated in your textbook are not duplicated here.

F. (L.O. 1)   Note: At year end, an adjusting entry must be made for any unrealized exchange gains or losses on outstanding receivables or payables that are to be settled in a foreign currency.

G. (L.O. 4)   Long-Term Investments   XX (purchase price)
         Cash   XX (purchase price)
           Purchased long-term investment in stock

H. (L.O. 4)   Unrealized Loss on Long-Term Investments   XX (amount of decline)
         Allowance to Adjust Long-Term Investments to Market   XX (amount of decline)
           To record reduction of long-term investment to market

I. (L.O. 4)   Cash   XX (amount received)
         Loss on Sale of Investment   XX (the difference)
           Long-Term Investments   XX (purchase price)
           To record sale of shares of stock (Note: had a gain on sale arisen, it would have been credited)

J. (L.O. 4)   Cash   XX (amount received)
         Dividend Income   XX (amount received)
           Receipt of cash dividend; cost adjusted to market method assumed

K. (L.O. 4)   Allowance to Adjust Long-Term Investments to Market   XX (amount of recovery)
         Unrealized Loss on Long-Term Investments   XX (amount of recovery)
           To record the adjustment in long-term investment so it is reported at market

L. (L.O. 4)   Investment in XYZ Corporation   XX (amount paid)
            Cash   XX (amount paid)
                Investment in XYZ Corporation common stock

M. (L.O. 4)   Investment in XYZ Corporation   XX (equity percentage)
            Income, XYZ Corporation Investment   XX (equity percentage)
                Recognition of percentage of income reported by investee;
                equity method assumed

N. (L.O. 4)   Cash   XX (amount received)
            Investment in XYZ Corporation   XX (amount received)
                Cash dividend received; equity method assumed

O. (L.O. 6a)   Investment in XYZ Corporation   XX (book value)
             Cash   XX (amount paid)
                 Purchase of 100 percent of XYZ Corporation at book value

P. (L.O. 6a)   Common Stock (subsidiary)   XX (current balance)
             Retained Earnings (subsidiary)   XX (current balance)
                 Investment in XYZ Corporation   XX (current balance)
                   Work sheet entry to eliminate intercompany investment at
                   acquisition date, subsidiary wholly owned

Q. (L.O. 6b)   Common Stock (subsidiary)   XX (current balance)
            Retained Earnings (subsidiary)   XX (current balance)
              Investment in XYZ Corporation   XX (current balance)
              Minority Interest   XX (equity percentage)
                 Work sheet entry to eliminate intercompany investment at
                 acquisition date, subsidiary less than 100 percent owned

R. (L.O. 6b)   Other Long-Term Assets   XX (excess allocated)
            Goodwill   XX (excess allocated)
            Common Stock (subsidiary)   XX (current balance)
            Retained Earnings (subsidiary)   XX (current balance)
              Investment in XYZ Corporation   XX (current balance)
                 Work sheet entry to eliminate intercompany investment at
                 acquisition date; cost exceeds book value

S. (L.O. 6b)   Accounts Payable   XX (intercompany amount)
            Accounts Receivable   XX (intercompany amount)
              Work sheet entry to eliminate intercompany receivables
              and payables

T. (L.O. 7)   Sales   XX (intercompany amount)
            Cost of Goods Sold (Purchases)   XX (intercompany amount)
              Work sheet entry to eliminate intercompany sales and
              purchases

U. (L.O. 7)   Interest Revenue (Other Revenue)   XX (intercompany amount)
            Interest Expense (Other Expense)   XX (intercompany amount)
              Work sheet entry to eliminate intercompany interest

International Accounting and Intercompany Investments

TESTING YOUR KNOWLEDGE

Matching

Match each term with its definition by writing the appropriate letter in the blank.

_____ 1. Cost adjusted to market method
_____ 2. Equity method
_____ 3. Parent company
_____ 4. Subsidiary
_____ 5. Consolidated financial statements
_____ 6. Purchase method
_____ 7. Significant influence
_____ 8. Minority interest
_____ 9. Control
_____ 10. Eliminations
_____ 11. Restatement
_____ 12. Exchange rate
_____ 13. Reporting currency
_____ 14. Functional currency
_____ 15. Multinational (transnational) corporation
_____ 16. Insider trading

a. A business that operates in more than one country
b. The method used to account for noninfluential and noncontrolling investments
c. Buying and selling stock based on information not yet public
d. The consolidation method used when the parent owns more than 50 percent of the subsidiary's voting stock and did not acquire it through an exchange of stock
e. The type of money in which a given set of consolidated financial statements is presented
f. The method used to account for influential or controlling investments
g. A company that is controlled by another company
h. Expressing one currency in terms of another
i. A company that has a controlling interest in another company
j. Combined statements of the parent and its subsidiaries
k. Usually, ownership of 20 to 50 percent of another company's voting stock
l. Ownership of more than 50 percent of the voting stock of another corporation
m. The type of money with which a company transacts most of its business
n. Entries that appear on a consolidated work sheet
o. The value of one currency in terms of another
p. Outside ownership of a subsidiary

Short Answer

Use the lines provided to answer each item.

1. List the three classifications for long-term investments in stocks, as well as the method that should be used after purchase to account for each investment.

    Classification

    _____

    _____

    _____

    Method

    _____

    _____

    _____

2. Briefly explain the accounting treatment for dividends received under the cost adjusted to market method and under the equity method.

    _____

    _____

    _____

    _____

3. Under what circumstance should goodwill be recorded in a consolidated balance sheet?

    _____

    _____

    _____

4. Why must certain items be eliminated when consolidated financial statements are prepared?

    _____

    _____

    _____

    _____

    _____

5. Under what circumstances would a company record an exchange gain or loss?

    _____

    _____

    _____

    _____

True-False

Circle T if the statement is true, F if it is false. Please provide explanations for the false answers, using the blank lines at the end of the section.

T F 1. When one company has an influential but noncontrolling interest in another company, it would use the equity method to account for the investment.

T F 2. Under the cost adjusted to market method, the investor records investment income for a percentage (based on percentage ownership) of the investee's periodic net income.

T F 3. When one company owns at least 20 percent of another company, consolidated financial statements should be prepared.

T F 4. When consolidated financial statements are prepared, the parent's investment in the subsidiary must be eliminated.

T F 5. Under the purchase method of consolidation, the subsidiary's earnings for the entire year of acquisition are included in the consolidated financial statements.

T F 6. Under the equity method, the investor records a cash dividend by debiting Cash and crediting the investment account.

T F 7. A minority interest should be reported as an asset in the consolidated balance sheet.

T F 8. Goodwill from consolidation does not appear on the unconsolidated balance sheet of the parent or subsidiary, but may appear on the consolidated balance sheet.

International Accounting and Intercompany Investments 183

T F 9. When Company A transacts business with foreign Company B in the currency of Company A, Company A will not record an exchange gain or loss even if the exchange rate has changed between the transaction date and the date of payment.

T F 10. Given the data in question 9, Company B should record an exchange gain or loss.

T F 11. When a given exchange rate remains constant over a period of time, no transaction involving the two currencies will result in an exchange gain or loss over that period.

T F 12. The calculation of net income should include any unrealized exchange gains and losses that arose during the period.

T F 13. When preparing consolidated financial statements, purchases of goods and services from outsiders should be eliminated.

T F 14. When the book value of the net assets purchased equals their cost, the assets and liabilities purchased should appear at cost on the consolidated balance sheet.

Multiple Choice

Circle the letter of the best answer.

1. The journal entry to record the receipt of a dividend under the cost adjusted to market method would include a
   a. debit to the investment account.
   b. credit to Dividend Income.
   c. debit to Goodwill.
   d. credit to the investment account.

2. When the book value of the net assets purchased exceeds their purchase cost,
   a. goodwill exists.
   b. the entire excess should appear as negative goodwill in the consolidated balance sheet.
   c. the subsidiary's long-term assets should be increased until the extra amount is eliminated.
   d. the subsidiary's long-term assets should be reduced until the extra amount is eliminated.

3. The elimination of an intercompany investment cannot include a
   a. debit to the investment account.
   b. debit to Goodwill.
   c. debit to Retained Earnings.
   d. credit to minority interest.

4. The unconsolidated financial statements of a parent company may not include
   a. purchases from its subsidiary.
   b. goodwill from consolidation.
   c. an account reflecting the investment in its subsidiary.
   d. purchases from outsiders.

5. Which of the following items would not be eliminated when consolidated financial statements are prepared, assuming that the subsidiary is 100 percent owned?
   a. The subsidiary's capital stock
   b. The parent's investment in the subsidiary
   c. Interest owned to the subsidiary from the parent
   d. Profit on goods sold by the subsidiary to outsiders

6. Morse Company uses the cost adjusted to market method to account for its three long-term investments. The total cost of the investments is $95,000, and the total market value of the investments at the end of 19xx is $60,000. The account Allowance to Adjust Long-Term Investments to Market has a credit balance of $10,000 before the 19xx adjusting entry is made. The year-end adjusting entry for 19xx would include a
   a. debit to Unrealized Loss on Long-Term Investments for $35,000.
   b. debit to Allowance to Adjust Long-Term Investments to Market for $10,000.
   c. credit to Allowance to Adjust Long-Term Investments to Market for $60,000.
   d. debit to Unrealized Loss on Long-Term Investments for $25,000.

7. For available-for-sale equity securities, the account Unrealized Loss on Long-Term Investments appears
   a. as a footnote only.
   b. on the balance sheet as a contra-asset account.
   c. on the income statement as a loss.
   d. on the balance sheet as a contra-stockholders' equity account.

8. When an American company purchases goods from France and the transaction involves francs, what would the American company record on the date of payment if the value of the franc declined relative to the dollar between the purchase date and the payment date?
   a. An unrealized exchange gain
   b. An exchange loss
   c. An exchange gain
   d. No exchange gain or loss

International Accounting and Intercompany Investments

APPLYING YOUR KNOWLEDGE

Exercises

1. Weber Corporation purchased 80 percent of the common stock of Carter Corporation for $165,000. Carter's stockholders' equity included common stock of $60,000 and retained earnings of $90,000. On the lines provided, show the debits, credits, and amounts for the eliminating entry that would be made on the work sheet for consolidating the balance sheets of Weber and Carter. Assume that up to $10,000 of any excess of cost over carrying value is allocated to the building purchased.

Account Debited	Amount	Account Credited	Amount
_____	$ _____	_____	$ _____
_____	$ _____	_____	$ _____
_____	$ _____		
_____	$ _____		

2. Fairfax Corporation owns 15 percent of the voting stock of Andrews Company and 30 percent of the voting stock of Wilkins Company. Both are long-term investments. During a given year, Andrews paid total dividends of $80,000 and earned $110,000, and Wilkins paid total dividends of $50,000 and earned $65,000. In the journal, prepare Fairfax's entries to reflect the above facts. Leave the date column empty, as no dates have been specified.

		General Journal		
Date		Description	Debit	Credit

3. Randy Corporation, an American company, sold merchandise on credit to a Mexican company for 100,000 pesos. On the sale date, the exchange rate was $.05 per peso. On the payment date, the value of the peso had declined to $.045. Prepare the entries in the journal to record Randy Corporation's sale and receipt of payment. Leave the date column empty, as no dates have been specified.

Date	Description	Debit	Credit

Crossword Puzzle
for Chapters 14, 15, and 16

ACROSS

2. Ratio indicating investor confidence in a company (2 words)
4. Analysis resulting in 9-Across
6. Quarterly financial statement, e.g.
7. Statement of cash _____
8. Financial statement _____
9. Statement showing percentage relationships (hyphenated)
13. _____ analysis, a variation of horizontal analysis
15. Method to account for long-term investments
16. An operating-activity outflow
17. Analysis involving dollar and percentage changes

DOWN

1. Relationship between debt and equity
2. Group of investments or loans
3. An operating-activity inflow or outflow
5. Dividends _____
9. With 14-Down, a measure of liquidity
10. Number used in 13-Across
11. Majority ownership of voting stock
12. Method for 7-Across
14. See 9-Down

APPENDIX B THE MERCHANDISING WORK SHEET AND CLOSING ENTRIES

REVIEWING THE APPENDIX

Objective 1: Prepare a work sheet and closing entries for a merchandising concern using the periodic inventory system (pp. 794–799).

1. Under the periodic inventory system, the objectives of dealing with inventory at the end of the period are to (a) remove the beginning balance from the Merchandise Inventory account, (b) enter the ending balance into the Merchandise Inventory account, and (c) enter the beginning inventory as a debit and the ending inventory as a credit to the Income Summary account to calculate net income.

2. The work sheet for a merchandising company is prepared a bit differently from that of a service company. The main difference is the inclusion of accounts such as Merchandise Inventory, Sales, and Freight In. In addition, work sheet preparation will differ depending upon whether the periodic or the perpetual inventory system is being used.

3. Under the periodic inventory system, beginning inventory appears as a debit in the Income Statement column. Ending inventory appears as a credit in the Income Statement column and as a debit in the Balance Sheet column. A Cost of Goods Sold account will *not* appear in the work sheet, though it will under the perpetual inventory system. Under either inventory system, an Adjusted Trial Balance column may be eliminated if only a few adjustments are necessary.

4. Data for closing entries may be obtained from the completed work sheet. Below is a summary of the closing entries prepared when using a periodic inventory system:

Income Summary   XX (sum of credits)
   Merchandise Inventory   XX (beginning amount)
   Sales Returns and Allowances   XX (current debit balance)
   Sales Discounts   XX (current debit balance)
   Purchases   XX (current debit balance)
   Freight In   XX (current debit balance)
   All other expenses   XX (current debit balances)
     Closing entry 1: To close temporary expense and revenue accounts with debit balances and to remove the beginning inventory

Merchandise Inventory   XX (ending amount)
Sales   XX (current credit balance)
Purchases Returns and Allowances   XX (current credit balance)
Purchases Discounts   XX (current credit balance)
   Income Summary   XX (sum of debits)
     Closing entry 2: To close temporary expense and revenue accounts with credit balances and to establish the ending inventory

Income Summary	XX	(current credit balance)
Retained Earnings		XX (net income amount)
Closing entry 3: To close the Income Summary account		
Retained Earnings	XX	(amount declared)
Dividends		XX (amount declared)
Closing entry 4: To close the Dividends account		

Objective 2: Prepare a work sheet and closing entries for a merchandising concern using the perpetual inventory system (pp. 799–801).

5. Under the perpetual inventory system, the Merchandise Inventory account is up to date at the end of the accounting period. This occurs because the account is updated whenever there is a purchase, sale, or return. Therefore, Merchandise Inventory is not involved in the closing process. On the work sheet, the Trial Balance and Balance Sheet columns both reflect the ending balance.

6. As inventory is sold (under the perpetual inventory system), the cost is transferred from the Merchandise Inventory account to Cost of Goods Sold. Therefore, Cost of Goods Sold will appear in the work sheet and in the closing entries along with all the other expenses.

7. Data for closing entries may be obtained from the completed work sheet. Below is a summary of the closing entries prepared when using a perpetual inventory system:

Income Summary	XX	(sum of credits)
Sales Returns and Allowances		XX (current debit balance)
Sales Discounts		XX (current debit balance)
Cost of Goods Sold		XX (current debit balance)
Freight In		XX (current debit balance)
All other expenses		XX (current debit balances)
Closing entry 1: To close temporary expense and revenue accounts with debit balances		
Sales	XX	(current credit balance)
Income Summary		XX (sales amount)
Closing entry 2: To close temporary revenue account with credit balance		
Income Summary	XX	(current credit balance)
Retained Earnings		XX (net income amount)
Closing entry 3: To close the Income Summary account		
Retained Earnings	XX	(amount declared)
Dividends		XX (amount declared)
Closing entry 4: To close the Dividends account		

APPLYING YOUR KNOWLEDGE

Exercises

1. The work sheet for Mammoth Mart, Inc., has been started, as shown on the next page. Use the following information to complete the work sheet (remember to key the adjustments). Assume use of the *periodic* inventory system. You will notice that the Adjusted Trial Balance column has been provided, even though it is not absolutely necessary.
   a. Expired rent, $250
   b. Accrued salaries, $500
   c. Depreciation on equipment, $375
   d. Ending merchandise inventory, $620
   e. Accrued income taxes expense, $180

Mammoth Mart, Inc.
Work Sheet
For the Month Ended March 31, 19xx

Account Name	Trial Balance Debit	Trial Balance Credit	Adjustments Debit	Adjustments Credit	Adjusted Trial Balance Debit	Adjusted Trial Balance Credit	Income Statement Debit	Income Statement Credit	Balance Sheet Debit	Balance Sheet Credit
Cash	1,000									
Accounts Receivable	700									
Merchandise Inventory	400									
Prepaid Rent	750									
Equipment	4,200									
Accounts Payable		900								
Common Stock		3,000								
Retained Earnings		1,200								
Sales		9,800								
Sales Discounts	300									
Purchases	3,700									
Purchases Returns and Allowances		150								
Freight In	400									
Salaries Expense	3,000									
Advertising Expense	600									
	15,050	15,050								

2. Following are the accounts and data needed to prepare the 19xx closing entries for Martin Manufacturing Company. Assume a normal account balance for each, as well as use of the *perpetual* inventory system. Omit explanations.

Cost of Goods Sold	$52,700
Freight In	3,200
General and Administrative Expenses	24,800
Income Taxes Expense	6,500
Sales	244,100
Sales Returns and Allowances	5,300
Selling Expenses	39,400

In addition, dividends of $50,000 were declared and paid during the year.

\multicolumn{4}{c}{General Journal}			
Date	Description	Debit	Credit

The Merchandising Work Sheet and Closing Entries

APPENDIX C SPECIAL-PURPOSE JOURNALS

REVIEWING THE APPENDIX

Objective 1: Explain the objectives and uses of special-purpose journals (pp. 805–806).

1. Companies using manual data processing (keeping handwritten accounting records) record an entry in one or more journals. A company can record all its transactions in the general journal. However, companies with a large number of transactions also use **special-purpose journals** for efficiency, economy, and control.

2. Most business transactions fall into one of four types, and are recorded in one of four special-purpose journals, as follows:
   a. Sales of merchandise on credit are recorded in the sales journal.
   b. Purchases of merchandise on credit are recorded in the purchases journal.
   c. Receipts of cash are recorded in the cash receipts journal.
   d. Disbursements of cash are recorded in the cash payments journal.

Objective 2: Construct and use the following types of special-purpose journals: sales journal, purchases journal, cash receipts journal, cash payments journal, and others as needed (pp. 806–817).

3. The **sales journal,** used only to handle credit sales, saves times because (a) each entry requires only one line; (b) account names need not be written out, since frequently occurring accounts are used as column headings; (c) an explanation is not needed; and (d) only total sales for the month are posted to the Sales account, not each individual sale. Postings are made daily, however, to customer accounts (in the accounts receivable subsidiary ledger). Similar time-saving principles apply to the other special-purpose journals.

4. The **purchases journal** is used to record purchases on credit. A single-column purchases journal records the purchases of merchandise only. However, a multicolumn purchases journal will accommodate purchases of more than just merchandise. Only total purchases for the month are posted to the Purchases account; however, postings are made daily to creditor accounts (in the accounts payable subsidiary ledger).

5. All receipts of cash are recorded in the **cash receipts journal.** Typically, a cash receipts journal would include debit columns for Cash and Sales Discounts and credit columns for Sales, Accounts Receivable, and "Other Accounts." Postings to customer accounts and "Other Accounts" are made on a daily basis. All column totals, except for Other Accounts, are posted to the general ledger at the end of the month.

6. All payments of cash are recorded in the **cash payments journal.** Typically, a cash payments journal would include debit columns for "Other Accounts" and Accounts Payable, and credit columns for Cash and Purchases Discounts. Postings to creditor accounts and Other Accounts are made daily. All column totals, except for Other Accounts, are posted to the general ledger at the end of the month.

7. Transactions that cannot be recorded in a special-purpose journal, such as the purchase of office equipment on credit (assuming a single-column purchases journal), are recorded in the general journal. Closing entries and adjusting entries are also made in the general journal. Postings are made at the end of each day, and in the case of Accounts Receivable and Accounts Payable, postings are made to both the controlling account and the subsidiary account.

8. Special-purpose journals of businesses may differ slightly from those used in the textbook, because the types of transactions may vary. However, an understanding of the general concepts and mechanics of special-purpose journals makes adapting to a different system relatively easy.

Objective 3: Explain the purposes and relationships of controlling accounts and subsidiary ledgers (pp. 806–818).

9. Most companies that sell to customers on credit keep an accounts receivable record for each customer. In this way the company can determine how much a given customer owes at any time. All customer accounts are filed alphabetically or by account number in the accounts receivable **subsidiary ledger.**

10. The general ledger, however, contains an Accounts Receivable **controlling** (or *control*) **account.** The controlling account is updated at the end of each month and keeps a running total of *all* accounts receivable. Its balance must equal the sum of all the accounts in the accounts receivable subsidiary ledger.

11. Most companies also use an Accounts Payable controlling account and subsidiary ledger, which function much like the Accounts Receivable controlling account and subsidiary ledger.

TESTING YOUR KNOWLEDGE

Matching

Match each term with its definition by writing the appropriate letter in the blank.

_____ 1. Special-purpose journal
_____ 2. Subsidiary ledger
_____ 3. Subsidiary account
_____ 4. Controlling account
_____ 5. Schedule of accounts receivable or accounts payable

a. Any journal except the general journal
b. A formal listing of the balances of customers or creditors
c. The record of a customer or creditor in a subsidiary ledger
d. Where the customer or creditor accounts are kept
e. Any general ledger account that has a related subsidiary ledger

APPLYING YOUR KNOWLEDGE

Exercises

1. In the spaces provided, indicate the symbol of the journal that should be used by Targum Appliance Store.

    S   = Sales journal
    P   = Purchases journal (single-column)
    CR = Cash receipts journal
    CP = Cash payments journal
    J   = General journal

    _____ a. Goods that had been purchased by Targum on credit are returned.
    _____ b. Goods that had been purchased by Targum for cash are returned for a cash refund.
    _____ c. Toasters are purchased on credit by Targum.
    _____ d. The same toasters are paid for.
    _____ e. A blender is sold on credit.
    _____ f. The electric bill is paid.
    _____ g. Adjusting entries are made.
    _____ h. Office furniture is purchased by Targum on credit.
    _____ i. Closing entries are made.
    _____ j. Targum pays for half of the office furniture.
    _____ k. A customer pays a bill and receives a discount.

2. Enter the following transactions of Riley Liquidators, Inc., into the cash receipts journal provided below. Complete the Post. Ref. column as though the entries had been posted daily. Also, make the proper posting notations in the journals as though the end-of-month postings had been made. Accounts Receivable is account no. 114, Sales is account no. 411, Sales Discounts is account no. 412, and Cash is account no. 111.

    Feb. 3 Received payment of $500 less a 2 percent discount from Frank Simpson for merchandise previously purchased on credit.
    9 Sold equipment (account no. 135) for $8,000 cash.
    14 Issued $10,000 more in common stock (account no. 311).
    23 Stanley Hall paid Riley $150 for merchandise he had purchased on credit.
    28 Cash sales for the month totaled $25,000.

Cash Receipts Journal								
				Debits			Credits	
Date	Account Debited/Credited	Post. Ref.	Cash	Sales Disc.	Other Accts.	Accts. Receiv.	Sales	Other Accts.

3. A page from a special-purpose journal is provided below.

Date	Ck. No.	Payee	Account Credited/ Debited	Post. Ref.	Credits Cash	Credits Purchases Discounts	Credits Other Accts.	Debits Accts. Payable	Debits Other Accts.
May 1	114	Vincennes Supply Co.		✓	784	16		800	
7	115	Jeppson Bus. Equip.	Office Equipment	167	2000				2000
13	116	Daily Planet	Advertising Expense	512	350				350
19	117	Olsen Motors		✓	420			420	
					3554	16		1220	2350
					(111)	(413)		(211)	(315)

The following questions relate to this journal.

a. What type of journal is this? _____

b. What error was made in this journal? _____

c. Provide an explanation for the four transactions.

May 1 _____

May 7 _____

May 13 _____

May 19 _____

d. Explain the following:

1. The check marks in the Post. Ref. column _____

2. The numbers 167 and 512 in the Post. Ref. column _____

3. The numbers below the column totals _____

Special-Purpose Journals

APPENDIX D ACCOUNTING FOR UNINCORPORATED BUSINESSES

REVIEWING THE APPENDIX

Objective 1: Record the basic transactions affecting the owner's equity of a sole proprietorship (pp. 822–823).

1. A **sole proprietorship** is a business owned by one person. In accounting, it is considered an entity separate from its owner, but for legal purposes, the owner and proprietorship are considered one and the same (that is, the owner is personally liable for all debts of the business). A cash investment is recorded as a debit to Cash and a credit to the owner's capital account. A cash withdrawal is recorded as a debit to the owner's withdrawals account and a credit to Cash. Closing entries for a sole proprietorship are the same as for a corporation, except that Income Summary is closed to the owner's capital account, as is the owner's withdrawals account (an account that does not exist for a corporation).

Objective 2: Identify the major characteristics of a partnership (pp. 823–825).

2. According to the Uniform Partnership Act, a **partnership** is "an association of two or more persons to carry on as co-owners of a business for profit." Its chief characteristics are as follows:
   a. Voluntary association: Partners choose each other when they form their business.
   b. **Partnership agreement:** Partners may have either an oral or a written agreement.
   c. **Limited life:** Certain events may dissolve the partnership.
   d. **Mutual agency:** Each partner may bind the partnership to outside contracts.
   e. **Unlimited liability:** Each partner is personally liable for all debts of the partnership.
   f. Co-ownership of partnership property: Business property is jointly owned by all partners.
   g. Participation in partnership income: Each partner shares income and losses of the business.

Objective 3: Record investments of cash and of other assets by the partners in forming a partnership (pp. 825–826).

3. The owners' equity section of a partnership's balance sheet is called **partners' equity,** and separate capital and withdrawals accounts must be maintained for each partner. When a partner makes an investment, the assets contributed are debited at their fair market value, and the partner's capital account is credited.

Objective 4: Compute and record the income or losses that partners share, based on stated ratios, capital balance ratios, and partners' salaries and interest (pp. 826–832).

4. The method of distributing partnership income and losses should be specified in the partnership agreement. If the agreement does not mention the distribution of income and losses, the law requires that they be shared equally. The most common methods base distribution on (a) a stated ratio only, (b) a capital balance ratio only, or (c) a combination of salaries, interest on each partner's capital, and the stated ratio. Net income is distributed to partners' equity by debiting Income Summary and crediting each partner's capital account; the reverse is done for a net loss.

5. When income and losses are based on a stated ratio only, partnership income or loss for the period is multiplied by each partner's ratio

(stated as a fraction or percentage) to arrive at each partner's share.

6. When income and losses are based on a **capital balance** ratio only, partnership income or loss for the period is multiplied by each partner's proportion of (a) the capital balance at the beginning of the period or (b) the average capital during the period.

7. When income and losses are based on salaries, interest, and a stated ratio, a procedure must be followed. First, salaries and interest must be allocated to the partners regardless of the net income figure for the period. Then, any net income left over after the salaries and interest must be allocated to the partners in the stated ratio. On the other hand, if salaries and interest are greater than net income, the excess must be deducted from each partner's allocation, in the stated ratio.

Objective 5: Record the admission of a new partner (pp. 832–835).

8. When a partnership is legally dissolved, it loses the authority to continue business as a going concern. **Dissolution** of a partnership occurs on (a) the admission of a new partner, (b) the withdrawal of a partner, or (c) the death of a partner.

9. A new partner can be admitted into a partnership by either (a) purchasing an interest in the partnership from one or more of the original partners or (b) investing assets into the partnership.
    a. When a new partner purchases an interest from another partner, the selling partner's capital account is debited and the buying partner's account credited for the interest in the business sold. The purchase price is ignored in making this entry.
    b. When a new partner invests his or her own assets into the partnership, the contributed assets are debited and the new partner's capital account is credited. The amount of the debit and credit may or may not equal the value of the assets. It depends on the value of the business and the method applied. When the partners feel that a share of their business is worth more than the value of the assets being contributed, they generally ask the entering partner to pay them a **bonus**. Under the opposite set of circumstances, a partnership may give the new partner a greater interest in the business than the value of the assets contributed.

Objective 6: Describe the implications of the withdrawal or death of a partner and of the liquidation of a partnership (pp. 835–836).

10. A partner may withdraw from (leave) a partnership in one of two ways. (a) The partner may take assets from the partnership that are greater than, less than, or equal to his or her capital investment. (b) The partner may sell his or her interest to new or existing partners. In addition, when a partner dies, the partnership is thereby dissolved. Accordingly, certain immediate steps must be taken to settle with the heirs of the deceased partner.

11. **Liquidation** of a partnership is the process of (a) selling partnership assets, (b) paying off partnership liabilities, and (c) distributing the remaining assets to the partners according to their capital balances.

TESTING YOUR KNOWLEDGE

Matching

Match each term with its definition by writing the appropriate letter in the blank.

_____ 1. Sole proprietorship
_____ 2. Partnership
_____ 3. Voluntary association
_____ 4. Partnership agreement
_____ 5. Limited life
_____ 6. Mutual agency
_____ 7. Unlimited liability
_____ 8. Dissolution
_____ 9. Liquidation
_____ 10. Partners' equity

a. The sale of partnership assets, and payment to creditors and owners
b. The fact that any change in partners will cause the business to dissolve
c. The power of each partner to enter into contracts that are within the normal scope of the business
d. The balance sheet section that lists the partners' capital accounts
e. A business owned by one person
f. An association of two or more persons to carry on as co-owners of a business for profit
g. Creditors' claim to the partners' personal assets if the partnership cannot pay its debts
h. The end of a partnership as a going concern
i. The specifics of how the partnership is to operate
j. The partners' consent to join one another in forming a partnership

Accounting for Unincorporated Businesses

APPLYING YOUR KNOWLEDGE

Exercises

1. Partners A, B, and C each receive a $10,000 salary, as well as 5 percent interest on their respective investments of $60,000, $40,000, and $50,000. If they share income and losses in a 3:2:1 ratio, how much net income or loss would be allocated to each under the following circumstances?
    a. A net income of $40,500

    A = $ _____

    B = $ _____

    C = $ _____

    b. A net income of $25,500

    A = $ _____

    B = $ _____

    C = $ _____

    c. A net loss of $4,500

    A = $ _____

    B = $ _____

    C = $ _____

2. Partners G, H, and I have capital balances of $10,000 each, and share income and losses in a 2:2:1 ratio. They agree to allow J to purchase a one-third interest in the business. If they use the bonus method to record the transaction, provide the proper journal entry under each of the following assumptions:
    a. J contributes $12,000 in cash.
    b. J contributes $15,000 in cash.
    c. J contributes $21,000 in cash.

Date	Description	Debit	Credit

General Journal

APPENDIX E OVERVIEW OF GOVERNMENTAL AND NOT-FOR-PROFIT ACCOUNTING

REVIEWING THE APPENDIX

Objective 1: Explain and differentiate some basic concepts related to governmental and not-for-profit accounting (pp. 839–840).

1. Appendix E deals with accounting for state and local governments, colleges and universities, hospitals, and voluntary health and welfare organizations. The first four learning objectives relate to accounting for state and local governments, and the last relates to accounting for the other not-for-profit groups listed above.

2. The development of governmental accounting standards is currently the responsibility of the Governmental Accounting Standards Board (GASB). Formerly, it was the responsibility of the National Council on Governmental Accounting (NCGA). These standards are developed, not to measure profit, but to measure the changes in the funds available for governmental activities. Of primary importance is the control the governmental unit exercises over the funds made available, many for specific purposes. In governmental accounting, a **fund** is defined as a fiscal and accounting entity, and it is generally based on **modified accrual accounting** (defined in paragraph 5).

Objective 2: Describe the types of funds used in governmental accounting (pp. 840–841).

3. State and local governments use a variety of funds, each of which must show (a) the financial position and results of operations for the period, and (b) compliance with legal provisions of state or local government.
   a. The general fund accounts for financial resources, such as police, fire, and sanitation, that are not accounted for in any other fund.
   b. Special revenue funds account for revenues that are legally restricted to specific purposes.
   c. Capital projects funds account for the acquisition and construction of major capital projects, such as buildings, highways, and sewer systems.
   d. The debt service fund accounts for resources to pay principal and interest on long-term debt.
   e. Enterprise funds account for activities, such as golf courses and utilities, that charge the public for goods or services.
   f. Internal service funds account for goods or services that one governmental agency provides to another (within the same governmental unit).
   g. Trust and agency funds account for assets held for individuals, private organizations, or other funds.

4. The funds discussed in paragraph 3a–d are described as **governmental funds;** the enterprise and internal service funds are described as **proprietary funds;** and trust and agency funds are described as **fiduciary funds.** State and local governments also use a general fixed assets **account group** and a general long-term debt group to account for fixed assets and long-term liabilities, respectively, that are not related to specific proprietary or trust funds.

Objective 3: Explain the modified accrual basis of accounting used by state and local governments (pp. 841–843).

5. Modified accrual accounting differs from accrual accounting in (a) the method of measuring and recognizing revenues and expenditures, (b) the

incorporation of the budget into the accounting records, and (c) the use of **encumbrance accounting** to account for purchases. In governmental accounting, **revenues** are increases in fund resources (other than from interfund transactions or proceeds of long-term debt), and are recognized when measurable and available. **Expenditures** are decreases in fund resources (other than from interfund transfers). Whereas business accounting emphasizes the matching of revenues and expenses to obtain net income, governmental accounting focuses on the inflows and outflows of fund resources. Examples of general fund journal entries follow.

a. The budget is incorporated into the accounts with a debit to Estimated Revenues, a credit to Appropriations, and a credit to Fund Balance (assuming that revenues are expected to exceed expenditures). The Appropriations account will enable the governmental unit to exercise control over its expenditures. Also, the Fund Balance occupies the equity section of governmental and nonprofit balance sheets.

b. When a governmental unit purchases an asset that is to be received in several weeks or months, the general fund debits Encumbrances and credits Reserve for Encumbrances. This entry will ensure that the governmental unit adheres to its spending limit.

c. When the above asset is received, two entries are made into the general fund. First, the encumbrance entry is reversed. Second, a debit to Expenditures and a credit to Cash or Vouchers Payable are made. The encumbered amount will not necessarily be equal to the amount of the expenditure.

Objective 4: Describe the financial reporting system used in governmental accounting (p. 843).

6. Financial statements of a governmental unit include (a) a combined balance sheet, (b) two types of combined statements of revenues, expenditures, and changes in fund balances, (c) a combined statement of revenues, expenses, and changes in retained earnings (or equity), and (d) a combined statement of changes in financial position.

Objective 5: Provide a brief introduction to other types of not-for-profit accounting (pp. 844–845).

7. Not-for-profit organizations such as colleges and hospitals are similar to governmental units in their use of several types of funds and in the absence of the profit motive. However, they differ in their use of full accrual accounting and in their inability to impose a tax as a source of revenue. Also, many of the funds obtained by not-for-profit organizations are restricted to specific purposes by the donors.

a. Colleges and universities prepare (1) a statement of current funds, revenues, expenditures, and other changes, (2) a combined balance sheet, and (3) a statement of changes in fund balances.

b. In not-for-profit hospital accounting, revenues are classified by source, and expenses by function.

c. Voluntary health and welfare organizations, such as the American Cancer Society and the Sierra Club, use funds like those used by colleges and universities.

d. The FASB requires all not-for-profit organizations to recognize as revenue, and list as assets, all gifts that have been promised unconditionally. Also, these organizations must prepare a statement of financial position, a statement of activities, and a statement of cash flows.

TESTING YOUR KNOWLEDGE

Matching

Match each term with its definition by writing the appropriate letter in the blank.

_____ 1. Fund
_____ 2. Modified accrual accounting
_____ 3. Governmental Accounting Standards Board (GASB)
_____ 4. General fund
_____ 5. Special revenue funds
_____ 6. Capital projects funds
_____ 7. Debt service fund
_____ 8. Restricted fund
_____ 9. Enterprise funds
_____ 10. Internal service funds
_____ 11. Trust and agency funds
_____ 12. Proprietary funds
_____ 13. Fiduciary funds
_____ 14. Revenues
_____ 15. Expenditures
_____ 16. Appropriations
_____ 17. Fund balance
_____ 18. Encumbrances
_____ 19. Unrestricted fund

a. A fund to be used only for a specific purpose
b. A fund to account for resources to pay principal and interest on long-term debt
c. The body responsible for developing governmental GAAP
d. The budgetary account used to control or limit expenditures for the period
e. Funds to account for goods or services that one governmental agency provides to another
f. Decreases in fund resources (other than from interfund transfers)
g. Funds to account for services or public improvements to special properties
h. A descriptive term for trust and agency funds
i. The account to reflect anticipated expenditures on the books
j. A fiscal and accounting entity
k. A fund for general operating activities
l. Funds to account for assets held for individuals, private organizations, or other funds
m. The fund to account for financial resources that are not accounted for in any other fund
n. Funds to account for activities that resemble private business activities
o. Increases in fund resources (other than from interfund transactions or proceeds of long-term debt)
p. A descriptive term for the enterprise and internal service funds
q. The basis of accounting for governmental units
r. In fund accounting, the equity section of the balance sheet
s. Funds to account for the acquisition and construction of buildings, streets, etc.

APPLYING YOUR KNOWLEDGE

Exercises

1. Transactions for the year ended December 31, 19xx for the town of Sharon are presented here. For each, prepare the journal entry that would appear in Sharon's General Fund. Omit explanations.
   a. On January 1, the town adopted its budget for the year with estimated revenues of $950,000 and appropriations of $935,000.
   b. On March 15, property taxes of $900,000 were levied. It is estimated that 1% will prove uncollectible.
   c. On March 25, goods were ordered for an estimated cost of $50,000.
   d. On May 9, a new bus was purchased for $30,000 cash.
   e. By June 15, property tax collections totaled $893,000. The remaining $7,000 was written off as uncollectible.
   f. On June 27, the goods ordered on March 25 were received. The supplier's invoice was for $51,000. A voucher was prepared, to be paid next week.
   g. On July 5, the voucher of June 27 was paid.
   h. By December 31, actual revenues totaled $955,000 and actual expenditures totaled $947,000. No encumbrances existed at year end.

Date	Description	Debit	Credit

APPENDIX F ACCOUNTING FOR BOND INVESTMENTS

REVIEWING THE APPENDIX

Objective 1: Account for the purchase of bonds between interest dates (pp. 847–848).

1. When bonds are purchased as long-term investments, the investment account is debited at cost (which includes the broker's commission). Interest Income is debited for accrued interest since the last interest date, and Cash is credited for cash paid.

Objective 2: Amortize the premium or discount of a bond (pp. 848–849).

2. When interest is received on a bond investment, Cash is debited for cash received, Interest Income is credited for cash received plus the amortization of a bond discount or minus the amortization of a bond premium, and the investment account is debited (when there is a discount) or credited (when there is a premium) to balance the entry. Prior entries to accrue interest may slightly alter the above entry. Under this method of amortization, a bond discount or bond premium account is not used.

Objective 3: Account for the sale of bonds (pp. 849–850).

3. At the maturity date, the bond investment account should equal the maturity value. However, if the bonds are sold prior to maturity, a gain or loss should be recorded for the difference between cash received and the bonds' carrying value.

APPLYING YOUR KNOWLEDGE

Exercises

1. On March 1, 19x1, Alt Company purchased ten $1,000 Pamco bonds at 94 plus a broker's commission of $200 plus accrued interest. The bonds had a face interest of 8-4/10 percent and paid interest each January 1 and July 1. In the journal provided, prepare Alt Company's journal entries based on the following facts (advice: keep a running T account for Investment in Bonds):

March 1, 19x1	Purchased the bonds.
July 1, 19x1	Received the interest and amortized the discount or premium. Assume a 9 percent effective interest rate.
Dec. 31, 19x1	Recorded accrued interest and amortized the discount or premium.
Jan. 1, 19x2	Received the interest.
March 1, 19x2	Sold all ten bonds at 95 less a $200 commission.

General Journal			
Date	Description	Debit	Credit

SPECIMEN FINANCIAL STATEMENTS: THE COCA-COLA COMPANY

SPECIMEN FINANCIAL STATEMENTS

The Financial Report from the 1991 Annual Report of the Coca-Cola Company is provided as a real example of the financial statement section of a major corporation. This complete set of financial statements, together with management's discussion and analysis, notes to the financial statements, report of the independent auditors, and other information, are for students to see the end product of the accounting process. They can be used by instructors and students for discussion and illustration of the concepts, techniques, and statements presented in *Financial Accounting,* Fifth Edition.

Financial Report

46	Financial Review Incorporating Management's Discussion and Analysis
54	Selected Financial Data
56	Consolidated Balance Sheets
58	Consolidated Statements of Income
59	Consolidated Statements of Cash Flows
60	Consolidated Statements of Share-Owners' Equity
61	Notes to Consolidated Financial Statements
71	Report of Independent Auditors
72	Report of Management
73	Quarterly Data
73	Financial Glossary

Financial Review Incorporating
Management's Discussion and Analysis The Coca-Cola Company and Subsidiaries

Management's primary objective is to maximize share-owner value over time. To accomplish this objective, The Coca-Cola Company and subsidiaries (the Company) have developed a comprehensive business strategy that emphasizes maximizing long-term cash flow by increasing gallon sales, optimizing profit margins, expanding global business systems through investment in areas offering attractive returns and maintaining an appropriate capital structure. The success of this strategy is evidenced by the growth in the Company's cash flow and earnings, its increased returns on total capital and equity and the total return to its share owners.

Global Business Systems: The Company distributes its products in more than 185 countries. In 1991, the Coca-Cola system continued to expand into new markets, including joint ventures in Hungary, Romania and Indonesia, and investments in production and distribution infrastructure in eastern Germany and Poland. Per capita consumption of Company products increased in most markets. With effective global systems in place, the Company is well positioned to capitalize on investment opportunities as they arise.

Investments: Management seeks investments that strategically enhance existing operations and offer cash returns that exceed the Company's long-term weighted average cost of capital, estimated by management to be approximately 12 percent after taxes. Capital expenditures in 1991 amounted to approximately $678 million in the Company's soft drink business, $57 million in its foods sector and $57 million in its corporate operations.

The Company's soft drink business provides an attractive area for investment due to its inherent high returns. Most soft drink markets are relatively undeveloped compared to the United States market. International per capita consumption of Company products is still only 13 percent of the United States level. As a result, attractive investment opportunities exist to expand the production, distribution and marketing systems in these markets. Additional strategic investments are also required in the relatively more developed markets to increase product availability, enhance marketing focus and improve efficiency. Efficiencies have been gained through the continued consolidation of production and distribution networks and investment in the latest technology and information systems.

A significant element of the Company's financial framework is bottling investments. The principal objective of these investments is to ensure the strongest and most efficient production, distribution and marketing systems possible, in order to maximize long-term growth in volume, cash flow and share-owner value of the bottler and the Company.

When considered appropriate, the Company makes equity investments in bottling companies (typically between 20 percent and 50 percent). Through these investments, the Company is able to help focus and improve sales and marketing programs, assist in the development of effective business and information systems and help establish capital structures appropriate for these respective operations.

Capital Expenditures by Geographic Area
- United States
- Latin America
- European Community
- Northeast Europe/Africa
- Pacific & Canada

Millions	89	90	91
Pacific & Canada	7%	4%	7%
Northeast Europe/Africa	6%	7%	8%
European Community	32%	39%	45%
Latin America	7%	11%	15%
United States	48%	39%	25%

214 Specimen Financial Statements

Financial Review Incorporating
Management's Discussion and Analysis   The Coca-Cola Company and Subsidiaries

In certain situations, management believes it is advantageous to own a controlling interest in bottling operations. For example, in eastern Germany, the Company's objective is to establish a modern soft drink business quickly. Due to the limited local resources, this is being accomplished through a wholly-owned bottling subsidiary.

In connection with restructuring the bottling system, the Company periodically participates in bottler ownership changes or takes temporary ownership positions in bottlers. The length of ownership is influenced by various factors, including operational changes, management changes or other restructuring that may be taking place at the bottler itself, and the process of identifying appropriate new investors.

At December 31, 1991, the Company owned approximately 51 percent of Coca-Cola Amatil Limited (CCA), an Australian-based bottler of Company products and manufacturer of snack foods. The Company expects to reduce its ownership interest to below 50 percent within the next 3 years. Accordingly, the investment has been accounted for by the equity method of accounting. If valued at the December 31, 1991, quoted closing price of the publicly traded CCA common shares, the calculated value of the Company's investment in CCA exceeded its $571 million carrying value by approximately $201 million at December 31, 1991.

At December 31, 1991, the Company had an additional $279 million of investments that represented majority interests in companies that were not consolidated. These investments were accounted for by the cost or equity methods, depending on the circumstances. Approximately $170 million related to recent acquisitions that will be consolidated in 1992 when alignment of financial reporting systems is complete. The remainder related primarily to a temporary majority interest in The Coca-Cola Bottling Company of New York, Inc., which management expects to reduce to below 50 percent within the next 2 years. Based on management's estimates, the market values of these majority-owned investments exceeded their carrying values at December 31, 1991.

The Company's consolidated bottling subsidiaries produced and distributed approximately 5 percent of worldwide bottle/can unit case sales and generated approximately $1.5 billion in revenues in 1991. Equity investee bottlers produced and distributed an additional 33 percent of worldwide bottle/can unit case sales.

Gallon Sales and Margins: The Company's emphasis on profitable gallon-sales growth is reflected in its level of reinvestment in the form of increased advertising. Advertising expenditures increased to $988 million in 1991, compared to $932 million in 1990 and $888 million in 1989. These expenditures position and enhance the Company's products as industry leaders.

Gallon sales and profits have benefited from the Company's ownership of and investments in bottling operations. While the bottling business has relatively lower margins on sales revenue compared to the concentrate business, aggressive investment in soft drink infrastructure has resulted in growth in share and unit case sales at the bottler level, which in turn generates gallon-sales gains for the concentrate business.

The Company manages its concentrate and bottling operations so as to optimize profit margins while at the same time increasing gallon-sales growth and its share of soft drink sales. Through cost control and efficient marketing, the Company has generally been able to maintain or improve margins in 1991 despite declining economic conditions in several key markets.

Capital Structure: The Company utilizes prudent debt levels to lower its overall cost of capital and increase its total return to share owners. The Company operates under a self-imposed net-debt-to-net-capital ratio ceiling of 35 percent, excluding the Company's finance subsidiary. Net debt represented 20.9 percent of net capital at December 31, 1991, compared with 22.8 percent at December 31, 1990. Net debt and net capital are net of $.8 billion and $1.2 billion of cash, cash equivalents and current marketable securities in excess of operating requirements at December 31, 1991 and 1990, respectively.

The Coca-Cola Company

**Financial Review Incorporating
Management's Discussion and Analysis** The Coca-Cola Company and Subsidiaries

Additional borrowing capacity within the 35 percent net debt ceiling was approximately $1.2 billion at December 31, 1991, excluding the Company's finance subsidiary. The Company anticipates using this additional borrowing capacity principally to fund investment opportunities that meet its strategic and financial objectives and, as a second priority, to fund the share repurchase program.

In October 1989, the Board of Directors approved a plan to repurchase up to an additional 40 million shares of the Company's common stock. Under this program, approximately 24.8 million shares (including 6.9 million shares in 1991) have been repurchased at an aggregate cost of approximately $1 billion (including $397 million in 1991). Since the introduction of share repurchase programs in 1984, the Company has repurchased 192.6 million shares at an aggregate cost of approximately $4 billion. This represents nearly a quarter of the Company's common shares that were outstanding in 1984. If these shares were valued based on the December 31, 1991, quoted closing price of the Company's common stock traded on the New York Stock Exchange, the result would be approximately $15.5 billion.

In February 1991, the Company completed the redemption of the remaining $75 million of its initial $300 million of Cumulative Money Market Preferred Stock (MMP). In 1990, the Company redeemed $225 million of the MMP.

The Company's capital structure and financial policies have resulted in long-term credit ratings of "AA" from Standard & Poor's and "Aa2" from Moody's, as well as the highest credit ratings available for its commercial paper programs. The Company's strong financial position and cash flow allow it opportunistic access to financing in financial markets around the world.

Economic Profit and Economic Value Added: A significant portion of the increase in the rate of growth of the Company's earnings, returns and cash flows can be attributed to the Company taking actions to (a) increase share and gallon-sales growth for its products, (b) increase its investments in the high-margin, high-return soft drink business and (c) manage its existing asset base effectively and efficiently. Economic Profit and Economic Value Added provide a management framework to measure the impact of these value-oriented actions. Economic Profit is defined as net operating profit after taxes in excess of capital charges for average operating capital employed. Economic Value Added represents the growth in Economic Profit from year to year.

Economic Profit and Economic Value Added vs. Stock Price Appreciation

**Financial Review Incorporating
Management's Discussion and Analysis** The Coca-Cola Company and Subsidiaries

Common Stock Dividends

▨ Cash Payout Ratio
■ Cash Dividend per Share

[Chart showing Cash Payout Ratio declining from 59.5% to 39.5% and Cash Dividend per Share rising from $.39 to $.96 between 1981 and 1991]

Over the last five years, Economic Profit has grown more than 3 times, resulting in Economic Value Added to the Company of $732 million. Over the same period, the Company's stock price has increased more than 4 times. Management believes that, over the long term, growth in Economic Profit, or Economic Value Added, will have a positive impact on the growth in share-owner value.

Return to Share Owners: During the past decade, the share owners of the Company have enjoyed an excellent return on their investment. A $100 investment in the Company's common stock at December 31, 1981, together with reinvested dividends, would be worth approximately $1,902 at December 31, 1991—an average annual compounded return of 34.3 percent.

Strong earnings growth has enabled the Company to reduce the dividend payout ratio while increasing the cash dividend per common share by an average annual compounded growth rate of 9.4 percent since December 31, 1981. The annual common stock dividend was $.96 per share, $.80 per share and $.68 per share in 1991, 1990 and 1989, respectively. At its February 1992 meeting, the Board of Directors increased the quarterly dividend per common share to $.28, equivalent to a full-year common dividend of $1.12 in 1992. This is the 30th consecutive year in which the Board of Directors has approved common stock dividend increases.

With approval from the Board of Directors, management plans to maintain a common stock dividend payout ratio of approximately 40 percent of earnings available to common share owners. The 1991 dividend payout ratio was 46.9 percent based on prior year earnings available to common share owners and 39.5 percent based on current year results.

The Coca-Cola Company

Financial Review Incorporating
Management's Discussion and Analysis The Coca-Cola Company and Subsidiaries

Management's Discussion and Analysis

Lines of Business

The Company operates in two major lines of business: soft drinks and foods (principally juice and juice-drink products).

Soft Drinks: The Company is the largest manufacturer, marketer and distributor of soft drink concentrates and syrups in the world. It manufactures soft drink concentrates and syrups, which it sells to bottling and canning operations, and manufactures fountain/post-mix soft drink syrups, which it sells to authorized fountain wholesalers and some fountain retailers. The Company has substantial equity investments in numerous soft drink bottling and canning operations, and it owns and operates certain bottling and canning operations outside the United States.

Foods: The foods business sector's principal business is processing and marketing citrus and other juice and juice-drink products, primarily orange juice. It is the world's largest marketer of packaged citrus products.

Operating Results

Soft Drinks: Worldwide revenues and operating income for the Company's soft drink business increased in 1991 primarily due to gallon-sales growth, price increases and continued expansion of bottling and canning operations. In 1990, revenues and operating income increased due to gallon-sales growth, price increases and the positive exchange effects of a weaker dollar.

Gallon sales of concentrates and syrups increased 5 percent and 6 percent in 1991 and 1990, respectively. Operating income increased 18 percent in 1991 compared to 16 percent in 1990, excluding nonrecurring items. Operating income in both years was favorably affected by system efficiencies and a more favorable product mix.

In the United States, gallon sales increased more than 2 percent in 1991, compared to an increase of just over 3 percent in 1990. The increase in 1991 was due in part to full-year results from significant fountain customers added in 1990. The Company's growth in the United States outpaced the growth of the rest of the industry in both 1991 and 1990.

Soft drink gallon sales outside the United States increased 6 percent in 1991 and 8 percent in 1990. Approximately 68 percent of soft drink gallon sales were generated outside the United States in 1991 and 1990.

In 1991, international performance was led by strong results in Latin America, where gallon sales advanced 8 percent. Gallon sales increased 6 percent in the European Community, 4 percent in the Pacific and 3 percent in Northeast Europe/Africa.

1991 Operating Income by Geographic Area

- United States 21%
- Latin America 15%
- European Community 28%
- Northeast Europe/Africa 7%
- Pacific & Canada 29%

Financial Review Incorporating
Management's Discussion and Analysis The Coca-Cola Company and Subsidiaries

In 1990, gallon sales increased 14 percent in the European Community, 11 percent in the Pacific, 8 percent in Northeast Europe/Africa and 4 percent in Latin America.

Foods: In the foods business sector, 1991 revenues increased 2 percent and operating income increased 11 percent, primarily due to a 12 percent volume increase, partially offset by price decreases. The volume increase reflects 17 percent and 29 percent growth in the Company's retail chilled and frozen orange juice categories, respectively. The volume increase for chilled orange juice benefited from a 38 percent volume gain for Minute Maid Premium Choice not-from-concentrate orange juice.

In 1990, revenues increased 1 percent, primarily due to price increases, offset by volume decreases. Revenues in 1990 increased 3 percent after adjustments for business disposals in 1989.

Selling, Administrative and General Expenses

Selling expenses were $3.5 billion in 1991, $3.2 billion in 1990 and $2.6 billion in 1989. The increases in 1991 and 1990 were due primarily to higher marketing investments in line with expansion of the business.

Administrative and general expenses increased 24 percent and 20 percent in 1991 and 1990, respectively. The 1991 increase was due to the growth of the business and stock-related employee benefits. The 1990 increase was due to the growth of the business and the inclusion of a full year of administrative and general expenses of the French bottling operation acquired in 1989. Administrative and general expenses, as a percentage of net operating revenues, were approximately 9 percent in 1991 and 8 percent in 1990 and 1989.

Interest Income and Interest Expense

Interest expense declined in 1991 due primarily to lower interest rates. Interest income in 1991 remained consistent with 1990 levels.

Interest income and interest expense decreased in 1990 due primarily to lower average invested balances and borrowings and lower interest rates.

Equity Income

Equity income decreased $70 million in 1991 due primarily to a decrease in earnings of Coca-Cola Enterprises Inc. (CCE). CCE's 1991 results were less than prior year earnings due to pretax restructuring charges of $152 million, a pretax charge of $15 million to increase insurance reserves and a nonrecurring gain that was recorded by CCE in 1990. The 1991 decrease in equity income was partially offset by improved results of the Company's United Kingdom equity investee, Coca-Cola & Schweppes Beverages Ltd. (CC&SB), which implemented a cost reduction program during 1991.

In 1990, equity income increased approximately $35 million due primarily to the inclusion of a full year of equity earnings from CCA and growth in earnings of CCE and CC&SB. CCE's 1990 earnings included a pretax gain of approximately $56 million on the sale of two bottling operations to Johnston Coca-Cola Bottling Group, Inc. (Johnston), a bottling company that, at the time of the sale, was 22 percent owned by the Company. CCE's 1990 results also included nonrecurring charges of $19 million.

The Coca-Cola Company

Financial Review Incorporating
Management's Discussion and Analysis *The Coca-Cola Company and Subsidiaries*

Other Income—Net

The $28 million favorable change in other income—net in 1991 results from a pretax gain of $69 million on the sale of property no longer required as a result of a consolidation of concentrate operations in Japan and a pretax gain of $27 million on the sale of the Company's 22 percent ownership interest in Johnston to CCE. This favorable change was partially offset by an increase in net foreign exchange costs (including certain hedging costs) and a nonrecurring gain that was recorded in the prior year.

The $52 million unfavorable change in other income—net in 1990 is due to a $61 million pretax gain recorded in 1989 related to the sale of Belmont Springs Water Co., Inc. and net foreign exchange costs in 1990 compared to net foreign exchange gains in 1989. This unfavorable change was partially offset by a 1990 pretax gain of $52 million on the Company's investment in BCI Securities L.P. (BCI) resulting from BCI's sale of Beatrice Company stock.

Discontinued Operation

In November 1989, the Company sold its common and preferred stock investments in Columbia Pictures Entertainment, Inc. (CPE) for approximately $1.6 billion in cash. The sale resulted in a pretax gain of approximately $930 million. On an after-tax basis, the gain was approximately $509 million or $.74 per common share. CPE has been reported as a discontinued operation, and, accordingly, the gain from the sale of CPE stock and the Company's equity income from CPE have been reported separately from continuing operations.

Liquidity and Capital Resources

The Company generates a significant amount of cash from operations. Normalized free cash flow (defined as operating cash flow less capital expenditures) was $1.3 billion in 1991, $691 million in 1990 and $672 million in 1989.

In 1991, primary sources of cash were from operations, issuances of debt and the sale of the Company's 22 percent ownership interest in Johnston. Primary uses of cash were payments of debt, capital expenditures, dividends, purchases of common stock for treasury and acquisitions of businesses.

In 1990, primary sources of cash were from operations, issuances of debt, the sale of a temporary investment and the sale of CCE stock to CCE under a share repurchase program. Major uses of cash were capital expenditures, dividends, estimated tax payments related to the 1989 gain on the sale of CPE stock, purchases of common stock for treasury and the redemption of preferred stock.

At December 31, 1991, the Company had $753 million in lines of credit and other short-term credit facilities contractually available, under which $111 million was outstanding. The lines included $505 million designated to support commercial paper and other borrowings, of which no amounts were outstanding at December 31, 1991.

The Company's ratio of earnings to fixed charges was 11.6 in 1991, 8.5 in 1990 and 6.2 in 1989. The Company aggressively manages its mix of short-term versus long-term debt to lower its overall cost of borrowing, resulting in current liabilities exceeding current assets at December 31, 1990.

The increase in prepaid expenses and other assets in 1991 was primarily due to growth in the business, increases in prepaid marketing expenses and amounts due from the sale of assets.

While total debt decreased in 1991, the Company increased its long-term debt levels. During 1991, the Company issued $250 million of 7 3/4 percent five-year notes due in 1996 and $250 million of 7 7/8 percent seven-year notes due in 1998. The proceeds were used to pay current loans and notes payable and replace $86 million of 11 3/8 percent notes that matured in 1991.

Financial Review Incorporating
Management's Discussion and Analysis The Coca-Cola Company and Subsidiaries

In 1990, working capital accounts, including trade accounts receivable, inventories and accounts payable, increased due primarily to the expansion of French bottling operations and entry into the eastern German market. Prepaid expenses and other assets decreased in 1990 due to the sale of a temporary investment to CCE.

The 1990 decrease in accrued taxes reflects estimated tax payments related to the gain on the November 1989 sale of the Company's investment in CPE. The estimated tax payments resulted in an increase in loans and notes payable. The 1990 increase in loans and notes payable was also attributable to capital investments, the redemption of preferred stock and the share repurchase program.

International Operations

Approximately 79 percent of total operating income in 1991 was generated by operations outside the United States. International operations are subject to certain opportunities and risks, including currency fluctuations and government actions. The Company closely monitors its methods of operating in each country and adopts strategies responsive to changing economic and political environments. In addition, the Company engages in various hedging activities to minimize potential losses on cash flows denominated in foreign currencies.

The Company uses approximately 40 functional currencies. For the Company, the weighted average annual exchange rates of foreign hard currencies, compared to the U.S. dollar, weakened slightly during 1991 and strengthened approximately 5 percent in 1990. In 1991, 1990 and 1989, weighted average exchange rates for certain key foreign currencies strengthened (weakened) against the U.S. dollar as follows:

	1991	1990	1989
Australian dollar	1 %	0 %	1 %
British pound	(1)%	10 %	(9)%
Canadian dollar	1 %	2 %	4 %
German mark	(3)%	17 %	(6)%
Japanese yen	8 %	(5)%	(7)%

Exchange effects recorded in other income—net were $(22) million in 1991, $(.5) million in 1990 and $20 million in 1989. Exchange effects include costs of hedging certain balance sheet, translation and transaction exposures, net gains or losses on foreign currency transactions and the remeasurement of foreign currencies into functional currencies.

Impact of Inflation and Changing Prices

Inflation is a factor in many markets around the world and consequently impacts the way the Company operates. In general, management believes that the Company is able to adjust prices to counteract the effects of increasing costs and generate sufficient cash flow to maintain its productive capability.

In highly inflationary countries, the Company has benefited from its net monetary liability position in recent years. This position is viewed as a hedge against the effects of inflation, since net liabilities would ultimately be paid with devalued currency.

Additional Information

For additional information concerning the Company's operations, cash flow, liquidity and capital resources, this analysis should be read in conjunction with the information on pages 56 through 72 of this Annual Report. Additional information concerning operations in different lines of business and geographic areas is presented on pages 69 and 70.

The Coca-Cola Company

Selected Financial Data
The Coca-Cola Company and Subsidiaries

Year Ended December 31, (In millions except per share data and ratios)	**1991**	1990	1989	1988
Summary of Operations				
Net operating revenues	**$11,572**	$10,236	$8,622	$8,065
Cost of goods sold	**4,649**	4,208	3,548	3,429
Gross profit	**6,923**	6,028	5,074	4,636
Selling, administrative and general expenses	**4,604**	4,076	3,348	3,038
Provisions for restructured operations and disinvestment	**—**	—	—	—
Operating income	**2,319**	1,952	1,726	1,598
Interest income	**175**	170	205	199
Interest expense	**192**	231	308	230
Equity income	**40**[1]	110	75	92
Other income (deductions)—net	**41**	13	66	(33)
Income from continuing operations before income taxes	**2,383**	2,014	1,764	1,626
Income taxes	**765**	632	571	537
Income from continuing operations	**$ 1,618**	$ 1,382	$1,193	$1,089
Net income	**$ 1,618**	$ 1,382	$1,724	$1,045
Preferred stock dividends	**1**	18	22	7
Net income available to common share owners	**$ 1,617**	$ 1,364	$1,702[2]	$1,038
Depreciation	**$ 254**	$ 236	$ 181	$ 167
Capital expenditures	**$ 792**	$ 593	$ 462	$ 387
Average common shares outstanding	**666**	669	692	729
Per Common Share Data				
Income from continuing operations	**$ 2.43**	$ 2.04	$ 1.69	$ 1.48
Net income	**2.43**	2.04	2.46[2]	1.42
Cash dividends	**.96**	.80	.68	.60
Market price at December 31	**80.25**	46.50	38.63	22.31
Balance Sheet Data				
Cash, cash equivalents and marketable securities	**$ 1,117**	$ 1,492	$1,182	$1,231
Property, plant and equipment—net	**2,890**	2,386	2,021	1,759
Total assets	**10,222**	9,278	8,283	7,451
Long-term debt	**985**	536	549	761
Total debt	**2,287**	2,537	1,981	2,124
Share-owners' equity	**4,426**	3,849	3,485	3,345
Total capital[3]	**6,713**	6,386	5,466	5,469
Other Key Financial Measures[3]				
Return on common equity	**39.5%**	39.2%	37.6%	34.7%
Return on capital	**26.7%**	26.0%	25.6%	21.3%
Economic profit	**$ 1,043**	$ 918	$ 819	$ 748
Total-debt-to-total-capital	**34.1%**	39.7%	36.2%	38.8%
Net-debt-to-net-capital	**20.9%**	22.8%	14.0%	18.9%
Dividend payout ratio	**39.5%**	39.2%	27.6%[2]	42.1%

[1] Equity income in 1991 includes a reduction of $44 million related to restructuring charges recorded by Coca-Cola Enterprises Inc.
[2] Net income available to common share owners in 1989 includes after-tax gains of $545 million ($.79 per common share) from the sale of the Company's equity interest in Columbia Pictures Entertainment, Inc. and the Company's bottled water business. Excluding these gains, the dividend payout ratio in 1989 was 41 percent.

1987	1986	1985	1984	1983	1982[4]	1981
$7,658	$6,977	$5,879	$5,442	$5,056	$4,760	$4,836
3,633	3,454	2,909	2,738	2,580	2,472	2,675
4,025	3,523	2,970	2,704	2,476	2,288	2,161
2,665	2,446	2,163	1,855	1,648	1,515	1,441
36	180	—	—	—	—	—
1,324	897	807	849	828	773	720
232	154	151	133	90	119	85
297	208	196	128	77	76	34
64	45	52	42	35	25	20
40	410	69	13	2	11	(20)
1,363	1,298	883	909	878	852	771
496	471	314	360	374	379	339
$ 867	$ 827	$ 569	$ 549	$ 504	$ 473	$ 432
$ 916	$ 934	$ 722	$ 629	$ 559	$ 512	$ 482
—	—	—	—	—	—	—
$ 916	$ 934	$ 722	$ 629	$ 559	$ 512	$ 482
$ 152	$ 151	$ 130	$ 119	$ 111	$ 104	$ 94
$ 304	$ 346	$ 412	$ 300	$ 324	$ 273	$ 279
755	774	787	793	817	779	742
$ 1.15	$ 1.07	$ .72	$ .69	$ .62	$ .61	$ .58
1.21	1.21	.92	.79	.68	.66	.65
.56	.52	.49	.46	.45	.41	.39
19.06	18.88	14.08	10.40	8.92	8.67	5.79
$1,489	$ 895	$ 843	$ 768	$ 559	$ 254	$ 344
1,602	1,538	1,483	1,284	1,247	1,233	1,160
8,606	7,675	6,341	5,241	4,540	4,212	3,373
909	996	801	631	428	423	132
2,995	1,848	1,280	1,310	520	493	227
3,187	3,479	2,948	2,751	2,912	2,779	2,271
6,182	5,327	4,228	4,061	3,432	3,272	2,498
26.0%	25.7%	20.0%	19.4%	17.7%	18.7%	19.9%
18.3%	20.1%	16.8%	16.7%	16.4%	17.9%	18.8%
$ 417	$ 311	$ 269	$ 268	$ 138	$ 61	$ 98
48.4%	34.7%	30.3%	32.3%	15.2%	15.1%	9.1%
15.4%	10.9%	15.6%	19.7%	5.6%	13.6%	2.9%
46.0%	43.1%	53.8%	57.9%	65.3%	62.8%	59.5%

[3] See Financial Glossary on page 73.
[4] In 1982, the Company adopted SFAS No. 52, "Foreign Currency Translation."

Operating Income

Compound Growth Rates

10 year 12%*
5 year 17%*

Income from Continuing Operations

Compound Growth Rates

10 year 14%*
5 year 18%*

Income from Continuing Operations per Common Share

Compound Growth Rates

10 year 15%*
5 year 22%*

* Excludes unusual items

The Coca-Cola Company

Consolidated Balance Sheets *The Coca-Cola Company and Subsidiaries*

December 31, (In thousands except share data)	1991	1990
Assets		
Current		
Cash and cash equivalents	$ 1,058,250	$1,429,555
Marketable securities, at cost (approximates market)	58,946	62,569
	1,117,196	1,492,124
Trade accounts receivable, less allowances of $34,567 in 1991 and $29,510 in 1990	933,448	913,541
Finance subsidiary—receivables	36,172	38,199
Inventories	987,764	982,313
Prepaid expenses and other assets	1,069,664	716,601
Total Current Assets	4,144,244	4,142,778
Investments and Other Assets		
Investments		
Coca-Cola Enterprises Inc. (CCE)	602,776	666,847
Coca-Cola Amatil Limited	570,774	569,057
Other, principally bottling companies	980,465	788,718
Finance subsidiary—receivables	288,471	128,119
Long-term receivables and other assets	442,135	321,977
	2,884,621	2,474,718
Property, Plant and Equipment		
Land	172,781	147,057
Buildings and improvements	1,200,672	1,059,969
Machinery and equipment	2,680,446	2,204,188
Containers	390,737	374,526
	4,444,636	3,785,740
Less allowances for depreciation	1,554,754	1,400,175
	2,889,882	2,385,565
Goodwill and Other Intangible Assets	303,681	275,126
	$10,222,428	$9,278,187

December 31, 1991 1990

Liabilities and Share-Owners' Equity

Current
Accounts payable and accrued expenses	$ 1,914,379	$1,576,426
Loans and notes payable	845,823	1,742,179
Finance subsidiary—notes payable	346,767	161,432
Current maturities of long-term debt	109,707	97,272
Accrued taxes	900,884	719,182
Total Current Liabilities	4,117,560	4,296,491
Long-Term Debt	985,258	535,861
Other Liabilities	493,765	332,060
Deferred Income Taxes	200,027	264,611

Share-Owners' Equity

Preferred stock, $1 par value—		
Authorized: 100,000,000 shares; Issued: 3,000 shares of Cumulative Money Market Preferred Stock in 1991 and 1990; Outstanding: No shares in 1991; 750 shares in 1990, stated at aggregate liquidation preference	—	75,000
Common stock, $.50 par value—		
Authorized: 1,400,000,000 shares; Issued: 843,675,547 shares in 1991; 840,487,486 shares in 1990	421,838	420,244
Capital surplus	639,990	512,703
Reinvested earnings	7,425,514	6,447,576
Unearned compensation related to outstanding restricted stock	(114,909)	(67,760)
Foreign currency translation adjustment	(4,909)	4,031
	8,367,524	7,391,794
Less treasury stock, at cost (179,195,464 common shares in 1991; 172,248,315 common shares in 1990)	3,941,706	3,542,630
	4,425,818	3,849,164
	$10,222,428	$9,278,187

See Notes to Consolidated Financial Statements.

The Coca-Cola Company

Consolidated Statements of Income
The Coca-Cola Company and Subsidiaries

Year Ended December 31, (In thousands except per share data)	1991	1990	1989
Net Operating Revenues	$11,571,614	$10,236,350	$8,622,287
Cost of goods sold	4,648,385	4,208,850	3,548,570
Gross Profit	6,923,229	6,027,500	5,073,717
Selling, administrative and general expenses	4,604,184	4,075,936	3,347,932
Operating Income	2,319,045	1,951,564	1,725,785
Interest income	175,406	169,985	205,035
Interest expense	192,515	230,979	308,034
Equity income (1991 reduced by $44 million related to restructuring charges recorded by CCE)	39,975	110,139	75,490
Other income—net	41,368	13,727	66,034
Income from Continuing Operations before Income Taxes	2,383,279	2,014,436	1,764,310
Income taxes	765,277	632,532	571,471
Income from Continuing Operations	1,618,002	1,381,904	1,192,839
Equity income from discontinued operation	—	—	21,537
Gain on sale of discontinued operation (net of income taxes of $421,021)	—	—	509,449
Net Income	1,618,002	1,381,904	1,723,825
Preferred stock dividends	521	18,158	21,392
Net Income Available to Common Share Owners	$ 1,617,481	$ 1,363,746	$1,702,433
Income per Common Share			
Continuing operations	$ 2.43	$ 2.04	$ 1.69
Discontinued operation	—	—	.77
Net Income per Common Share	$ 2.43	$ 2.04	$ 2.46
Average Common Shares Outstanding	666,472	668,570	691,962

See Notes to Consolidated Financial Statements

Consolidated Statements of Cash Flows
The Coca-Cola Company and Subsidiaries

Year Ended December 31, (In thousands)	1991	1990	1989
Operating Activities			
Net income	$1,618,002	$1,381,904	$1,723,825
Depreciation and amortization	261,427	243,888	183,765
Deferred income taxes	(66,147)	(30,254)	37,036
Equity income, net of dividends	(16,013)	(93,816)	(76,088)
Foreign currency adjustments	65,534	(77,068)	(31,043)
Gain on sale of businesses and investments before income taxes	(34,577)	(60,277)	(1,006,664)
Other noncash items	33,338	97,752	24,360
Net change in operating assets and liabilities	222,837	(178,202)	279,382
Net cash provided by operating activities	2,084,401	1,283,927	1,134,573
Investing Activities			
Additions to finance subsidiary receivables	(210,267)	(31,551)	(57,006)
Collections of finance subsidiary receivables	51,942	58,243	188,810
Purchases of investments and other assets	(399,183)	(186,631)	(858,510)
Proceeds from disposals of investments and other assets	180,058	149,807	126,850
Proceeds from sale of businesses	—	—	1,680,073
Decrease (increase) in marketable securities	2,735	16,733	(3,889)
Purchases of property, plant and equipment	(791,677)	(592,971)	(462,466)
Proceeds from disposals of property, plant and equipment	43,958	19,208	60,665
Purchases of temporary investments and other	(2,246)	(113,875)	(145,009)
Proceeds from disposals of temporary investments	—	241,373	—
Net cash provided by (used in) investing activities	(1,124,680)	(439,664)	529,518
Net cash provided by operations after reinvestment	959,721	844,263	1,664,091
Financing Activities			
Issuances of debt	989,926	592,417	336,370
Payments of debt	(1,246,664)	(81,594)	(410,690)
Preferred stock redeemed	(75,000)	(225,000)	—
Common stock issued	39,394	29,904	41,395
Purchases of common stock for treasury	(399,076)	(306,667)	(1,166,941)
Dividends (common and preferred)	(640,064)	(552,640)	(490,655)
Net cash used in financing activities	(1,331,484)	(543,580)	(1,690,521)
Effect of Exchange Rate Changes on Cash and Cash Equivalents	458	32,852	(22,896)
Cash and Cash Equivalents			
Net increase (decrease) during the year	(371,305)	333,535	(49,326)
Balance at beginning of year	1,429,555	1,096,020	1,145,346
Balance at end of year	$1,058,250	$1,429,555	$1,096,020

See Notes to Consolidated Financial Statements

The Coca-Cola Company

Consolidated Statements of Share-Owners' Equity The Coca-Cola Company and Subsidiaries

Three Years Ended December 31, 1991 (In thousands except per share data)	Preferred Stock	Common Stock	Capital Surplus	Reinvested Earnings	Unearned Restricted Stock	Foreign Currency Translation	Treasury Stock
Balance December 31, 1988	$300,000	$417,395	$380,264	$4,385,142	$(51,467)	$(17,010)	$(2,069,022)
Sales to employees exercising stock options	—	1,481	39,914	—	—	—	(3,804)
Tax benefit from employees' stock option and restricted stock plans	—	—	14,811	—	—	—	—
Translation adjustments (net of income taxes of $900)	—	—	—	—	—	9,804	—
Stock issued under restricted stock plans, less amortization of $7,944	—	34	2,335	—	5,575	—	—
Purchases of common stock for treasury	—	—	—	—	—	—	(1,163,137)
Net income	—	—	—	1,723,825	—	—	—
Dividends							
Preferred	—	—	—	(21,392)	—	—	—
Common (per share—$.68)	—	—	—	(469,263)	—	—	—
Balance December 31, 1989	300,000	418,910	437,324	5,618,312	(45,892)	(7,206)	(3,235,963)
Sales to employees exercising stock options	—	905	28,999	—	—	—	(2,762)
Tax benefit from employees' stock option and restricted stock plans	—	—	13,286	—	—	—	—
Translation adjustments (net of income taxes of $573)	—	—	—	—	—	11,237	—
Stock issued under restricted stock plans, less amortization of $11,655	—	429	33,094	—	(21,868)	—	—
Purchases of common stock for treasury	—	—	—	—	—	—	(303,905)
Redemption of preferred stock	(225,000)	—	—	—	—	—	—
Net income	—	—	—	1,381,904	—	—	—
Dividends							
Preferred	—	—	—	(18,158)	—	—	—
Common (per share—$.80)	—	—	—	(534,482)	—	—	—
Balance December 31, 1990	75,000	420,244	512,703	6,447,576	(67,760)	4,031	(3,542,630)
Sales to employees exercising stock options	—	972	38,422	—	—	—	(2,421)
Tax benefit from employees' stock option and restricted stock plans	—	—	20,015	—	—	—	—
Translation adjustments (net of income taxes of $958)	—	—	—	—	—	(8,940)	—
Stock issued under restricted stock plans, less amortization of $22,323	—	622	68,850	—	(47,149)	—	—
Purchases of common stock for treasury	—	—	—	—	—	—	(396,655)
Redemption of preferred stock	(75,000)	—	—	—	—	—	—
Net income	—	—	—	1,618,002	—	—	—
Dividends							
Preferred	—	—	—	(521)	—	—	—
Common (per share—$.96)	—	—	—	(639,543)	—	—	—
Balance December 31, 1991	$ —	$421,838	$639,990	$7,425,514	$(114,909)	$(4,909)	$(3,941,706)

See Notes to Consolidated Financial Statements

Notes to Consolidated Financial Statements *The Coca-Cola Company and Subsidiaries*

1. Accounting Policies

The significant accounting policies and practices followed by The Coca-Cola Company and subsidiaries (the Company) are as follows:

Consolidation

The consolidated financial statements include the accounts of the Company and all subsidiaries where control is not temporary. The Company's investments in companies in which it has the ability to exercise significant influence over operating and financial policies, including certain investments where there is a temporary majority interest, are accounted for by the equity method. Accordingly, the Company's share of the net earnings of these companies is included in consolidated net income. The Company's investments in other companies are carried at cost. All significant intercompany accounts and transactions are eliminated.

Certain amounts in the prior years' financial statements have been reclassified to conform to the current year presentation.

Net Income per Common Share

Net income per common share is computed by dividing net income less dividends on preferred stock by the weighted average number of common shares outstanding.

Cash Equivalents

Marketable securities that are highly liquid and have maturities of three months or less at the date of purchase are classified as cash equivalents.

Inventories

Inventories are valued at the lower of cost or market. In general, inventories are valued on the basis of average cost or first-in, first-out methods. However, certain soft drink and citrus inventories are valued on the last-in, first-out (LIFO) method. The excess of current costs over LIFO stated values amounted to approximately $27 million and $42 million at December 31, 1991 and 1990, respectively.

Property, Plant and Equipment

Property, plant and equipment are stated at cost, less allowances for depreciation. Property, plant and equipment are depreciated principally by the straight-line method over the estimated useful lives of the assets.

Goodwill and Other Intangible Assets

Goodwill and other intangible assets are stated on the basis of cost and are being amortized, principally on a straight-line basis, over the estimated future periods to be benefited (not exceeding 40 years). Accumulated amortization was approximately $16 million and $10 million at December 31, 1991 and 1990, respectively.

Income Taxes

Income tax amounts and balances have been computed in accordance with APB Opinion No. 11, "Accounting for Income Taxes."

In 1987, the Financial Accounting Standards Board (FASB) issued Statement of Financial Accounting Standards No. 96, "Accounting for Income Taxes" (SFAS 96). In 1991, the FASB issued an Exposure Draft, which would further modify accounting for income taxes. The Company's required adoption date is January 1, 1993. Based on preliminary studies and evaluations, accounting for income taxes under SFAS 96 or the Exposure Draft would not have a material impact on the Company's results of operations or financial position.

2. Inventories

Inventories consist of the following (in thousands):

December 31,	1991	1990
Raw materials and supplies	$615,459	$567,694
Work in process	23,475	18,451
Finished goods	348,830	396,168
	$987,764	$982,313

3. Bottling Investments

The Company invests in bottling companies to ensure the strongest and most efficient production, distribution and marketing systems possible, in order to maximize long-term growth in volume, cash flow and share-owner value of the bottler and the Company.

The Coca-Cola Company

Notes to Consolidated Financial Statements *The Coca-Cola Company and Subsidiaries*

Coca-Cola Enterprises Inc.

Coca-Cola Enterprises Inc. (CCE) is the largest bottler of Company products in the United States. The Company owns approximately 44 percent of the outstanding common stock of CCE and, accordingly, accounts for its investment by the equity method of accounting. A summary of financial information for CCE is as follows (in thousands):

	December 31, 1991	December 28, 1990
Current assets	$ 706,298	$ 495,341
Noncurrent assets	5,970,297	4,525,255
Total assets	$6,676,595	$5,020,596
Current liabilities	$1,385,445	$1,054,791
Noncurrent liabilities	3,848,519	2,339,326
Total liabilities	$5,233,964	$3,394,117
Share-owners' equity	$1,442,631	$1,626,479
Company equity investment	$ 602,776	$ 666,847

Year Ended	December 31, 1991	December 28, 1990	December 29, 1989
Net operating revenues	$4,050,798	$4,034,043	$3,881,947
Cost of goods sold	2,380,258	2,359,267	2,313,032
Gross profit	$1,670,540	$1,674,776	$1,568,915
Operating income	$ 120,178	$ 325,548	$ 310,067
Operating cash flow[1]	$ 538,422	$ 592,391	$ 539,086
Income (loss) before income taxes	$ (91,140)	$ 184,247	$ 137,931
Net income (loss) available to common share owners	$ (91,675)	$ 77,148	$ 53,507
Company equity income (loss)	$ (39,732)	$ 34,429	$ 26,218

[1] Excludes nonrecurring charges

CCE's 1991 results include pretax restructuring charges of $152 million and a pretax charge of $15 million to increase insurance reserves.

In a December 18, 1991, merger, CCE acquired Johnston Coca-Cola Bottling Group, Inc. (Johnston) for approximately $196 million and 13 million shares of CCE common stock. The Company exchanged its 22 percent ownership interest in Johnston for approximately $81 million in cash and 50,000 shares of CCE common stock, resulting in a pretax gain of $27 million to the Company. The Company's ownership interest in CCE was reduced from 49 percent to 44 percent as a result of this transaction.

Net concentrate/syrup sales to CCE were $626 million in 1991, $602 million in 1990 and $569 million in 1989. CCE purchases sweeteners through the Company under a pass-through arrangement, and, accordingly, related collections from CCE and payments to suppliers are not included in the Company's consolidated statements of income. These transactions amounted to $185 million in 1991 and 1990 and $195 million in 1989. The Company also provides certain administrative and other services to CCE under negotiated fee arrangements.

The Company engages in a wide range of marketing programs, media advertising and other similar arrangements to promote the sale of Company products in territories in which CCE operates. The Company's direct support for certain CCE marketing activities and participation with CCE in cooperative advertising and other marketing programs, net of fees charged for services provided, amounted to approximately $199 million, $181 million and $178 million in 1991, 1990 and 1989, respectively.

During 1990, the Company sold 4 million shares of CCE common stock to CCE for $60 million under a share repurchase program.

In June 1990, the Company sold a temporary investment, Coca-Cola Holdings (Arkansas) Inc. (CCHA), to CCE for approximately $241 million and assumed indebtedness, which approximated the Company's original 1989 investment, plus carrying costs.

In June 1990, CCE recorded a pretax gain of approximately $56 million from the sale of two of its bottling subsidiaries. The purchaser of these former CCE bottling subsidiaries was Johnston, which, at the time of the sale, was 22 percent owned by the Company.

If valued at the December 31, 1991, quoted closing price of the publicly traded CCE shares, the calculated value of the Company's investment in CCE common stock would have exceeded the Company's carrying value by approximately $263 million.

Other Equity Investments

The Company owns approximately 51 percent of Coca-Cola Amatil Limited (CCA), an Australian-based bottler of Company products and manufacturer of snack foods. In August 1989, the Company acquired an initial 59.5 percent ownership interest in CCA for approximately $491 million (including certain acquisition-related costs). In separate transactions during 1990, CCA acquired an independent Australian bottler and the Company's 50 percent interest in a New Zealand bottling joint venture in exchange for consideration that included previously unissued common stock of CCA, resulting in a net reduction of the Company's owner-

Notes to Consolidated Financial Statements *The Coca-Cola Company and Subsidiaries*

ship interest to its present level. The Company intends to reduce its ownership interest in CCA to below 50 percent. Accordingly, the investment has been accounted for by the equity method of accounting.

At December 31, 1991, the excess of the Company's investment over its equity in the underlying net assets of CCA was approximately $283 million, which is being amortized primarily over 40 years. The Company recorded equity income from CCA of $15 million, $17 million and $6 million in 1991, 1990 and 1989, respectively. These amounts are net of the amortization charges discussed above.

Operating results include the Company's proportionate share of income from equity investments since the respective dates of investment. A summary of financial information for the Company's equity investments, other than CCE, is as follows (in thousands):

December 31,	1991	1990
Current assets	$1,797,396	$1,658,341
Noncurrent assets	3,794,114	4,431,810
Total assets	$5,591,510	$6,090,151
Current liabilities	$1,947,025	$1,696,796
Noncurrent liabilities	1,594,696	2,518,902
Total liabilities	$3,541,721	$4,215,698
Share-owners' equity	$2,049,789	$1,874,453
Company equity investments	$1,456,959	$1,310,209

Year Ended December 31,	1991	1990	1989
Net operating revenues	$7,876,737	$7,312,904	$5,598,946
Cost of goods sold	5,243,943	4,609,004	3,633,647
Gross profit	$2,632,794	$2,703,900	$1,965,299
Operating income	$ 559,885	$ 574,712	$ 431,915
Operating cash flow	$ 979,232	$ 940,244	$ 679,552
Income before income taxes	$ 315,231	$ 327,784	$ 199,255
Net income	$ 214,144	$ 205,436	$ 123,752
Company equity income	$ 79,707	$ 75,710	$ 49,272

Equity investments also include certain non-bottling investees

Net sales to equity investees, other than CCE, were $1.3 billion in 1991 and $1.2 billion in 1990. The Company participates in various marketing, promotional and other activities with these investees, the majority of which are located outside the United States.

If valued at the December 31, 1991, quoted closing prices of shares actively traded on stock markets, the net calculated value of the Company's investment in publicly traded bottlers, other than CCE, would have exceeded the Company's carrying value by approximately $189 million.

The balance sheet caption "Other, principally bottling companies" also includes various investments that are accounted for by the cost method.

4 Finance Subsidiary

Coca-Cola Financial Corporation (CCFC) provides loans and other forms of financing to Coca-Cola bottlers and customers for the acquisition of sales-related equipment and for other business purposes. The approximate contractual maturities of finance receivables for the five years succeeding December 31, 1991, are as follows (in thousands):

1992	$ 36,172
1993	23,325
1994	169,317
1995	10,414
1996	19,620

These amounts do not reflect possible prepayments or renewals.

In connection with the December 1991 acquisition of Sunbelt Coca-Cola Bottling Company, Inc. by Coca-Cola Bottling Co. Consolidated (Consolidated), CCFC purchased 25,000 shares of Consolidated preferred stock for $50 million, provided to Consolidated a $153 million bridge loan and issued a $77 million letter of credit on Consolidated's behalf. The Company beneficially owns a 30 percent economic interest and a 23 percent voting interest in Consolidated.

Finance receivables also include amounts due from CCE (substantially all of which were assumed by CCE upon its acquisition of Johnston) of $68 million and $56 million at December 31, 1991 and 1990, respectively.

5 Short-Term Borrowings and Credit Arrangements

Loans and notes payable consist primarily of commercial paper issued in the United States. At December 31, 1991, the Company had $753 million in lines of credit and other short-term credit facilities contractually available, under which $111 million was outstanding. The lines included $505 million designated to support commercial paper and other borrowings, of which no amounts were outstanding at December 31, 1991. These facilities are subject to normal banking terms and conditions. Some of the financial arrangements require compensating balances, none of which are presently significant to the Company.

Notes to Consolidated Financial Statements *The Coca-Cola Company and Subsidiaries*

6. Accrued Taxes

Accrued taxes consist of the following (in thousands):

December 31,	1991	1990
Income taxes	$789,632	$618,590
Sales, payroll and miscellaneous taxes	111,252	100,592
	$900,884	$719,182

7. Long-Term Debt

Long-term debt consists of the following (in thousands):

December 31,	1991	1990
9 7/8% U.S. dollar notes due 1992	$ 89,565	$ 59,667
7 3/4% U.S. dollar notes due 1996	249,890	—
5 3/4% Japanese yen notes due 1996[1]	239,987	222,977
5 3/4% German mark notes due 1998[1]	165,206	166,953
7 7/8% U.S. dollar notes due 1998	249,372	—
11 3/8% U.S. dollar notes due 1991	—	85,675
Other, due 1992 to 2013[2]	100,945	97,861
	1,094,965	633,133
Less current portion	109,707	97,272
	$ 985,258	$535,861

[1] Portions of these notes have been swapped for liabilities denominated in other currencies.
[2] Interest on a portion of this debt varies with the changes in the prime rate, and the weighted average interest rate applicable to the remainder is approximately 12.3 percent.

Maturities of long-term debt for the five years succeeding December 31, 1991, are as follows (in thousands):

1992	$109,707
1993	28,396
1994	17,601
1995	7,932
1996	494,264

The above notes include various restrictions, none of which are presently significant to the Company.

Interest paid was approximately $160 million, $233 million and $319 million in 1991, 1990 and 1989, respectively.

8. Financial Instruments

The Company has entered into foreign currency hedging transactions to reduce its exposure to adverse fluctuations in foreign exchange rates. While the hedging instruments are subject to the risk of loss from changes in exchange rates, these losses would generally be offset by gains on the exposures being hedged. The Company had $2.6 billion and $1.4 billion of foreign currency hedging instruments outstanding at December 31, 1991 and 1990, respectively. The contracts are transacted with creditworthy financial institutions and generally mature within one year.

At December 31, 1991, the Company is contingently liable for guarantees of indebtedness owed by third parties of $117 million, of which $54 million is related to independent bottling licensees.

9. Preferred Stock

In February 1991, the Company completed the redemption of the remaining $75 million of its initial $300 million of Cumulative Money Market Preferred Stock (MMP). The Company redeemed $225 million of the MMP in 1990. Prior to redemption, the weighted average dividend rate (per annum) for the MMP was approximately 6 percent in 1991 and 1990.

10. Common Stock

Common shares outstanding and related changes for the three years ended December 31, 1991, are as follows (in thousands):

	1991	1990	1989
Outstanding at January 1,	668,239	674,030	709,578
Issued to employees exercising stock options	1,943	1,810	2,962
Issued under restricted stock plans	1,245	858	68
Purchases of common stock for treasury	(6,947)	(8,459)	(38,578)
Outstanding at December 31,	664,480	668,239	674,030

11. Restricted Stock, Stock Options and Other Stock Plans

The Company sponsors restricted stock award plans, stock option plans, Incentive Unit Agreements and Performance Unit Agreements.

Under the amended 1989 Restricted Stock Award Plan and the amended 1983 Restricted Stock Award Plan (the Plans), 10 million and 6 million shares of restricted common stock, respectively, may be granted to certain officers and key employees of the Company.

In 1991, 1990 and 1989, 1,245,000 shares, 858,000 shares and 68,000 shares, respectively, were granted under the Plans. At December 31, 1991, 8.7 million shares were available for grant under the Plans. The participant is entitled to vote and receive dividends on the shares, and, under the

Notes to Consolidated Financial Statements The Coca-Cola Company and Subsidiaries

1983 Restricted Stock Award Plan, the participant is reimbursed by the Company for income taxes imposed on the award. The shares are subject to certain transfer restrictions and may be forfeited if the participant leaves the Company for reasons other than retirement, disability or death, absent a change in control of the Company. On July 18, 1991, the Plans were amended to specify age 62 as the minimum retirement age. In addition, the 1983 Restricted Stock Award Plan was further amended to conform to the terms of the 1989 Restricted Stock Award Plan by requiring a minimum of five years of service prior to retirement. The amendments affect shares granted subsequent to July 18, 1991.

Under the Company's 1991 Stock Option Plan (the Option Plan), a maximum of 30 million shares of the Company's common stock may be issued or transferred to certain officers and employees pursuant to stock options and stock appreciation rights granted under the Option Plan. The stock appreciation rights permit the holder, upon surrendering all or part of the related stock option, to receive cash, common stock or a combination thereof, in an amount up to 100 percent of the difference between the market price and the option price. No stock appreciation rights have been granted since April 1990, and the Company does not presently intend to grant additional stock appreciation rights in the future. Options outstanding at December 31, 1991, also include various options granted under previous plans. Further information relating to options is as follows (in thousands, except per share amounts):

	1991	1990	1989
Outstanding at January 1,	16,532	13,504	17,315
Granted	3,996	5,196	32
Exercised	(1,943)	(1,810)	(2,962)
Canceled	(394)	(358)	(881)
Outstanding at December 31,	18,191	16,532	13,504
Exercisable at December 31,	12,026	9,569	8,561
Shares available at December 31, for options that may be granted	27,689	1,559	6,643
Prices per share			
Exercised	$6–$56	$5–$39	$5–$23
Unexercised at December 31,	$8–$59	$6–$48	$5–$24

In 1988, the Company entered into Incentive Unit Agreements, whereby certain officers will be granted cash awards based on the market value of 600,000 shares of the Company's common stock at the measurement dates. The Incentive Unit Agreements provide for a cash payment for income taxes when the value of the units is paid.

In 1985, the Company entered into Performance Unit Agreements, whereby certain officers will be granted cash awards based on the difference in the market value of approximately 1.1 million shares of the Company's common stock at the measurement dates and the base price of $10.31, the market value as of January 2, 1985.

12. Pensions and Other Postretirement Benefits

In the United States, the Company sponsors and/or contributes to pension plans covering substantially all U.S. employees and certain employees in international locations. The benefits are primarily based on years of service and the employees' compensation for certain periods during the last years of employment. Pension costs are generally funded currently, subject to regulatory funding limitations. The Company also sponsors nonqualified, unfunded defined benefit plans for certain officers and other employees. In addition, the Company and its subsidiaries have various pension plans and other forms of postretirement arrangements outside the United States.

Total pension expense amounted to approximately $42 million in 1991, $30 million in 1990 and $23 million in 1989. Net periodic pension cost for the Company's defined benefit plans in 1991, 1990 and 1989 consists of the following (in thousands):

The Coca-Cola Company

Notes to Consolidated Financial Statements *The Coca-Cola Company and Subsidiaries*

	U.S. Plans			International Plans		
Year Ended December 31,	1991	1990	1989	1991	1990	1989
Service cost—benefits earned during the period	$ 12,475	$ 10,684	$ 9,830	$ 15,894	$ 12,902	$ 12,133
Interest cost on projected benefit obligation	45,860	41,786	35,393	18,523	14,720	12,539
Actual return on plan assets	(112,530)	(9,121)	(95,254)	(17,498)	(3,811)	(16,108)
Net amortization and deferral	71,090	(31,168)	56,548	555	(11,273)	2,240
Net periodic pension cost	$ 16,895	$ 12,181	$ 6,517	$ 17,474	$ 12,538	$ 10,804

The following table sets forth the funded status for the Company's defined benefit plans at December 31, 1991 and 1990 (in thousands):

	U.S. Plans				International Plans			
	Assets Exceed Accumulated Benefits		Accumulated Benefits Exceed Assets		Assets Exceed Accumulated Benefits		Accumulated Benefits Exceed Assets	
December 31,	1991	1990	1991	1990	1991	1990	1991	1990
Actuarial present value of benefit obligations								
Vested benefit obligation	$359,857	$340,598	$ 66,907	$ 53,386	$ 96,074	$ 84,890	$ 81,609	$ 70,044
Accumulated benefit obligation	$383,972	$362,724	$ 72,610	$ 57,372	$106,286	$ 89,263	$ 91,208	$ 72,938
Projected benefit obligation	$455,357	$424,118	$ 82,251	$ 65,703	$145,435	$129,435	$144,245	$113,842
Plan assets at fair value[1]	583,819	508,267	—	811	175,392	160,945	74,640	62,335
Plan assets in excess of (less than) projected benefit obligation	128,462	84,149	(82,251)[2]	(64,892)[2]	29,957	31,510	(69,605)	(51,507)
Unrecognized net (asset) liability at transition	(40,764)	(44,317)	21,292	23,416	(29,229)	(32,076)	40,908	38,121
Unrecognized prior service cost	25,756	28,302	2,795	1,175	105	2,017	5,243	—
Unrecognized net (gain) loss	(114,934)	(64,617)	14,506	5,647	10,265	5,171	(1,672)	58
Adjustment required to recognize minimum liability	—	—	(28,952)	(21,941)	—	—	(453)	(167)
Accrued pension asset (liability) included in the consolidated balance sheet	$ (1,480)	$ 3,517	$(72,610)	$(56,595)	$ 11,098	$ 6,622	$ (25,579)	$ (13,495)

[1] Primarily listed stocks, bonds and government securities.
[2] Substantially all of this amount relates to nonqualified, unfunded defined benefit plans.

The assumptions used in computing the above information are as follows:

	U.S. Plans			International Plans (weighted average rates)		
	1991	1990	1989	1991	1990	1989
Discount rates	9%	9%	9%	7½%	8%	7%
Rates of increase in compensation levels	6%	6%	6%	6%	6%	4%
Expected long-term rates of return on assets	9½%	9½%	9%	7½%	8%	8%

234 **Specimen Financial Statements**

Notes to Consolidated Financial Statements *The Coca-Cola Company and Subsidiaries*

The Company also has plans that provide postretirement health care and life insurance benefits to substantially all U.S. employees and certain international employees who retire with a minimum of five years of service. The annual cash cost of these benefits is not significant. In 1990, the FASB issued Statement of Financial Accounting Standards No. 106, "Employers' Accounting for Postretirement Benefits Other than Pensions" (SFAS 106). SFAS 106 will require companies to accrue the cost of postretirement health care and life insurance benefits within employees' active service periods. The Company's required adoption date for SFAS 106 is January 1, 1993.

SFAS 106 allows companies to either recognize their full accumulated postretirement benefit obligation at the date of adoption or amortize it as a component of postretirement benefits expense over a period of up to twenty years. The Company is currently evaluating these options.

Based on preliminary studies and evaluations, the Company's accumulated postretirement benefit obligation at January 1, 1993, will be approximately $200 million, before related income tax benefits. The increase in annual pretax postretirement benefits expense after adoption of SFAS 106 is expected to be in the range of $20 million to $30 million.

13. Income Taxes

The components of income before income taxes for both continuing and discontinued operations consist of the following (in thousands):

Year Ended December 31,	1991	1990	1989
United States	$ 648,471	$ 494,544	$1,459,213
International	1,734,808	1,519,892	1,257,104
	$2,383,279	$2,014,436	$2,716,317

Income taxes for continuing and discontinued operations consist of the following (in thousands):

Year Ended December 31,	United States	State & Local	International	Total
1991				
Current	$204,781	$30,981	$595,662	$831,424
Deferred	(61,229)	(5,267)	349	(66,147)
1990				
Current	$134,973	$26,515	$501,298	$662,786
Deferred	(49,387)	(2,596)	21,729	(30,254)
1989				
Current	$478,004	$84,072	$393,380	$955,456
Deferred	(8,025)	160	44,901	37,036

The Company made income tax payments of approximately $672 million, $803 million and $537 million in 1991, 1990 and 1989, respectively.

A reconciliation of the statutory U.S. federal rate and effective rates for continuing operations is as follows:

Year Ended December 31,	1991	1990	1989
Statutory U.S. federal rate	34.0%	34.0%	34.0%
State income taxes—net of federal benefit	1.0	1.0	1.0
Earnings in jurisdictions taxed at rates different from the statutory U.S. federal rate	(3.1)	(2.6)	(1.6)
Equity income	(.6)	(1.8)	(1.5)
Other—net	.8	.8	.5
	32.1%	31.4%	32.4%

Deferred taxes are provided principally for depreciation, certain employee compensation-related expenses and certain capital transactions that are recognized in different years for financial statement and income tax purposes. The Company has manufacturing facilities in Puerto Rico that operate under a negotiated exemption grant that expires December 31, 2009.

Appropriate U.S. and international taxes have been provided for earnings of subsidiary companies that are expected to be remitted to the parent company. Accumulated unremitted earnings of international subsidiaries that are expected to be required for use in the international operations were approximately $373 million at December 31, 1991, exclusive of amounts that, if remitted, would result in little or no tax.

The Coca-Cola Company

Notes to Consolidated Financial Statements The Coca-Cola Company and Subsidiaries

14. Net Change in Operating Assets and Liabilities

The changes in operating assets and liabilities, net of effects of acquisitions and divestitures of businesses and unrealized exchange gains/losses, are as follows (in thousands):

Year Ended December 31,	1991	1990	1989
Increase in trade accounts receivable	$ (31,826)	$ (87,749)	$ (99,496)
Increase in inventories	(3,020)	(169,442)	(34,709)
Increase in prepaid expenses and other assets	(325,595)	(65,758)	(204,222)
Increase in accounts payable and accrued expenses	266,684	198,631	88,940
Increase (decrease) in accrued taxes	215,877	(111,014)	456,544
Increase in other liabilities	100,717	57,130	72,325
	$222,837	$(178,202)	$279,382

The net change in operating assets and liabilities in 1990 reflects estimated tax payments of approximately $300 million related to the 1989 gain on the sale of Columbia Pictures Entertainment, Inc. stock.

15. Acquisitions and Divestitures

The Company periodically engages in the acquisition and/or divestiture of bottling and other related companies. Significant transactions are discussed below.

In August 1989, the Company acquired all of the Coca-Cola bottling operations of Pernod Ricard. Pernod Ricard had operated the Coca-Cola bottling, canning and distribution business in six major territories in France. The fair values of assets acquired and liabilities assumed were $285 million and $145 million, respectively. The $140 million acquisition was accounted for by the purchase method. Operating results have been included in the consolidated statements of income from the date of acquisition.

In August 1989, the Company sold Belmont Springs Water Co., Inc., a bottled water operation, which resulted in a pretax gain of approximately $61 million.

See Note 3 for discussions of the equity investment in CCA, which was acquired in August 1989, and the temporary investment in CCHA, which was acquired in July 1989 and sold in June 1990. See Note 17 for a discussion of the sale of Columbia Pictures Entertainment, Inc. stock.

16. Other Nonrecurring Items

"Other income—net" in 1991 includes a $69 million pretax gain on the sale of property no longer required as a result of a consolidation of concentrate operations in Japan and a $27 million pretax gain on the sale of the Company's 22 percent ownership interest in Johnston to CCE. "Selling, administrative and general expenses" and "Interest expense" include 1991 pretax charges of $13 million and $8 million, respectively, for potential future costs related to bottler litigation. In addition, 1991 equity income has been reduced by $44 million related to restructuring charges recorded by CCE.

"Other income—net" in 1990 includes a pretax gain of $52 million on the Company's investment in BCI Securities L.P. (BCI) resulting from BCI's sale of Beatrice Company stock. "Selling, administrative and general expenses" in 1990 include nonrecurring pretax charges of $49 million related to the Company's United States soft drink business. These charges reflect accelerated amortization of certain software costs due to management plans to upgrade and standardize information systems and adjustments to the carrying value of certain fountain equipment and marketing-related items to amounts estimated to be recoverable in future periods.

17. Discontinued Operation

In 1989, the Company sold its entire equity interest in Columbia Pictures Entertainment, Inc. (CPE) for approximately $1.6 billion in cash. The equity interest consisted of approximately 49 percent of the outstanding common shares of CPE and 1,000 shares of preferred stock. The sale resulted in a pretax gain of approximately $930 million. On an after-tax basis, the gain was approximately $509 million or $.74 per common share. The effective tax rate of 45 percent on the gain on the sale of CPE stock differs from the statutory U.S. federal rate of 34 percent due primarily to differences between the book basis and tax basis of the Company's investment in CPE.

CPE has been reported as a discontinued operation, and, accordingly, the gain from the sale of CPE stock and the Company's equity income from CPE have been reported separately from continuing operations.

Notes to Consolidated Financial Statements The Coca-Cola Company and Subsidiaries

18 Lines of Business

The Company operates in two major lines of business: soft drinks and foods (principally juice and juice-drink products). Information concerning operations in these businesses at December 31, 1991, 1990 and 1989, and for the years then ended, is presented below (in millions):

1991	Soft Drinks United States	Soft Drinks International	Foods	Corporate	Consolidated
Net operating revenues	$2,645.2	$7,244.8	$1,635.7	$ 45.9	$11,571.6
Operating income	468.7	2,141.1	103.7	(394.5)	2,319.0
Identifiable operating assets	1,447.0	4,742.3	755.0	1,124.1[3]	8,068.4
Equity income				40.0[1]	40.0
Investments (principally bottling companies)				2,154.0	2,154.0
Capital expenditures	131.1	546.3	57.1	57.2	791.7
Depreciation and amortization	81.9	111.9	30.8	36.8	261.4

1990	Soft Drinks United States	Soft Drinks International	Foods	Corporate	Consolidated
Net operating revenues	$2,461.3	$6,125.4	$1,604.9	$ 44.8	$10,236.4
Operating income	358.1[2]	1,801.4	93.5	(301.4)	1,951.6
Identifiable operating assets	1,691.0	3,672.2	759.2	1,131.2[3]	7,253.6
Equity income				110.1	110.1
Investments (principally bottling companies)				2,024.6	2,024.6
Capital expenditures	138.4	321.4	68.2	65.0	593.0
Depreciation and amortization	88.5	94.4	28.3	32.7	243.9

1989	Soft Drinks United States	Soft Drinks International	Foods	Corporate	Consolidated
Net operating revenues	$2,222.2	$4,759.2	$1,583.3	$ 57.6	$ 8,622.3
Operating income	390.6	1,517.6	87.4	(269.8)	1,725.8
Identifiable operating assets	1,814.4	2,806.0	695.3	1,036.4[3]	6,352.1
Equity income				75.5	75.5
Investments (principally bottling companies)				1,930.4	1,930.4
Capital expenditures	136.3	215.6	61.6	49.0	462.5
Depreciation and amortization	73.9	48.4	30.7	30.8	183.8

Intercompany transfers between sectors are not material.

[1] *Reduced by $44 million related to restructuring charges recorded by CCE*
[2] *Includes nonrecurring charges of $49 million*
[3] *Corporate identifiable operating assets are composed principally of marketable securities and fixed assets.*

Net Operating Revenues by Line of Business *(In millions)*
- Soft Drinks - United States
- Soft Drinks - International
- Foods

Year	Soft Drinks - US	Soft Drinks - Intl	Foods
89	26%	56%	18%
90	24%	60%	16%
91	23%	63%	14%

Operating Income by Line of Business *(In millions)*
- Soft Drinks - United States
- Soft Drinks - International
- Foods

Year	Soft Drinks - US	Soft Drinks - Intl	Foods
89	20%	76%	4%
90	16%	80%	4%
91	17%	79%	4%

The Coca-Cola Company

Notes to Consolidated Financial Statements *The Coca-Cola Company and Subsidiaries*

19. Operations in Geographic Areas

Information about the Company's operations in different geographic areas at December 31, 1991, 1990 and 1989, and for the years then ended, is presented below (in millions):

1991	United States	Latin America	European Community	Northeast Europe/Africa	Pacific and Canada	Corporate	Consolidated
Net operating revenues	$4,124.8	$1,103.2	$3,338.3	$613.6	$2,345.8	$ 45.9	$11,571.6
Operating income	560.2	404.6	767.3	204.1	777.3	(394.5)	2,319.0
Identifiable operating assets	2,160.9	814.6	2,558.0	423.5	987.3	1,124.1[3]	8,068.4
Equity income						40.0[1]	40.0
Investments (principally bottling companies)						2,154.0	2,154.0
Capital expenditures	184.8	105.5	330.6	61.3	52.3	57.2	791.7
Depreciation and amortization	111.3	23.3	65.8	9.7	14.5	36.8	261.4

1990	United States	Latin America	European Community	Northeast Europe/Africa	Pacific and Canada	Corporate	Consolidated
Net operating revenues	$3,931.0	$ 813.0	$2,804.8	$562.8	$2,080.0	$ 44.8	$10,236.4
Operating income	440.4[2]	300.2	666.5	174.2	671.7	(301.4)	1,951.6
Identifiable operating assets	2,414.2	640.3	1,818.8	400.1	849.0	1,131.2[3]	7,253.6
Equity income						110.1	110.1
Investments (principally bottling companies)						2,024.6	2,024.6
Capital expenditures	204.0	59.7	203.5	38.8	22.0	65.0	593.0
Depreciation and amortization	115.6	18.0	54.5	7.6	15.5	32.7	243.9

1989	United States	Latin America	European Community	Northeast Europe/Africa	Pacific and Canada	Corporate	Consolidated
Net operating revenues	$3,678.7	$ 646.2	$1,855.1	$425.2	$1,959.5	$ 57.6	$ 8,622.3
Operating income	468.2	226.7	540.6	147.3	612.8	(269.8)	1,725.8
Identifiable operating assets	2,476.0	515.4	1,342.8	328.8	652.7	1,036.4[3]	6,352.1
Equity income						75.5	75.5
Investments (principally bottling companies)						1,930.4	1,930.4
Capital expenditures	196.4	30.7	133.9	24.6	27.9	49.0	462.5
Depreciation and amortization	103.5	11.8	18.0	4.9	14.8	30.8	183.8

Intercompany transfers between geographic areas are not material.
Identifiable liabilities of operations outside the United States amounted to approximately $1.7 billion, $1.5 billion and $1.1 billion at December 31, 1991, 1990 and 1989, respectively.

[1] Reduced by $44 million related to restructuring charges recorded by CCE.
[2] Includes nonrecurring charges of $49 million.
[3] Corporate identifiable operating assets are composed principally of marketable securities and fixed assets.

Report of Independent Auditors

Board of Directors and Share Owners
The Coca-Cola Company

We have audited the accompanying consolidated balance sheets of The Coca-Cola Company and subsidiaries as of December 31, 1991 and 1990, and the related consolidated statements of income, share-owners' equity and cash flows for each of the three years in the period ended December 31, 1991. These financial statements are the responsibility of the Company's management. Our responsibility is to express an opinion on these financial statements based on our audits.

We conducted our audits in accordance with generally accepted auditing standards. Those standards require that we plan and perform the audit to obtain reasonable assurance about whether the financial statements are free of material misstatement. An audit includes examining, on a test basis, evidence supporting the amounts and disclosures in the financial statements. An audit also includes assessing the accounting principles used and significant estimates made by management, as well as evaluating the overall financial statement presentation. We believe that our audits provide a reasonable basis for our opinion.

In our opinion, the financial statements referred to above present fairly, in all material respects, the consolidated financial position of The Coca-Cola Company and subsidiaries at December 31, 1991 and 1990, and the consolidated results of their operations and their cash flows for each of the three years in the period ended December 31, 1991, in conformity with generally accepted accounting principles.

Atlanta, Georgia
January 24, 1992

Ernst & Young

Report of Management *The Coca-Cola Company and Subsidiaries*

Management is responsible for the preparation and integrity of the consolidated financial statements appearing in this Annual Report. The financial statements were prepared in conformity with generally accepted accounting principles appropriate in the circumstances and, accordingly, include some amounts based on management's best judgments and estimates. Financial information in this Annual Report is consistent with that in the financial statements.

Management is responsible for maintaining a system of internal accounting controls and procedures to provide reasonable assurance, at an appropriate cost/benefit relationship, that assets are safeguarded and that transactions are authorized, recorded and reported properly. The internal accounting control system is augmented by a program of internal audits and appropriate reviews by management, written policies and guidelines, careful selection and training of qualified personnel and a written Code of Business Conduct adopted by the Board of Directors, applicable to all employees of the Company and its subsidiaries. Management believes that the Company's internal accounting controls provide reasonable assurance that assets are safeguarded against material loss from unauthorized use or disposition and that the financial records are reliable for preparing financial statements and other data and for maintaining accountability of assets.

The Audit Committee of the Board of Directors, composed solely of Directors who are not officers of the Company, meets with the independent auditors, management and internal auditors periodically to discuss internal accounting controls, auditing matters and financial reporting matters. The Committee reviews with the independent auditors the scope and results of the audit effort. The Committee also meets with the independent auditors and the chief internal auditor without management present to ensure that the independent auditors and the chief internal auditor have free access to the Committee.

The independent auditors, Ernst & Young, are recommended by the Audit Committee of the Board of Directors, selected by the Board of Directors and ratified by the share owners. Ernst & Young is engaged to audit the consolidated financial statements of The Coca-Cola Company and subsidiaries and conduct such tests and related procedures as they deem necessary in conformity with generally accepted auditing standards. The opinion of the independent auditors, based upon their audits of the consolidated financial statements, is contained in this Annual Report.

Roberto C. Goizueta
Chairman, Board of Directors,
and Chief Executive Officer

Jack L. Stahl
Senior Vice President
and Chief Financial Officer

Patrick M. Worsham
Vice President
and Controller

January 24, 1992

Quarterly Data (Unaudited) *The Coca-Cola Company and Subsidiaries*

Years Ended December 31, 1991 and 1990
(In millions except per share data)

1991	First Quarter	Second Quarter	Third Quarter	Fourth Quarter	Full Year
Net operating revenues	$2,481.0	$3,039.5	$3,172.1	$2,879.0	$11,571.6
Gross profit	1,516.9	1,853.8	1,864.9	1,687.6	6,923.2
Net income	320.9	482.4	456.3	358.4	1,618.0
Net income available to common share owners	320.4	482.4	456.3	358.4	1,617.5
Net income per common share	.48	.72	.69	.54	2.43

1990	First Quarter	Second Quarter	Third Quarter	Fourth Quarter	Full Year
Net operating revenues	$2,148.3	$2,739.3	$2,792.8	$2,556.0	$10,236.4
Gross profit	1,281.8	1,639.4	1,625.5	1,480.8	6,027.5
Net income	283.5	409.9	394.2	294.3	1,381.9
Net income available to common share owners	278.6	405.1	389.4	290.6	1,363.7
Net income per common share	.41	.61	.58	.44	2.04

The second quarter of 1991 includes a nonrecurring pretax charge of $21 million ($.02 per common share after income taxes) for potential future costs, including interest, related to bottler litigation.

The fourth quarter of 1991 includes a $69 million pretax gain ($.07 per common share after income taxes) on the sale of property in Japan, a $27 million pretax gain ($.03 per common share after income taxes) on the sale of a bottling investment to Coca-Cola Enterprises Inc. (CCE) and a reduction to equity income of $44 million ($.07 per common share after income taxes) related to restructuring charges recorded by CCE.

The third quarter of 1990 includes a $52 million pretax gain ($.05 per common share after income taxes) on the Company's investment in BCI Securities L.P. and nonrecurring pretax charges of $49 million ($.05 per common share after income taxes) related to the Company's United States soft drink business.

Financial Glossary

Total capital equals share-owners' equity plus total debt.

Return on common equity is calculated by dividing income from continuing operations less preferred stock dividends by average common share-owners' equity.

Return on capital is calculated by dividing income from continuing operations before interest expense by average total capital.

Economic profit represents net operating profit after taxes in excess of capital charges for average operating capital employed. Temporary investments and cash, cash equivalents and current marketable securities in excess of operating requirements, including interest income thereon, are excluded from the economic profit calculation.

Net debt and **net capital** are net of temporary investments and cash, cash equivalents and current marketable securities in excess of operating requirements. The net-debt-to-net-capital ratio excludes debt and excess cash of the Company's finance subsidiary.

The **dividend payout ratio** is calculated by dividing cash dividends on common stock by net income available to common share owners.

Corporate Officers

Roberto C. Goizueta[1]
Chairman, Board of Directors,
and Chief Executive Officer

Donald R. Keough[1]
President and Chief
Operating Officer

Senior Vice Presidents
Ralph H. Cooper[1]
Douglas N. Daft[1]
M.A. Gianturco
Joseph R. Gladden, Jr.[1]
John Hunter[1]
E. Neville Isdell[1]
M. Douglas Ivester[1]
Weldon H. Johnson[1]
Earl T. Leonard, Jr.[1]
Alex Malaspina
Peter S. Sealey[1]
Jack L. Stahl[1]
R.V. Waltemeyer[1]
Carl Ware

Vice Presidents
Anton Amon
William R. Buehler
Robert L. Callahan, Jr.
Philip J. Carswell, Jr.
Carlton L. Curtis
William J. Davis
Lance E. Disley
Thomas E. Floyd
Murray D. Friedman
Charles B. Fruit
C. Patrick Garner
John J. Gillin
George Gourlay
Robert D. Guy
Timothy J. Haas[1]
Gary P. Hite
Ingrid S. Jones
W. Glenn Kernel
Janmarie C. Prutting
Hugh K. Switzer
Michael W. Walters
Patrick M. Worsham[1]

Jack L. Stahl
Chief Financial Officer

Joseph R. Gladden, Jr.
General Counsel

Lance E. Disley
Treasurer

Patrick M. Worsham
Controller

Susan E. Shaw
Secretary

Executive Officers– Operating Units

North America Business Sector
M. Douglas Ivester
President

Coca-Cola USA
M. Douglas Ivester
President

Coca-Cola Foods
Timothy J. Haas
President

International Business Sector
John Hunter
President

Pacific Group
Douglas N. Daft
President

European Community Group
Ralph H. Cooper
President

Northeast Europe/ Africa Group
E. Neville Isdell
President

Latin America Group
Weldon H. Johnson
President

Board of Directors

Herbert A. Allen[3,4,5]
President and
Chief Executive Officer
The investment banking firm
Allen & Company Incorporated

Ronald W. Allen[4,6]
Chairman of the Board and
Chief Executive Officer
Delta Air Lines, Inc.

Warren E. Buffett[2,3]
Chairman of the Board
and Chief Executive Officer
The diversified holding company
Berkshire Hathaway Inc.

Charles W. Duncan, Jr.[2,4]
Private Investor

Roberto C. Goizueta[4]
Chairman, Board of Directors,
Chief Executive Officer
The Coca-Cola Company

Donald R. Keough[4]
President and
Chief Operating Officer
The Coca-Cola Company

Susan B. King[5,7]
Senior Vice President–
Corporate Affairs
Corning Incorporated

James T. Laney[7]
President
Emory University

Donald F. McHenry[2,6,7]
University Research
Professor of Diplomacy
and International Affairs
Georgetown University

Paul F. Oreffice[3,6]
Chairman of the Board
The Dow Chemical Company

James D. Robinson, III[6,7]
Chairman and
Chief Executive Officer
American Express Company

William B. Turner[3,4,5]
Chairman, Executive Committee
of Board of Directors
The diversified company
W.C. Bradley Co.
Chairman, Executive Committee
of Board of Directors
Synovus Financial Corp.
Chairman of the Board
Columbus Bank & Trust Company

Peter V. Ueberroth[2,5]
Investor,
Managing Director
The management company
The Contrarian Group, Inc.

James B. Williams[3,4]
Chairman and
Chief Executive Officer
SunTrust Banks, Inc.

---

[1] Officers subject to the reporting requirements of Section 16 of the Securities Exchange Act of 1934
[2] Audit Committee
[3] Finance Committee
[4] Executive Committee
[5] Compensation Committee
[6] Committee on Directors
[7] Public Issues Review Committee

Share-Owner Information

Common Stock
Ticker symbol: KO

The Coca-Cola Company is one of 30 companies in the Dow Jones Industrial Average.

Common stock of The Coca-Cola Company is listed and traded on the New York Stock Exchange, which is the principal market for the common stock, and also is traded on the Boston, Cincinnati, Midwest, Pacific and Philadelphia stock exchanges. Outside the United States, the Company's common stock is listed and traded on the German exchange in Frankfurt and on Swiss exchanges in Zurich, Geneva, Bern, Basel and Lausanne.

Share owners of record at year-end: 117,874

Shares outstanding at year-end: 664 million

Dividends
At its February 1992 meeting, the Company's Board of Directors increased the quarterly dividend to 28 cents per share, equivalent to an annual dividend of $1.12 per share. The Company has increased dividends each of the last 30 years.

The Coca-Cola Company normally pays dividends four times a year, usually on April 1, July 1, October 1 and December 15. The Company has paid 283 consecutive quarterly dividends, beginning in 1920.

Dividend and Cash Investment Plan
All share owners of record are invited to participate in the Dividend and Cash Investment Plan. The Plan provides a convenient, economical and systematic method of acquiring additional shares of the Company's common stock. The Plan permits share owners of record to reinvest dividends from Company stock in shares of The Coca-Cola Company. Share owners also may purchase Company stock through voluntary cash investments of up to $60,000 per year.

All costs and commissions associated with joining and participating in the Plan are paid by the Company.

The Plan's administrator, First Chicago Trust Company of New York, purchases stock for voluntary cash investments on or about the first of each month, and for dividend reinvestment on April 1, July 1, October 1 and December 15.

At year-end, 37 percent of share owners of record were participants in the Plan. In 1991, share owners invested $12.78 million in dividends and $16.35 million in cash in the Plan.

Stock Prices
Below are the New York Stock Exchange high, low and closing prices of The Coca-Cola Company stock for each quarter of 1991 and 1990, adjusted for a 2-for-1 stock split in May 1990.

Quarter	1991 High	Low	Close
Fourth	81.75	62.38	80.25
Third	66.50	54.50	64.50
Second	58.00	51.38	54.50
First	55.50	42.63	54.25

Quarter	1990 High	Low	Close
Fourth	49.00	39.75	46.50
Third	48.38	37.25	39.50
Second	46.88	37.13	44.38
First	39.00	32.63	37.38

Annual Meeting of Share Owners
April 15, 1992, at 9:00 a.m. local time
The Georgia World Congress Center Ballroom
285 International Boulevard, N.W.
Atlanta, Georgia

Publications
The Company's annual report on Form 10-K and quarterly report on Form 10-Q are available free of charge from the Office of the Secretary, The Coca-Cola Company, P.O. Drawer 1734, Atlanta, Georgia 30301.

A *Notice of Annual Meeting of Share Owners* and *Proxy Statement* are furnished to share owners in advance of the annual meeting. *Progress Reports*, containing financial results and other information, are distributed quarterly to share owners.

Also available from the Office of the Secretary are *Coca-Cola, A Business System Toward 2000: Our Mission in the 1990s*, *The Chronicle of Coca-Cola Since 1886* and other booklets about the Company and its products.

Equal Opportunity Policy
The Coca-Cola Company employs 28,900 people worldwide and maintains a long-standing commitment to equal opportunity and affirmative action. The Company strives to create a working environment free of discrimination and harassment with respect to race, sex, color, national origin, religion, age, disability or being a veteran of the Vietnam era as well as to make reasonable accommodations in the employment of qualified individuals with disabilities. The Company continued to increase minority and female representation in 1991. In addition, the Company provides fair marketing opportunities to all suppliers and maintains programs to increase transactions with firms that are owned and operated by minorities and women.

The Coca-Cola Company

ANSWERS

Chapter 1

Matching

1. h	7. s	13. u	19. d
2. f	8. c	14. e	20. g
3. o	9. j	15. l	21. a
4. r	10. v	16. q	22. p
5. w	11. i	17. m	23. k
6. n	12. b	18. t	

Short Answer

1. (L.O. 6) Alpha Corporation
   Income Statement
   For the Year Ended June 30, 19xx
2. (L.O. 1) Bookkeeping deals only with the mechanical and repetitive recordkeeping process. Accounting involves bookkeeping as well as the design of an accounting system, its use, and the analysis of its output.
3. (L.O. 8)
   a. *Integrity*—The accountant is honest, regardless of consequences.
   b. *Objectivity*—The accountant is impartial in performing his or her job.
   c. *Independence*—The accountant avoids all relationships or situations that could impair his or her objectivity.
   d. *Due care*—The accountant carries out his or her responsibilities with competence and diligence.
4. (L.O. 2) Management, outsiders with a direct financial interest, and outsiders with an indirect financial interest
5. (L.O. 1) To earn a satisfactory profit to hold investor capital; to maintain sufficient funds to pay debts as they fall due
6. (L.O. 6)

   Statement
   a. Balance sheet
   b. Income statement
   c. Statement of cash flows
   d. Statement of retained earnings

   Purpose
   a. Shows financial position at a point in time
   b. Measures net income during a certain period
   c. Discloses operating, financing, and investing activities during the period
   d. Shows how retained earnings changed during the period

True-False

1. F (L.O. 5) It is the balance sheet that shows financial position.
2. F (L.O. 7) The IRS interprets and enforces tax laws.
3. T (L.O. 5)
4. T (L.O. 5)
5. F (L.O. 5) It indicates that the company has one or more debtors.
6. T (L.O. 5)
7. F (L.O. 3) The measurement stage refers to the recording of business transactions.
8. F (L.O. 6) Dividends are a deduction in the statement of retained earnings.
9. T (L.O. 7)
10. T (L.O. 4)
11. T (L.O. 6)
12. T (L.O. 6)
13. F (L.O. 7) That is the GASB's responsibility.
14. F (L.O. 4) A corporation is managed by its board of directors.
15. T (L.O. 7)
16. F (L.O. 5) Net assets equal assets *minus* liabilities.
17. F (L.O. 6) Balance sheets do not list revenues and expenses.
18. F (L.O. 3) Nonexchange transactions, such as the accumulation of interest, do exist.
19. T (L.O. 1)
20. T (L.O. 6)
21. T (L.O. 3)
22. F (L.O. 2) Economic planners have an indirect financial interest in accounting information.
23. T (L.O. 5)

Multiple Choice

1. a (L.O. 6) The answer "Wages Expense" is correct because it is the account title, of the possible choices, that would appear on the income statement. The income statement is the financial statement that reports revenues and expenses.
2. c (L.O. 7) The SEC (Securities and Exchange Commission) is the organization that regulates financial trading. Its role is to help protect the public from incomplete information. The SEC requires that certain financial information be made available so that the public will be able to make informed investment decisions.
3. b (L.O. 4) The stock of a corporation is easily transferred from one investor to another. Corporations are owned through ownership of shares of stock.
4. b (L.O. 6) The balance sheet is a "snapshot" of the business, in a financial sense, on a given date. The account balances, as they appear on the balance sheet, are a report of the ultimate effect of financial transactions during an accounting period, not a report of the actual transactions.
5. a (L.O. 7) An audit is used to verify the information presented by the management of a firm in its financial statements. The term "fairness" refers to the ability of users of the financial statements to rely on the information as presented.
6. d (L.O. 5) Collection on an account receivable is simply an exchange of one asset (the account receivable) for another asset (cash). As a result, there is no effect on the accounting equation.
7. d (L.O. 4) The partners *are* the partnership. There is no separate legal entity in this form of organization. When a partner leaves the partnership, the original partnership is dissolved, although a new partnership may be formed by replacing the exiting partner.
8. a (L.O. 6) "Assets" is a major heading found in the balance sheet. Accounts Receivable is merely a type of asset.
9. c (L.O. 5) The payment of a liability will reduce both sides of the accounting equation equally. The transaction is a reduction in assets and a reduction in liabilities in equal amounts.
10. d (L.O. 5) The purchase of an asset for cash is an exchange of one asset for another. It is an increase and a decrease, in equal amounts, on one side of the accounting equation. Therefore, it has no effect on total assets, liabilities, or owner's equity.
11. b (L.O. 6) The statement of cash flows does not acknowledge anything called "funding activities."

Exercises

1. (L.O. 2, 7)
   a. Potential investors need all recent financial statements to assess the future profitability of a company and thus whether they should invest in it.
   b. The principal goal of the SEC is to protect the public. Insisting that Lindlay make its statements public as well as examining the statements for propriety certainly will help the public make decisions regarding Lindlay.
   c. The bank will have difficulty in determining Lindlay's ability to repay the loan if it does not have access to Lindlay's most recent financial statements.
   d. Present stockholders will wish to see the statements in order to decide whether to sell, maintain, or increase their investments.
   e. Management will want to see the statements because the statements should help them pinpoint the weaknesses that caused the year's loss.

2. (L.O. 5) $35,000

3. (L.O. 6)

Acme TV Repair Corporation
Balance Sheet
December 31, 19xx

Assets

Cash	$ 950
Accounts Receivable	1,500
Equipment	850
Land	1,000
Building	10,000
Truck	4,500
	$18,800

Liabilities

Accounts Payable	$ 1,300

Stockholders' Equity

Common Stock	14,500
Retained Earnings	3,000
	$18,800

4. (L.O. 5)

	Assets				Liabilities	Stockholders' Equity	
Transaction	Cash	Accounts Receivable	Supplies and Equipment	Trucks	Accounts Payable	Common Stock	Retained Earnings
a	+$20,000					+$20,000	
b	−650		+$650				
c				+$5,200	+$5,200		
d	+525						+$525
e	−2,600				−2,600		
f		+$150					+150
g	−250						−250
h	+150	−150					
i		+20	−20				
j	−200						−200
Balance at end of month	$16,975	$20	$630	$5,200	$2,600	$20,000	$225

Solution to Crossword Puzzle

(Chapter 1)

				¹L		²F	³I	N	A	N	C	I	⁴A	L	
			⁵S	O	L	E		E					U		
				S				T		⁶P			D		⁷C
	⁸A	S	S	E	T	⁹S		¹⁰C	R	E	D	I	T	O	R
						E				O					R
¹¹B	A	¹²L	A	N	C	E				F		¹³A	I	C	P	A
O		I								I		N			O
O		¹⁴A	C	C	O	U	N	T	I	N	G			¹⁵T	A	X
K		B								A					T
K		I		¹⁶E						B					I
E		¹⁷L	I	Q	U	I	D	I	T	Y		¹⁸M	I	S
E		I		U						L		O		
P		T		I						I		N		
E		Y		¹⁹E	N	T	I	T	Y					
R				Y										

248   Answers: Chapter 1

Chapter 2

Matching

1. k	7. a	13. e	19. d
2. f	8. m	14. n	
3. q	9. l	15. p	
4. o	10. s	16. h	
5. b	11. j	17. c	
6. g	12. r	18. i	

Short Answer

1. (L.O. 3) Determine the transaction's effect on the accounts, apply the rules of double entry, make the entry (journalize), post the entry to the ledger, and prepare a trial balance.
2. (L.O. 1)
   a. July 14
   b. $150
   c. Cash and Accounts Receivable
3. (L.O. 4) Two examples are the purchase of any asset for cash and the collection on an account receivable.
4. (L.O. 4) One example is the payment of an account payable.
5. (L.O. 2) Revenues, expenses, and dividends

True-False

1. F (L.O. 1) A sale should be recorded when it takes place.
2. T (L.O. 1)
3. T (L.O. 2)
4. F (L.O. 3) The credit side of an account does not imply anything favorable or unfavorable.
5. F (L.O. 3) Only those accounts with zero balances have equal debits and credits.
6. F (L.O. 6) One quickly can determine cash on hand by referring to the ledger.
7. T (L.O. 2)
8. F (L.O. 2) Notes Payable is the proper account title; the liability is evidenced by the existence of a promissory note.
9. T (L.O. 2)
10. T (L.O. 3)
11. F (L.O. 3) It is possible to have all increases or all decreases in a journal entry.
12. F (L.O. 5) Journal entries are made before transactions are posted to the ledger.
13. F (L.O. 5) Liabilities and stockholders' equity accounts are indented only when credited.
14. T (L.O. 5)
15. T (L.O. 6)
16. T (L.O. 6)
17. T (L.O. 6)
18. F (L.O. 2) It is a table of contents to the general ledger.
19. F (L.O. 7) Unearned Revenue has a normal credit balance.
20. F (L.O. 2) Retained earnings is not cash and should be shown in the stockholders' equity section.
21. T (L.O. 2)

Multiple Choice

1. c (L.O. 1) Summarization of accounting data occurs at the end of the accounting cycle. Journal entries are prepared throughout the accounting period.
2. d (L.O. 4) When a liability is paid, each side of the accounting equation is reduced in equal proportion. The transaction results in a reduction in an asset and a corresponding reduction in a liability.
3. c (L.O. 5) The explanation accompanying a journal entry is a brief statement as to the reason for the entire transaction. Debits and credits are elements of the recorded transaction. The explanation is entered after all debit and credit entries have been made.
4. d (L.O. 6) The final step in the posting process is the transfer of the ledger account number to the Post. Ref. column of the general journal. This last step is an indication that all other steps in the process are complete.
5. c (L.O. 7) If only part of a journal entry has been posted, the omitted information would usually be either a debit or a credit. As a result, total debits would not equal total credits in the general ledger accounts. Therefore, the trial balance would be out of balance.
6. b (L.O. 3) In the transaction described, the receipt of cash in payment of an account receivable, an exchange of one asset for another has occurred. Therefore, total assets would remain unchanged.
7. a (L.O. 3) The Dividends account ultimately causes a reduction in Retained Earnings, a stockholders' equity account. A decrease in stockholders' equity is recorded with a debit.
8. b (L.O. 2) Of the accounts listed, Prepaid Rent is the only one that is classified as an asset. Unearned Revenue is a liability; Retained Earnings is a stockholders' equity account; and Fees Earned is a revenue account.
9. a (L.O. 2) Of the accounts listed, only Interest Payable would represent an amount owing.
10. b (L.O. 4) Unearned Rent would represent a liability on the accounting records of the *lessor*. The question refers to the possible entries of the *lessee*, which include entries into Prepaid Rent, Rent Payable, and Rent Expense.
11. c (L.O. 3) Sales is a revenue account. Revenues increase with a credit entry, and therefore Sales is referred to as having a *normal credit balance*. Revenues ultimately cause an increase in Retained Earnings, which also has a normal credit balance.

Exercises

1. (L.O. 5)

\multicolumn{5}{	c	}{General Journal}
\multicolumn{2}{|c|}{Date}	Description	Debit	Credit

May	2	Cash
		    Common Stock
		        To record the stockholders' original investment
			28,000	28,000

	3	Prepaid Rent
		    Cash
		        Paid 3 months' rent in advance
			900	900

	5	Printing Press
		Photographic Equipment
		    Cash
		    Accounts Payable
		        Purchased a press and equipment from Irvin Press, Inc.
			10,000
			3,000
				2,000
				11,000

	8	No entry		

	9	Cash
		    Unearned Revenue
		        Received payment in advance from Doherty's Department Store for brochures to be printed
			1,200	1,200

	11	Office Supplies
		    Notes Payable
		        Purchased paper from Pulp Supply Co.
			800	800

	14	Cash
		Accounts Receivable
		    Revenue from Services
		        Completed job for Sullivan Shoes
			250
			250
				500

	14	Salaries Expense
		    Cash
		        Paid the pressman his weekly salary
			200	200

	15	Accounts Payable
		    Cash
		        Payment on account owed to Irvin Press, Inc.
			1,000	1,000

	18	Cash
		    Accounts Receivable
		        Sullivan Shoes paid its debt in full
			250	250

	20	Dividends
		    Cash
		        The board of directors declared and paid a $700 cash dividend
			700	700

	24	Utilities Expense
		    Accounts Payable
		        To record electric bill
			45	45

	30	Accounts Payable
		    Cash
		        To record payment of electric bill
			45	45

2. (L.O. 3)
  a. $1,750 debit balance
  b. $1,000 credit balance
  c. $14,600 debit balance

3. (L.O. 6)

General Journal					Page 7
Date		Description	Post. Ref.	Debit	Credit
Apr.	3	Cash	11	1,000	
		Revenue from Services	41		1,000
		Received payment from Malden Company for services			
	5	Accounts Payable	21	300	
		Cash	11		300
		Paid Douglas Supply Company for supplies purchased on March 31 on credit			

Cash — Account No. 11

Date		Item	Post. Ref.	Debit	Credit	Balance Debit	Balance Credit
Apr.	3		7	1,000		1,000	
	5		7		300	700	

Accounts Payable — Account No. 21

Date		Item	Post. Ref.	Debit	Credit	Balance* Debit	Balance* Credit
Apr.	5		7	300		300	

Revenue from Services — Account No. 41

Date		Item	Post. Ref.	Debit	Credit	Balance Debit	Balance Credit
Apr.	3		7		1,000		1,000

*Previous postings have been omitted, resulting in an improbable debit balance in Accounts Payable.

Chapter 3

Matching

1. i	6. q	11. a	16. j
2. d	7. f	12. h	17. b
3. n	8. k	13. m	18. g
4. r	9. e	14. p	19. t
5. c	10. o	15. l	20. s

Short Answer

1. (L.O. 4) Dividing recorded expenses between two or more accounting periods; dividing recorded revenues between two or more accounting periods; recording unrecorded expenses; and recording unrecorded revenues
2. (L.O. 2) The matching rule means that revenues should be recorded in the period in which they are earned, and that all expenses related to those revenues also should be recorded in that period.
3. (L.O. 5) Depreciation is the allocation of the cost of a long-lived asset to the periods benefiting from the asset.
4. (L.O. 5) Prepaid expenses are expenses paid for in advance; they initially are recorded as assets. Unearned revenues represent payment received in advance of providing goods or services; they initially are recorded as liabilities.

True-False

1. T (L.O. 1)
2. T (L.O. 1)
3. F (L.O. 2) The calendar year lasts specifically from January 1 to December 31.
4. T (L.O. 2)
5. F (L.O. 3) Under accrual accounting, the timing of cash exchanges is irrelevant in recording revenues and expenses.
6. F (L.O. 6) Adjusting entries are made before the financial statements are prepared.
7. T (L.O. 5)
8. F (L.O. 5) It is debited for the amount consumed during the period (the amount available during the period less ending inventory).
9. F (L.O. 5) Accumulated Depreciation (a contra account) has a credit balance, even though it appears on the left side of the balance sheet.
10. T (L.O. 5)
11. F (L.O. 5) Unearned Revenues is a liability account.
12. F (L.O. 4) The credit is to a liability account.
13. T (L.O. 6)
14. F (L.O. 5) If payment has not yet been received, the debit is to Accounts Receivable.
15. T (L.O. 5)
16. T (L.O. 3, 4)

Multiple Choice

1. c (L.O. 1) Temporary accounts are those that appear on the income statement. They also are referred to as *nominal accounts*.
2. b (L.O. 5) The use of office supplies is recorded as an expense. Adjustments to Office Supplies are the result of reconciling the ending inventory of office supplies to a cumulative total in the Office Supplies account. This cumulative total is a result of the addition of office supplies to the beginning office supplies inventory balance throughout the accounting period.
3. b (L.O. 5) Unearned Fees is used to record the firm's liability for amounts received but not yet earned. The use of this system of recognition is required so that revenue amounts can be represented properly and allocated in the appropriate accounting period. As the revenues are earned, the proper amounts are transferred from lia-

bilities to revenues. Between the time those future revenues are received and the time they actually are earned, one accounting period may have ended and another accounting period begun.
4. a (L.O. 5) Depreciation is the allocation of the cost of an asset over the expected useful life of that asset. The matching rule requires the gradual allocation of the cost while the asset is in use in the revenue-generating activities of a firm.
5. c (L.O. 6) Net income is the result of the calculation that nets revenues and expenses. The adjusted trial balance contains summary balances of each general ledger account after adjusting entries have been made.
6. d (L.O. 5) The adjustment debiting Interest Receivable and crediting Interest Income is required so that interest income for the period is allocated, even though the interest has not been received as yet. This income recognition is necessary for compliance with the matching rule.
7. a (L.O. 2) Estimates are involved in the preparation of account balances used to report net income. An example of this kind of estimate is the recording of depreciation expense. Although not exact, the reported net income of one accounting period can be compared with the net income of other accounting periods, providing a basis for conclusions about the firm.
8. d (L.O. 5) Until such time as Prepaid Rent is expired, and through adjustments is recorded as an expense, it remains an asset on the books of a firm.
9. b (L.O. 4) The Cash account balance represents a dollar amount at the time the balance sheet is prepared. Cash is *never* involved in the end-of-period adjustments.

Exercises

1. (L.O. 6)

Mass Transit Company
Partial Balance Sheet
December 31, 19x3

Assets

Cash		$ 5,000
Accounts Receivable		3,000
Company Vehicles	$24,000	
Less Accumulated Depreciation	9,000	15,000
Total Assets		$23,000

2. (L.O. 5)
  a. $970
  b. $1,750
  c. $450

3. (L.O. 5)

Date*	Description	Debit	Credit

a.	Supplies Expense
	    Supplies
	        To record supplies consumed during the period
		125	125

b.	Wages Expense
	    Wages Payable
	        To record accrued wages
		2,000	2,000

c.	Unearned Revenues
	    Revenues from Services
	        To record earned revenues
		600	600

d.	Depreciation Expense, Buildings
	    Accumulated Depreciation, Buildings
	        To record depreciation on buildings
		4,500	4,500

e.	Advertising Expense
	    Prepaid Advertising
	        To record advertising used up during the year
		2,000	2,000

f.	Insurance Expense
	    Prepaid Insurance
	        To record insurance expired during the year
		250	250

g.	Accounts Receivable
	    Revenues from Services
	        To record revenues earned for which payment has not been received
		2,200	2,200

h.	Interest Expense
	    Interest Payable
	        To record accrued interest on a note payable
		52	52

i.	Income Taxes Expense
	    Income Taxes Payable
	        To record accrued income tax expense
		21,700	21,700

*In reality, all of the adjusting entries would be dated December 31.

4. (S.O. 7)
   a. $6,200 ($1,200 + $8,700 − $3,700)
   b. $35,400 ($900 + $35,000 − $500)
   c. $3,000 ($1,800 + $3,600 − $2,400)

Solution to Crossword Puzzle

(Chapters 2 and 3)

	1				2				3					4
	C	O	N	T	R	A			I	N	C	O	M	E
	O				E			5W						X
	S		6D	E	F	E	R	R	A	L		7L		P
	T							G		8R				I
				9L	E	D	G	10E	R	E				R
11J	12M							13S	E	R	V	I	14C	E
O	A		15V						■	E	■	R		
U	16T	R	I	A	L	B	17A	L	A	N	C	E		
R	C		L				C			U	■	D		
N	H		U			18D	E	B	I	T				
A	I		19S	A	L	A	R	Y		■	S	■	T	
20L	A	N	D		T		U			21N				
I		G			I		A		22N	O				
Z			23D	O	U	B	L	E	E	N	T	R	Y	
24E	A	R	N		N				T		E			

256   Answers: Chapter 3

Chapter 4

Matching

1. e   4. b   7. c
2. g   5. h   8. a
3. d   6. f

Short Answer

1. (L.O. 3) Revenue accounts, expense accounts, Income Summary, Dividends
2. (S.O. 6) Trial Balance, Adjustments, Adjusted Trial Balance, Income Statement, Balance Sheet
3. (L.O. 4) Assets, liabilities, and owners' equity accounts will appear. Revenue and expense accounts, Income Summary, and the Dividends account will not appear.
4. (S.O. 5) Reversing entries enable the bookkeeper to continue making simple, routine journal entries rather than more complicated ones.
5. (L.O. 1) The steps should be numbered as follows: 3, 5, 1, 4, 2, 6.

True-False

1. T (S.O. 6)
2. T (S.O. 6)
3. T (S.O. 6)
4. T (S.O. 7)
5. F (L.O. 2) Income Summary does not appear in any statement.
6. F (L.O. 2) Only nominal accounts are closed.
7. T (L.O. 3)
8. F (L.O. 3) The Dividends account is closed to Retained Earnings.
9. F (L.O. 3) When there is a net loss, Income Summary will be credited.
10. T (S.O. 5)
11. F (S.O. 6) The work sheet is never published.
12. F (S.O. 6) The key letter is in the *Adjustments* columns to relate debits and credits of the same entry.
13. T (S.O. 6)
14. F (L.O. 4) It will not include the Dividends account, because that account will have a zero balance.
15. F (S.O. 5) Reversing entries, dated the first day of the new accounting period, serve to simplify the bookkeeping process.

Multiple Choice

1. c (L.O. 4) Of the accounts listed, Retained Earnings is the only account that remains open after the closing procedures are complete at the end of the accounting cycle. The post-closing trial balance is a listing of such accounts, along with their account balances.
2. d (S.O. 7) Of the choices given, this is the only sequence that it is possible to complete in order. In the proper sequence of steps in the accounting cycle, during the end-of-period process, the financial statements are prepared prior to entering the closing entries in the general journal.
3. b (S.O. 5) Reversing entries "undo" some of the effects of certain adjusting entries. Therefore, they could be referred to as "opposite to" adjusting entries.
4. a (S.O. 6) The amount used to balance the Income Statement columns of the work sheet and the Balance Sheet columns of the work sheet is the net income or loss. When the entry that is required to bring the Balance Sheet columns into balance on the work sheet is an entry to the credit column, there must have been a net income. The corresponding entry to bring the Income Statement columns into balance will be to the debit column.
5. a (L.O. 3) Of the accounts listed, Unearned Commissions is the only choice that is not involved in the closing process. Unearned Com-

Answers: Chapter 4

missions is a permanent balance sheet account and will remain open from one period to the next if it contains a balance.

6. b (L.O. 3) When, in the closing process (after revenues and expenses have been closed), Income Summary has a debit balance (expenses have exceeded revenues), the account will be closed by a credit entry equal to the debit balance. The corresponding debit will be an entry to Retained Earnings, reducing the balance of that account by an amount equal to the net loss for the period.

7. c (L.O. 2) The closing entries occur after the adjusting entries, during the end-of-period steps in the accounting cycle. The purpose of the adjusting entries is to update the revenue and expense accounts.

8. a (S.O. 7) All the components of a statement of retained earnings have been provided, except for net income or loss. A net income figure of $55,000 will correctly complete the statement.

Exercises

1. (L.O. 3)

General Journal

Date		Description	Debit	Credit

July	31	Revenue from Services
		    Income Summary
		        To close the revenue account
			4,700	4,700

	31	Income Summary
		    Rent Expense
		    Telephone Expense
		    Utility Expense
		        To close the expense accounts
			700	500
				50
				150

	31	Income Summary
		    Retained Earnings
		        To close the Income Summary account
			4,000	4,000

	31	Retained Earnings
		    Dividends
		        To close the dividends account
			2,500	2,500

2. (S.O. 7)

Barrett's Fix-It Services, Inc.
Statement of Retained Earnings
For the Month Ended July 31, 19xx

Retained Earnings, July 1, 19xx	$3,000
Add Net Income for July	4,000
Subtotal	$7,000
Less Dividends declared in July	2,500
Retained Earnings, July 31, 19xx	$4,500

3. (L.O. 1)

Steve's Maintenance, Inc.
Work Sheet
For the Year Ended December 31, 19xx

Account Name	Trial Balance Debit	Trial Balance Credit	Adjustments Debit	Adjustments Credit	Adjusted Trial Balance Debit	Adjusted Trial Balance Credit	Income Statement Debit	Income Statement Credit	Balance Sheet Debit	Balance Sheet Credit
Cash	2,560				2,560				2,560	
Accounts Receivable	880			(a) 550	930				930	
Prepaid Rent	750				200				200	
Lawn Supplies	250			(c) 150	100				100	
Lawn Equipment	10,000				10,000				10,000	
Accum. Deprec., Lawn Equip.		2,000		(b) 1,500		3,500				3,500
Accounts Payable		630				630				630
Unearned Landscaping Fees		300				180				180
Common Stock		5,000				5,000				5,000
Retained Earnings		1,000				1,000				1,000
Dividends	6,050				6,050				6,050	
Grass-Cutting Fees		15,000		(e) 50		15,050		15,050		
Wages Expense	3,300		(d) 280		3,580		3,580			
Gasoline Expense	140				140		140			
	23,930	23,930								
Rent Expense			(a) 550		550		550			
Depreciation Expense			(b) 1,500		1,500		1,500			
Lawn Supplies Expense			(c) 150		150		150			
Landscaping Fees Earned				(f) 120		120		120		
Wages Payable				(d) 280		280				280
Income Taxes Expense			(g) 1,570		1,570		1,570			
Income Taxes Payable				(g) 1,570		1,570				1,570
			4,220	4,220	27,330	27,330	7,490	15,170	19,840	12,160
Net Income							7,680			7,680
							15,170	15,170	19,840	19,840

Answers: Chapter 4 259

4. (S.O. 5)

\multicolumn{4}{c	}{General Journal}
Date	Description	Debit	Credit

Dec. 1	Cash
	    Notes Payable
	        To record 90-day bank note
		20,000	20,000

31	Interest Expense
	    Interest Payable
	        To record accrued interest on note
		200	200

31	Income Summary
	    Interest Expense
	        To close interest on note
		200	200

Jan. 1	Interest Payable
	    Interest Expense
	        To reverse adjusting entry for interest
		200	200

Mar. 1	Notes Payable
	Interest Expense
	    Cash
	        To record payment of note plus interest
		20,000
		600
			20,600

Chapter 5

Matching

1. c	5. l	9. i	13. f	17. t
2. h	6. k	10. d	14. p	18. o
3. j	7. s	11. m	15. n	19. q
4. e	8. g	12. a	16. r	20. b

Short Answer

1. (L.O. 2) Net sales
   − Cost of goods sold
   = Gross margin
   − Operating expenses
   = Income before income taxes
   − Income taxes
   = Net income
2. (L.O. 2) Beginning inventory
   + Net cost of purchases
   = Goods available for sale
   − Ending inventory
   = Cost of goods sold
3. (L.O. 2) (Gross) purchases
   − Purchases returns and allowances
   − Purchases discounts
   = Net purchases
   + Freight in
   = Net cost of purchases
4. (L.O. 2) Gross sales
   − Sales returns and allowances
   − Sales discounts
   = Net sales
5. (L.O. 5)
   a. *Control environment*—The overall attitude, awareness, and actions of the owners and management of a business
   b. *Accounting system*—The methods and records established to accomplish the objectives of internal control
   c. *Control procedures*—Actual steps taken to safeguard the business's assets and ensure the reliability of its records
6. (L.O. 5) Required authorization for certain transactions
   Recording of all transactions
   Design and use of adequate documents
   Limited access to assets
   Periodic, independent verification of records
   Separation of duties
   Sound personnel procedures
7. (L.O. 7) (Any six of the following would answer the question)
   Separate the authorization, recordkeeping, and custodianship of cash
   Limit access to cash
   Designate a person to handle cash
   Use banking facilities and minimize cash on hand
   Bond employees with access to cash
   Protect cash on hand with safes, cash registers, etc.
   Conduct surprise audits of cash on hand
   Record all cash receipts promptly
   Deposit all cash receipts promptly
   Make all payments by check
   Have a person who does not authorize, handle, or record cash transactions reconcile the Cash account.

True-False

1. F (L.O. 3) It will result in an understated net income.
2. F (L.O. 4) It means that payment is due 10 days after the end of the month.
3. T (L.O. 3)
4. F (L.O. 3) The dealer is more likely to use the perpetual inventory system.
5. T (L.O. 4)
6. F (S.O. 8) It is a contra account to *gross sales*.
7. T (L.O. 2)
8. T (L.O. 2)
9. T (L.O. 3)
10. T (L.O. 2)
11. F (L.O. 2) It normally has a debit balance.
12. F (L.O. 4) It requires a debit to Office Supplies, because it is not merchandise.
13. T (L.O. 2)
14. T (L.O. 2)
15. F (L.O. 4) Both are done at the end of the period.

16. F (L.O. 4) 2/10, n/30 is a sales discount, offered for early payment. A trade discount is a percentage off the list or catalog price.
17. F (L.O. 4) Title passes at the shipping point.
18. F (L.O. 5) It increases the probability of accuracy but will not guarantee it.
19. T (L.O. 6)
20. F (L.O. 7) This procedure could easily lead to theft.
21. F (L.O. 7) The supplier is sent a purchase *order*.
22. F (L.O. 5) Rotating employees is good internal control because it might uncover theft.

Multiple Choice

1. d (L.O. 4) According to the terms, Burns would be entitled to a 2 percent purchases discount of $10. In this example (after allowing for the purchase returns), the discount would be entered as a credit to balance the journal entry, which would also include a debit to Accounts Payable for the balance due ($500) and a credit to Cash for the balance due less the discount ($490).
2. c (L.O. 4) Purchase Returns and Allowances is a contra account to the Purchases account. Purchases has a normal debit balance. Its corresponding contra accounts have a normal credit balance.
3. d (L.O. 3) Counting ending inventory at a larger amount than actually exists would result in a larger deduction from goods available for sale. This would result in an understatement of cost of goods sold.
4. b (L.O. 2) Freight out is a selling expense. It is not considered to be an element of the cost of goods sold.
5. d (L.O. 7) The purchase requisition is the initial demand for goods. The purchase requisition is prepared by the individual who ultimately needs the inventory for sale or production. The requisition is then authorized by the appropriate person before the process of purchasing begins.
6. a (L.O. 7) Proper internal control procedures separate the functions of handling of assets and recordkeeping in hopes of preventing employee theft.
7. a (L.O. 2) Advertising Expense is considered a selling expense within the operating expenses section of the income statement. Sales Discounts appears as a contra account to Gross Sales, whereas Freight In and Purchases appear within the cost of goods sold section.
8. c (L.O. 4) Under the perpetual inventory system, purchases of merchandise are recorded in the Merchandise Inventory, not the Purchases, account.
9. b (L.O. 1) When inventory is paid for has no bearing on the length of the operating cycle.

Exercises

1. (L.O. 4; S.O. 8)

\multicolumn{3}{c	}{General Journal}		
\multicolumn{2}{c	}{Date}	Description	Debit	Credit

May	1	Purchases
		    Accounts Payable
		        Purchased merchandise on credit, terms 2/10, n/60
			500	500

	3	Accounts Receivable
		    Sales
		        Sold merchandise on credit, terms 2/10, 1/20, n/30
			500	500

	4	Freight In
		    Cash
		        Paid for freight charges
			42	42

	5	Office Supplies
		    Accounts Payable
		        Purchased office supplies on credit
			100	100

	6	Accounts Payable
		    Office Supplies
		        Returned office supplies from May 5 purchase
			20	20

	7	Accounts Payable
		    Purchases Returns and Allowances
		        Returned merchandise from May 1 purchase
			50	50

	9	Accounts Receivable
		    Sales
		        Sold merchandise on credit, terms 2/10, 1/15, n/30
			225	225

	10	Accounts Payable
		    Purchases Discounts
		    Cash
		        Paid for purchase of May 1
			450	9
				441

	14	Sales Returns and Allowances
		    Accounts Receivable
		        The customer of May 9 returned merchandise
			25	25

	22	Cash
		Sales Discounts
		    Accounts Receivable
		        The customer of May 9 paid
			198
			2
				200

	26	Cash
		    Accounts Receivable
		        The customer of May 3 paid for merchandise
			500	500

Answers: Chapter 5

2. (L.O. 2)

<table>
<tr><td colspan="4" align="center">Jefferson Merchandising Company
Partial Income Statement
For the Year 19xx</td></tr>
<tr><td>Gross Sales</td><td></td><td></td><td>$100,000</td></tr>
<tr><td>Less: Sales Discounts</td><td></td><td>$ 300</td><td></td></tr>
<tr><td>   Sales Returns and Allowances</td><td></td><td>200</td><td>500</td></tr>
<tr><td>Net Sales</td><td></td><td></td><td>$ 99,500</td></tr>
<tr><td>Less Cost of Goods Sold</td><td></td><td></td><td></td></tr>
<tr><td> Merchandise Inventory, Jan. 1</td><td></td><td>$10,000</td><td></td></tr>
<tr><td> Purchases</td><td>$50,000</td><td></td><td></td></tr>
<tr><td> Less: Purchases Discounts</td><td>500</td><td></td><td></td></tr>
<tr><td>   Purchases Returns and Allowances</td><td>500</td><td></td><td></td></tr>
<tr><td> Net Purchases</td><td>$49,000</td><td></td><td></td></tr>
<tr><td> Freight In</td><td>2,000</td><td></td><td></td></tr>
<tr><td> Net Cost of Purchases</td><td></td><td>51,000</td><td></td></tr>
<tr><td> Goods Available for Sale</td><td></td><td>$61,000</td><td></td></tr>
<tr><td> Less Merchandise Inventory, Dec. 31</td><td></td><td>8,000</td><td></td></tr>
<tr><td> Cost of Goods Sold</td><td></td><td></td><td>53,000</td></tr>
<tr><td>Gross Margin</td><td></td><td></td><td>$ 46,500</td></tr>
</table>

Note: See Chapter 6 for placement of interest income in this type of income statement.

Solution to Crossword Puzzle
(Chapters 4 and 5)

Across:
5. REVERSING
6. COST OF GOODS SOLD
8. PERPETUAL
9. PURCHASES
10. CROSSFOOT
12. DESTINATION

Down:
1. GROSS
2. DISCOUNT
3. WORKSHEET
4. INCOME SUMMARY
5. RETURN
7. CLOSING
8. PERIODIC
11. NDC

Chapter 6

Matching

1. g	6. s	11. q	16. b
2. n	7. m	12. l	17. k
3. r	8. d	13. j	18. f
4. e	9. o	14. a	19. p
5. i	10. h	15. c	

Short Answer

1. (L.O. 5)

Business Organization	Name for Stockholders' Equity Section
Sole Proprietorship	Owner's Equity
Partnership	Partners' Equity
Corporation	Stockholders' Equity

2. (L.O. 7) *Profit margin*—Shows net income in relation to net sales.
Asset turnover—Shows how efficiently assets are used to produce sales.
Return on assets—Shows net income in relation to average total assets.
Return on equity—Shows net income in relation to owner's investment.
Debt to equity ratio—Shows the proportion of a business financed by creditors and that financed by owners.

3. (L.O. 7) *Working capital*—Current assets minus current liabilities.
Current ratio—Current assets divided by current liabilities.

4. (L.O. 3) *Consistency and comparability*—Applying the same accounting procedures from one period to the next.
Materiality—The relative importance of an item or event.
Cost-benefit—The cost of providing additional accounting information should not exceed the benefits gained from it.
Conservatism—Choosing the accounting procedure that will be least likely to overstate assets and income.
Full disclosure—Showing all relevant information in the financial statements or in the footnotes.

True-False

1. F (L.O. 5) They are considered current assets if collection is expected within the normal operating cycle, even if that cycle is more than one year.
2. T (S.O. 8)
3. T (L.O. 6)
4. F (L.O. 6) Operating expenses are made up of selling expenses and general and administrative expenses only.
5. T (L.O. 2)
6. T (L.O. 7)
7. F (L.O. 5) Short-term investments in stock should be included in the current assets section of the balance sheet.
8. F (L.O. 7) *Liquidity* is what is being defined.
9. F (L.O. 5) The operating cycle can be less than one year.
10. F (L.O. 5) Net worth is merely another term for owner's equity, and does not necessarily equal net asset worth.
11. T (L.O. 6)
12. F (L.O. 6) The net income figures will be the same, although they are arrived at differently.
13. F (S.O. 8) It is the accountants' report that is divided into scope and opinion sections.
14. F (L.O. 7) Working capital equals current assets *minus* current liabilities.
15. T (L.O. 7)
16. F (L.O. 2) *Reliability* is what is being described.
17. T (S.O. 8)
18. F (L.O. 6; S.O. 8) Financial statements are condensed when they contain little detail; they are consolidated when they combine parent and subsidiary information.

Answers: Chapter 6

Multiple Choice

1. c (L.O. 5) The conversion of inventories to cash is the basis for a firm's operations. This conversion cycle (called the normal operating cycle) is frequently less than 12 months. However, if it is *greater* than 12 months, the inventory by definition is still classified as a current asset.

2. c (L.O. 6) The single-step income statement does not isolate gross margin from sales. Instead, cost of goods sold is combined with other operating expenses and then subtracted from total revenues to calculate income from operations.

3. b (L.O. 7) The current ratio gives management information about a firm's liquidity. Liquidity is important for anticipation of a company's capability to cover operations and current liabilities.

4. d (L.O. 5) The owner's capital account would appear on the balance sheet of a sole proprietorship or partnership only.

5. a (S.O. 8) An auditor's job is to examine the financial statements of a client firm to determine the fairness of the presentation of the accounting data. That determination is set forth as an ''opinion'' within the independent auditors' report.

6. a (L.O. 7) The ratio described is the profit margin, which describes the relationship between net income and net sales.

7. c (L.O. 6) ''Operating expenses'' is a broad term referring to expenses of running a company *other than the cost of goods sold.*

8. c (L.O. 3) Conservatism requires that losses experienced by a firm should be recognized in the period of the decline. Since inventories and short-term investments are subject to fluctuations in value, losses are recorded to reflect a negative economic impact on a firm from market conditions.

9. d (L.O. 1) Each choice except *d* describes an objective of FASB *Statement of Financial Accounting Concepts No. 1*. The FASB statement described is not a source of information to be used as an addendum to an independent auditors' report.

Exercises

1. (L.O. 5)

1. d	5. a	9. f	13. X
2. e	6. c	10. e	14. a
3. c	7. a	11. d	15. e
4. g	8. b	12. a	

2. (L.O. 7)

a. $40,000		d.	12.5%
b. 3:1		e.	16⅔%
c. 10%		f.	1.25 times

3. (L.O. 6)

a.

Confrey Corporation
Income Statement (Multistep)
For the Year Ended December 31, 19xx

Net Sales	$200,000
Less Cost of Goods Sold	150,000
Gross Margin	$ 50,000
Less Operating Expenses	30,000
Income from Operations	$ 20,000
Add Interest Revenues	2,000
Income Before Income Taxes	$ 22,000
Less Income Tax Expense	5,000
Net Income	$ 17,000
Earnings per share	$4.86/share

b.

Confrey Corporation
Income Statement (Single-Step)
For the Year Ended December 31, 19xx

Revenues		
Net Sales	$200,000	
Interest Revenues	2,000	$202,000
Expenses		
Cost of Goods Sold	$150,000	
Operating Expenses	30,000	180,000
Income Before Income Taxes		$ 22,000
Income Tax Expense	$ 5,000	
Net Income		$ 17,000
Earnings per share		$4.86/share

Chapter 7

Matching

1. j	6. e	11. c	16. n
2. g	7. r	12. o	17. q
3. f	8. l	13. t	18. a
4. m	9. i	14. h	19. b
5. p	10. k	15. d	20. s

Short Answer

1. (L.O. 4) Percentage of net sales method, accounts receivable aging method, and direct charge-off method
2. (L.O. 1) It means that the original payee, who discounts the note receivable, must make good on the note if the maker does not pay at maturity.
3. (L.O. 4) There would be a debit balance when more accounts are written off (in dollar amounts) than have been provided for in the adjusting entries for estimated uncollectible accounts.
4. (L.O. 3) Held-to-maturity securities, trading securities, and available-for-sale securities
5. (L.O. 2) Bank service charges; a customer's NSF check; bank charges for collecting and paying notes, stop payments, and printing checks; and an error in recording a check (only if underrecorded). (Any three would answer the question.)
6. (L.O. 1) Cash and cash equivalents, short-term investments, accounts receivable, and notes receivable

True-False

1. T (L.O. 4)
2. F (L.O. 4) It follows the matching rule.
3. F (L.O. 4) The balance must be taken into account.
4. T (L.O. 4)
5. T (L.O. 4)
6. T (L.O. 4)
7. F (L.O. 5) The computation is 700 × 5/100 × 90/360.
8. T (L.O. 4)
9. F (L.O. 1) The payee must make good if the maker defaults.
10. F (L.O. 5) It has a duration of 62 days.
11. T (L.O. 1)
12. F (L.O. 4) Total assets remain the same.
13. T (L.O. 5)
14. F (L.O. 4) The debit is to Allowance for Uncollectible Accounts.
15. T (L.O. 5)
16. T (L.O. 4)
17. F (L.O. 2) Accounts receivable are a short-term liquid asset but not a cash equivalent.
18. F (L.O. 1) Major credit cards involve factoring without recourse.
19. F (L.O. 1) It equals quick assets divided by current liabilities.
20. T (L.O. 2)
21. T (L.O. 2)
22. F (L.O. 2) No entries are made for outstanding checks.
23. F (L.O. 2) It begins with the September 30 balances.
24. T (L.O. 2)
25. T (L.O. 3)
26. F (L.O. 3) They appear at market value.
27. F (L.O. 4) They appear in the subsidiary ledger.

Multiple Choice

1. d (S.O. 6) The credit card company would deduct the 5% charge before remitting cash to the company.
2. b (L.O. 5) Principal × rate × time for *b* equals $12. Each of the other choices results in $6.
3. c (L.O. 4) Using the net sales method of calculating adjustments for Allowance for Uncollectible Accounts, the amount of the Uncollectible Accounts Expense is based on the sales during the period. Therefore, it is not

netted with an existing balance in the allowance account.

4. a (L.O. 1) Because the discounting bank has the right to extract funds from a firm's account if a note is dishonored, the firm carries that liability until such time as the note is paid to the bank. Once the note is paid, the contingent liability is eliminated.

5. b (L.O. 4) Under this method, Uncollectible Accounts Expense equals the amount deemed uncollectible ($850) minus the credit balance in Allowance for Uncollectible Accounts ($300), or $550.

6. c (L.O. 4) When an allowance account is established to record anticipated uncollectible accounts, the expense is recorded at the time the allowance is made. As a result, when the actual uncollectible account is known and written off, the allowance account is reduced, and Accounts Receivable is reduced by the same amount.

7. a (L.O. 5) The discount rate is used as an adjustment to the maturity value of a note to calculate the proceeds on discounting that note to the bank. The details of a note would not include the discount rate because it is not known at the time the note is originated. Additionally, whether a note is going to be discounted or not is irrelevant in determining the note arrangements.

8. b (L.O. 4) The direct charge-off method of handling uncollectible accounts often postpones the uncollectible accounts expense of a given accounting period to subsequent accounting periods. Usually, a significant period of time elapses between a credit sale and the determination that the corresponding receivable is uncollectible.

9. c (L.O. 1) Inventory is not considered a short-term liquid asset. The ability of a firm to convert its inventory to cash is the basis of the firm's operations. Short-term liquid assets, by definition, are assets that can be converted quickly to cash (or are cash or near cash) to cover operating expenses and immediate cash requirements.

10. d (L.O. 3) It appears as a contra account to Short-Term Investments in the balance sheet.

11. b (L.O. 2) The company presumably already has recorded the deposit in transit. However, it just learned of the bank service charge, the note collected by the bank, and the bank error when it received its bank statement, and, therefore, must adjust for those items.

12. c (L.O. 2) Interest earned would be a component of the balance per bank, but it would not yet have been placed on the books. Because it is interest earned, it should be added.

13. a (L.O. 2) The error would cause the balance per bank to be understated. Therefore, the $900 should be added.

Exercises

1. (L.O. 5)
   a. $16.00
   b. $910.00
   c. $43.17
   d. $4.00

2. (L.O. 2)
   | 1. d | 3. b | 5. a |
   | 2. c | 4. d | 6. d |

3. (L.O. 3)

\multicolumn{5}{c}{General Journal}
Date		Description	Debit	Credit

Nov.	17	Short-Term Investments
		    Cash
		        Purchased Simpson stock for trading
			60,000	60,000

Dec.	31	Unrealized Loss on Investments
		    Allowance to Adjust Short-Term Investments to Market
		        Year-end adjustment for market decline
			4,000	4,000

Jan.	12	Cash
		    Short-Term Investments
		    Realized Gain on Investments
		        To record sale of Simpson stock
			66,000	60,000
				6,000

4. (L.O. 4, 5; S.O. 6)

\multicolumn{5}{	c	}{General Journal}
\multicolumn{2}{|c|}{Date}	Description	Debit	Credit

Dec.	31	Interest Receivable
		    Interest Income
		        To record accrued interest on Notes Receivable
			75	75

	31	Uncollectible Accounts Expense
		    Allowance for Uncollectible Accounts
		        To record estimated bad debts
			24,000	24,000

Jan.	3	Notes Receivable
		    Accounts Receivable, Kohn
		        Kohn substituted a 30-day, 6% note for her debt
			10,000	10,000

	8	Allowance for Uncollectible Accounts
		    Accounts Receivable, O'Brien
		        To write off O'Brien's account
			1,000	1,000

	14	Accounts Receivable, MasterCard
		Credit Card Discount Expense
		    Sales
		        To record MasterCard sales for the first two weeks in January;
		        discount fee is 5 percent
			3,800
			200
				4,000

	24	Cash
		    Accounts Receivable, MasterCard
		        Received payment from MasterCard for invoices at 95 percent of face
		        value
			3,800	3,800

	25	Accounts Receivable, O'Brien
		    Allowance for Uncollectible Accounts
		        To reinstate O'Brien's account
			600	600

	28	Cash
		    Accounts Receivable, O'Brien
		        Received $200 from O'Brien
			200	200

Solution to Crossword Puzzle

(Chapters 6 and 7)

Across:
4. DISCOUNT
6. SCOPE
8. RETURNONASSETS
9. NOTE
10. PROPERTY
13. BAD
15. DURATION
17. LAND
18. SINGLESTEP
19. CASH

Down:
1. ACCRUAL
2. CYCLE
3. CURRENTRATIO
4. DEBENTURES
5. SHARE
7. CONSULR (CONSULTERS)
10. PLEDGE
11. EARNING
12. INTEREST
14. AGING
16. PREPAID

Answers: Chapter 7

Chapter 8

Matching

1.	m	5.	j	9.	c	13.	k
2.	h	6.	a	10.	l		
3.	d	7.	f	11.	e		
4.	g	8.	i	12.	b		

Short Answer

1. (L.O. 3) Specific identification; average-cost; first-in, first-out; and last-in, first out
2. (L.O. 6) Item-by-item, major category, and total inventory
3. (S.O. 7) Retail method and gross profit method
4. (L.O. 4) The periodic system does not keep detailed records of inventory; the perpetual system does. Under the periodic system, physical inventory is taken at the end of each period to determine the cost of goods sold.

True-False

1. T (L.O. 1)
2. T (L.O. 1)
3. T (L.O. 5)
4. T (L.O. 5)
5. F (L.O. 2) They belong in the buyer's ending inventory if the buyer has title to the goods.
6. T (L.O. 3)
7. F (L.O. 3) Not necessarily. The actual flow of goods is not known; the flow of costs is assumed.
8. F (L.O. 3) It results in the highest income.
9. F (S.O. 7) Items sold are recorded only at retail.
10. F (S.O. 7) The cost of goods sold is estimated by subtracting the gross margin percentage of sales from total sales.
11. T (L.O. 4)
12. F (L.O. 3) Average-cost results in a higher net income.
13. F (L.O. 5) The requirement is for LIFO, not FIFO.
14. F (L.O. 2) The consignee has possession but not title.

Multiple Choice

1. b (L.O. 2) The cost to store goods normally is considered too difficult to trace to specific inventory items, so it is expensed when incurred. The other costs listed are more closely related to the acquisition cost of inventory.
2. a (L.O. 5) Under rising prices, the FIFO inventory method matches current selling prices with the oldest, least expensive costs. Of the inventory methods listed, this method results in the highest net income.
3. c (L.O. 1) Forgetting to inventory a warehouse results in an understated ending inventory, which, in turn, produces an overstated cost of goods sold. An overstated cost of goods sold produces an understated net income and, therefore, an understated stockholders' equity.
4. c (L.O. 3) With low-volume, high-priced goods, it is especially necessary to match the selling price of a particular item with its cost in order to avoid distortion in the financial statements. Only specific identification directly matches cost and selling price.
5. b (S.O. 7) In performing the retail inventory calculation, freight in is incorporated at cost, not at retail. The other choices provided are included as stated.
6. a (L.O. 1) The matching rule states that a cost must be expensed in the period in which that cost helps to generate revenue. Therefore, the

cost of inventory is expensed in the period in which the inventory is sold.
7. d (L.O. 2) By definition, inventory should appear on the balance sheet of the company that has title to the goods (although not necessarily possession of them).
8. d (L.O. 6) *Market* means current replacement cost, or the amount a company would pay now for the same goods, purchased from the usual suppliers in the usual quantities.
9. d (S.O. 7) The gross profit method is a simple way to prove mathematically the approximate amount of inventory lost or destroyed by fire, theft, etc. It assumes a relatively consistent gross margin ratio over time.

Exercises

1. (L.O. 3)
   a. $6,600; $8,800
   b. $7,200; $8,200
   c. $6,820; $8,580

2. (S.O. 7)

	Cost	Retail
Beginning Inventory	$ 70,000	$125,000
Net Purchases	48,000	75,000
Freight In	2,000	—
Cost/Retail	$120,000 ÷ $200,000 = 60%	
Less Sales		156,000
Estimated Ending Inventory at Retail		$ 44,000
		× 60%
Estimated Cost of Ending Inventory		$ 26,400

3. (S.O. 7)

Beginning Inventory at Cost	$150,000
Purchases at Cost	120,000
Cost of Goods Available for Sale	$270,000
Less Estimated Cost of Goods Sold ($300,000 × 80%)	240,000
Estimated Cost of Ending Inventory	$ 30,000

4. (L.O. 4)

May					
1	Inventory	100 units @ $10		$1,000	
4	Purchase	60 units @ $12		720	
8	Sale	50 units @ $12		(600)	
8	Balance	100 units @ $10	$1,000		
		10 units @ $12	120	$1,120	
17	Purchase	70 units @ $11		770	
25	Sale	70 units @ $11	($770)		
		10 units @ $12	(120)		
		20 units @ $10	(200)	(1,090)	
25	Balance	80 units @ $10		$800	
	Cost of Goods Sold = $600 + $1,090			$1,690	

Chapter 9

Matching

1. e	5. l	9. v	13. u	17. g	21. p
2. f	6. t	10. j	14. c	18. a	22. q
3. n	7. r	11. b	15. k	19. i	
4. s	8. h	12. o	16. m	20. d	

Short Answer

1. (S.O. 9) Additions, like a new building wing, add to the physical layout. Betterments, like a new air-conditioning system, simply improve the existing layout.
2. (L.O. 5) When the cash received equals the carrying value of the asset sold
3. (L.O. 7) The cost of the well, the estimated residual value of the well, the estimated barrels to be extracted over the life of the well, and the actual barrels extracted and sold during the year.
4. (S.O. 9) Ordinary repairs (a paint job, a tune-up) merely maintain the asset in good operating condition. Extraordinary repairs—for example, a complete overhaul—increase the asset's estimated residual value or useful life.
5. (L.O. 1) Amortization, depreciation, and depletion
6. (L.O. 3) Physical deterioration and obsolescence

True-False

1. T (L.O. 1)
2. T (L.O. 5)
3. T (L.O. 1)
4. F (L.O. 3) Depreciation is a process of allocation, not valuation.
5. F (L.O. 3) The physical deterioration of a machine is irrelevant in computing depreciation.
6. T (L.O. 2)
7. T (S.O. 9)
8. T (L.O. 4)
9. F (L.O. 4) Depreciation expense will be $1,000 in the second year also.
10. T (S.O. 9)
11. T (L.O. 6)
12. F (L.O. 4) It results in more net income.
13. F (L.O. 3) Depreciable cost equals cost minus residual value.
14. F (L.O. 4) The carrying value theoretically never reaches zero under this method.
15. T (S.O. 9)
16. F (L.O. 8) A trademark is a name or symbol that can be used only by its owner.
17. T (L.O. 2)
18. F (S.O. 9) A betterment is a capital expenditure.
19. F (S.O. 9) The carrying value increases because the accumulated depreciation account is decreased (debited).
20. F (L.O. 5) The Accumulated Depreciation account always is debited when a depreciable asset is sold.
21. F (L.O. 2) *Capital expenditure* refers to the purchase of an asset; *expense* refers to the expiration of asset cost through the use or depreciation of an asset.
22. T (L.O. 6)
23. F (L.O. 5) Depreciation expense should be brought up to date before the sale.
24. T (L.O. 8)
25. T (L.O. 4)
26. T (L.O. 8)
27. F (L.O. 8) Research and development costs normally are charged as expenses in the year incurred.
28. T (L.O. 7)

Multiple Choice

1. c (L.O. 2) Because the relative values of the lump-sum purchase are known, a ratio can be determined and applied to the purchase price of both assets. The total value assigned to the land and building is $80,000. Of that $80,000, $20,000, or 25%, is apportioned to the land. So 25% of the purchase price for both assets, $16,500, would be allocated to land.

2. a (L.O. 3) The expired cost of an asset is its total accumulated depreciation to date. Depreciation is the allocation of the cost of an asset over its useful life.

3. d (L.O. 4) The declining-balance method would probably produce the greatest depreciation charge in the first year, although it is possible that the production method could instead. Therefore, more information is needed to answer the question.

4. c (S.O. 9) The change requires an adjustment to the depreciation schedule of the asset. The remaining depreciable cost would be spread over the remaining (new) estimated useful life of the machine.

5. c (L.O. 8) Although the life of an intangible asset can be difficult to estimate, GAAP set a "reasonable" limit on how long a firm can amortize the costs associated with intangible assets.

6. b (L.O. 2) Although land is not a depreciable asset, improvements to land (buildings, street lights, pavement, etc.) are. Each improvement has an estimated useful life over which the costs will be allocated.

7. d (L.O. 5) In order to eliminate the asset from the company's accounting records, existing accounts pertaining to the asset must be removed from the books as part of the transaction. Because the book value of the machine was $2,000 and the original cost was $9,000, accumulated depreciation must have been $7,000 (credit balance). To eliminate that account, a debit of $7,000 should be recorded to Accumulated Depreciation.

8. b (L.O. 2) A new roof has an economic life of more than a year. Therefore, the expenditure for a new roof is considered a capital expenditure.

9. d (L.O. 2) Understatement of net income results from expensing a capital expenditure. By definition, capital expenditures should be spread over the useful life of the acquisition (more than one period). If the entire cost is put into one period, expenses for that period will be overstated.

10. b (L.O. 7) Depletion costs assigned to a given period are the result of calculations based on expected total output over the life of an oil well. Total costs divided by total expected units of output equal the depletion cost per unit. If the expected units of output are overestimated, the unit cost will be underestimated.

11. a (L.O. 8) Up to a point at which the software is technologically feasible, its costs are treated as research and development and, therefore, must be expensed.

12. d (L.O. 8) Research and development costs are considered revenue expenditures and are recognized in the period incurred. It is a difficult problem to estimate the useful life of research and development.

Exercises

1. (L.O. 4)

	Depreciation Expense	*Accumulated Depreciation*	*Carrying Value*
a.	$4,800	$ 9,600	$16,400
b.	$6,240	$16,640	$ 9,360

2. (L.O. 4)

$2,250 $ $\left(\dfrac{\$35,000 - \$5,000}{100,000 \text{ toys}} \times 7,500 \text{ toys} \right)$

3. (L.O. 2)

a.	C	**d.**	C	**f.**	R	**h.**	C
b.	R	**e.**	C	**g.**	C	**i.**	R
c.	R						

4. (L.O. 6)

General Journal				
Date		Description	Debit	Credit

Jan	1	Merchandise (new)
		Accumulated Depreciation, Machinery
		Loss on Trade-in of Machinery
		    Cash
		    Machinery (old)
		        To record trade-in of machine, following GAAP
			23,000
			17,000
			500
				
				15,500
				25,000

	1	Machinery (new)
		Accumulated Depreciation, Machinery
		    Cash
		    Machinery (old)
		        To record trade-in of machine, following income tax rulings*
			23,500
			17,000
				
				15,500
				25,000

*For income tax purposes, neither gains nor losses are recognized on the exchange of similar assets.

5. (L.O. 7)

General Journal				
Date		Description	Debit	Credit

Dec.	31	Depletion Expense, Coal Deposits
		    Accumulated Depreciation, Coal Mine
		        To record depletion of coal mine for 19xx
			40,000	
				40,000

Solution to Crossword Puzzle

(Chapter 8 and 9)

```
                M
            S A L V A G E     D E P L E T E
            C     M       D   A       A
            R     O       E   T       N
            S     R       P   E       G
                B E T T E R M E N T    I
                      I   E       T    B
            C         Z   C            L
            O       D E C L I N I N G  E
            N       I     A       L    U
            S       S   C T     L A    S
            I       P   O     E X C H A N G E
            G R O S S       M     D    F
            N       S   T I M E        U
            E       A           R E T A I L
            D     L I F O
```

Across/Down answers shown: SALVAGE, DEPLETE, MACRS, AMOR, DEPREC, PATENTE, TANGIBLE, BETTERMENT, SIZE, CONSIGNED, DECLINING, DISPSA, COST, LAST, EXCHANGE, GROSS, TIME, RETAIL, LIFO

Chapter 10

Matching

1. n	**4.** d	**7.** o	**10.** j	**13.** e
2. k	**5.** l	**8.** g	**11.** h	**14.** i
3. f	**6.** m	**9.** c	**12.** a	**15.** b

Short Answer

1. (L.O. 2) Definitely determinable liabilities, estimated liabilities
2. (L.O. 3) Some examples of contingent liabilities are pending lawsuits, tax disputes, discounted notes receivable, the guarantee of another company's debt, and failure to follow government regulations.
3. (L.O. 2) Some examples of estimated liabilities are income taxes payable, property taxes payable, estimated warranty expense, and vacation pay.
4. (L.O. 2) Some examples of definitely determinable liabilities are trade accounts payable, short-term notes payable, dividends payable, sales tax payable, excise tax payable, current portion of long-term debt, accrued liabilities, payroll liabilities, and deferred revenues.
5. (L.O. 2) Social security taxes, Medicare taxes, federal income taxes, and state income taxes
6. (L.O. 2) Social security taxes, Medicare taxes, federal unemployment taxes, and state unemployment taxes

True-False

1. F (L.O. 2) Unearned revenue is a liability on the balance sheet representing an obligation to deliver goods or services.
2. T (L.O. 2)
3. T (L.O. 1)
4. T (L.O. 2)
5. F (L.O. 2) Sales Tax Payable is a definitely determinable liability.
6. F (L.O. 2) A warranty is an estimated liability.
7. T (L.O. 6)
8. F (L.O. 5) Payments associated with an ordinary annuity are made at the *end* of each period.
9. F (L.O. 6) The higher the interest rate, the *lower* the present value.
10. T (L.O. 3)
11. F (L.O. 2) The account is associated with notes whose interest is included in the face amount.
12. F (L.O. 2) An estimate should be recorded for Product Warranty Expense in year 1, the year of the sale.
13. F (L.O. 2) Wages Payable is credited for net (take-home) pay.
14. T (L.O. 2)
15. T (L.O. 2)

Multiple Choice

1. c (L.O. 2) Property tax bills are not available to a firm until months after the liability actually exists. Therefore, the accountant must estimate the property taxes due for the accounting period, and enter that estimate onto the books as a liability. Upon receipt of the actual tax bill, adjustments will be made. This method is required by the matching rule, which allows for estimates when perfect information is not available, to match expenses of a period to that accounting period.

2. d (L.O. 2) Pending lawsuits, and the settlement thereof, would be recorded as contingent liabilities, but only if the outcome against the company can be estimated and is probable.

3. c (L.O. 2) Under the matching rule, estimated liabilities for vacation pay as a result of current employee status must be recorded as an expense of the current period. Therefore, by the time the employee exercises the right to a paid vacation, the expense has been recorded by the use of a liability account, Estimated Liability for Vacation Pay. As the liability expires, it is reduced by a debit entry. This credit entry is to Cash for the disbursement of pay to the employee.

4. d (L.O. 2) The entry to record payment in advance of the property tax bill would be a debit to the Prepaid Property Taxes account and a credit to Cash. Then, as each monthly share of the prepaid amount expires, the entry would be a debit to Property Taxes Expense and a reduction (credit entry) to the corresponding prepaid (asset) account.

5. b (L.O. 5) When interest is calculated on a semiannual basis, the annual interest rate is cut in half, but the number of years must be doubled to arrive at the correct number of semiannual periods.

6. d (L.O. 6) To calculate the present value of a single sum due in the future, one must multiply the future amount by the present value of a single sum factor, using the assumed discount rate and number of periods.

7. c (L.O. 5, 6) One way to calculate the future value of a single sum invested now is to divide the single sum by the appropriate present value of a single sum factor.

8. a (L.O. 7) Even though the problem states that there is no interest borne by the note, a rate must be applied. The method for doing so would be to record the note, discounted at an appropriate rate. The principal of the note less the discount is the actual "cost" of the equipment to Marina Pools, Inc.

9. b (L.O. 2) With the passage of time, Discount on Notes Payable will be changed into Interest Expense, in accordance with the matching rule.

Exercises

1. (L.O. 2)

General Journal				
Date		Description	Debit	Credit

Dec.	31	Product Warranty Expense
		    Estimated Product Warranty Liability
		        To record estimated warranty expense for washing machines
			525	525

Apr.	9	Estimated Product Warranty Liability
		    Parts, Wages Expense, etc.
		        To record the repair of a washing machine
			48	48

2. (L.O. 5, 6)
    a. $747 ($1,000 × .747)
    b. $4,122 ($1,000 × 4.122)
    c. $1,126 ($1,000 × 1.126)
    d. $1,745.81 ($100,000/57.28)

3. (L.O. 7) Present value = $2,000 × 4.494 = $8,988
The purchase should not be made because the present value of future cash savings is less than the initial cost of the equipment.

4. (L.O. 7)

\multicolumn{4}{c	}{General Journal}
Date	Description	Debit	Credit
(a) Jan. 1	Equipment ($10,000 × .826) Discount on Notes Payable Notes Payable	8,260 1,740	 10,000
(b) 1	Interest Expense ($8,260 × .1) Discount on Notes Payable	826	 826

(c) 1	Interest Expense ($1,740 − $826)
	Notes Payable
	    Discount on Notes Payable
	    Cash
		914
		10,000
			
			914
			10,000

5. (L.O. 2)

\multicolumn{4}{c	}{General Journal}
Date	Description	Debit	Credit

May 11	Wages Expense
	    Social Security Taxes Payable
	    Medicare Taxes Payable
	    Union Dues Payable
	    State Income Taxes Payable
	    Federal Income Taxes Payable
	    Wages Payable
	        To record payroll liabilities and wages expense for Oswald Nelson
		260.00	
			16.12
			3.77
			5.00
			8.00
			52.00
			175.11

11	Payroll Taxes Expense
	    Social Security Taxes Payable
	    Medicare Taxes Payable
	    Federal Unemployment Taxes Payable
	    State Unemployment Taxes Payable
	        To record payroll taxes on Nelson's earnings
		36.01	
			16.12
			3.77
			2.08
			14.04

Answers: Chapter 10

Chapter 11

Matching

1. i	6. s	11. m	16. n	21. d
2. u	7. j	12. l	17. p	
3. q	8. f	13. b	18. h	
4. a	9. c	14. g	19. k	
5. o	10. e	15. r	20. t	

Short Answer

1. (L.O. 2) A debenture is an unsecured bond, whereas an indenture is the contract between the bondholder and the corporation.
2. (L.O. 3) A premium would probably be received when the bond's interest rate is higher than the market rate for similar bonds at the time of the issue.
3. (L.O. 3) Interest = principal × rate × time
4. (L.O. 4) The present value of periodic interest payments and the present value of the maturity value
5. (L.O. 1) Stockholders retain their level of control; interest is tax deductible; increased earnings accrue to stockholders.

True-False

1. F (L.O. 2) They are creditors.
2. T (L.O. 2)
3. F (L.O. 2) Bond interest must be paid on each interest date. It is not something that the board of directors declares.
4. T (L.O. 3)
5. F (L.O. 5) It will be less than the cash paid.
6. T (L.O. 5)
7. F (L.O. 6) Bond Interest Expense is credited.
8. T (L.O. 5)
9. F (L.O. 5) It equals interest payments *plus* the bond discount.
10. T (L.O. 7)
11. F (L.O. 5) The premium amortized increases each year.
12. T (L.O. 5)
13. F (L.O. 8) The statement describes capital leases.
14. T (L.O. 8)
15. F (L.O. 7) No gain or loss is recorded.
16. T (L.O. 3)
17. T (L.O. 8)
18. T (L.O. 1)

Multiple Choice

1. d (L.O. 6) When bonds are issued between interest dates, the amount the investor pays for the bond includes the accrued interest as of the date of issue. On the interest date, the full interest due for the entire period is paid out to each bondholder, including those who have held a bond for only a partial period. The issuing firm maintains the abnormal balance in the Bond Interest Expense account until the interest is paid to the bondholders.

2. a (L.O. 8) Interest expense on a mortgage is based on the unpaid balance. Over time, as the principal of the mortgage is reduced, the interest portion of a fixed payment becomes less. Therefore, the portion of the payment attributable to the reduction of the unpaid balance increases.

3. d (L.O. 3) Bonds issued at a premium have a carrying value above the face value. The Unamortized Bond Premium should be shown on the balance sheet under Long-Term Liabilities after the Bonds Payable line with the two items being totaled.
4. c (L.O. 6) Interest expense for the period must be recorded as an adjustment at year end. In recording interest expense for bonds that were sold at a discount, the calculation includes a reduction in Unamortized Bond Discount, which has a normal debit balance.
5. b (L.O. 5) Using the effective interest method, the calculation for interest expense is based on the current carrying value of the bonds. As the bond discount is amortized, that carrying value increases. As a result, the interest expense per period also increases.
6. b (L.O. 8) The lease described in *b* does not meet the requirements for a capital lease. The arrangement does not resemble a sale. It is, therefore, an operating lease.
7. c (L.O. 7) Early retirement of bonds is considered an extraordinary occurrence. Therefore, when a gain or loss results from the transaction, the results are presented on the income statement as an extraordinary item. In the transaction described, the company paid $204,000 ($200,000 × 102%) for bonds outstanding with a carrying value of $195,000. The difference between the carrying value and the amount paid ($9,000) is a loss.
8. c (L.O. 7) The carrying value of the bonds is $612,000. If one-third of the bonds are converted, the carrying value of the bonds payable will be reduced by $204,000 ($612,000/3).

Exercises

1. (L.O. 3, 5)
   a. $9,000 ($600,000 − $591,000)
   b. $21,000 ($600,000 × 7% × ½)
   c. $21,450 $\left(\$21,000 + \dfrac{\$9,000}{20}\right)$
   d. $593,700 ($600,000 − $6,300)

2. (L.O. 3, 5)
   a. $550,000 ($500,000 × 110%)
   b. $17,500 ($500,000 × 7% × ½)
   c. $16,500 ($550,000 × 6% × ½)
   d. $1,000 ($17,500 − $16,500)
   e. $549,000 ($550,000 − $1,000)

3. (L.O. 5)

Interest payments ($600,000 × 8% × 10)	$480,000
Premium on bonds payable ($600,000 × 6%)	36,000
Total interest costs	$444,000 ($44,400/year)

4. (L.O. 8)

General Journal				
Date		Description	Debit	Credit
19x1 Dec.	31	Cash	50,000	
		Notes Payable		50,000
		Borrowed $50,000 at 10% on 5-year note		
19x2 Dec.	31	Notes Payable	10,000	
		Interest Expense	5,000	
		Cash		15,000
		Made first installment payment		
19x3 Dec.	31	Notes Payable	10,000	
		Interest Expense	4,000	
		Cash		14,000
		Made second installment payment		

5. (L.O. 8)

General Journal				
Date		Description	Debit	Credit
19x1 Dec.	31	Cash	50,000	
		Notes Payable		50,000
		Borrowed $50,000 at 10% on 5-year note		
19x2 Dec.	31	Notes Payable	8,190	
		Interest Expense	5,000	
		Cash		13,190
		Made first installment payment		
19x3 Dec.	31	Notes Payable	9,009	
		Interest Expense	4,181	
		Cash		13,190
		Made second installment payment		

Solution to Crossword Puzzle

(Chapters 10 and 11)

¹P	E	N	S	I	O	N	P	²L	A	N		³S	
R								E				E		⁴R
E		⁵F	A	⁶C	E			A		⁷I		R		E
M				O		⁸D		⁹S	I	N	K	I	N	G
¹⁰I	N	¹¹D	E	N	T	U	R	E		T		A		I
U		E		T		E		S		E		L		S
M		F		I						R				T
		I		N		¹²I		¹³T	E	R	¹⁴M		E
	¹⁵A	N		G		N				S		O		R
N		I		E		C		¹⁶F		T		R		E
¹⁷N	E	T		N		O		U				T		D
U		¹⁸E	S	T	I	M	A	T	E	D		G		
I		L				E		U			¹⁹C	A	L	L
T		Y						R			G			
Y			²⁰S	I	M	P	L	E		²¹Z	E	R	O	

Chapter 12

Matching

1. f	6. m	11. d	16. q
2. k	7. g	12. h	17. i
3. p	8. a	13. c	18. r
4. l	9. o	14. s	19. j
5. e	10. n	15. t	20. b

Short Answer

1. (L.O. 1) Separate legal entity, limited liability, ease of capital generation, ease of transfer of ownership, lack of mutual agency, continuous existence, centralized authority and responsibility, and professional management
2. (L.O. 1) Government regulation, double taxation, limited liability, and separation of ownership and control
3. (L.O. 3) Contributed capital and retained earnings
4. (L.O. 5) When dividends are declared and when a corporation liquidates
5. (L.O. 3) When a corporation has bought back some of its issued stock. Treasury stock is stock that has been issued but is no longer outstanding.
6. (L.O. 7) Treasury stock is stock that has been issued and later repurchased by the corporation. Unissued stock has never been issued.

True-False

1. T (L.O. 1)
2. T (L.O. 3, 6)
3. T (L.O. 1)
4. F (L.O. 2) Organization costs normally are amortized over the early years of a corporation's life.
5. T (L.O. 3)
6. T (L.O. 3)
7. F (L.O. 5) It may.
8. T (L.O. 5)
9. F (L.O. 3) Par value does not necessarily relate to market value (worth).
10. T (L.O. 7)
11. F (L.O. 5) No stockholders are ever guaranteed dividends.
12. F (L.O. 3) Common stock is considered the residual equity of a corporation.
13. F (L.O. 8) The amount of compensation is measured on the date of grant.
14. F (L.O. 4) Total assets and total liabilities decrease.
15. F (L.O. 5) Dividends in arrears are not a liability until declared. Any arrearage normally appears as a footnote.
16. F (L.O. 7) Treasury Stock is listed in the stockholders' equity section as a deduction.
17. T (L.O. 3)
18. F (L.O. 7) Paid-in Capital, Treasury Stock is recorded for the excess of the issue price over the cost.

Multiple Choice

1. d (L.O. 7) When a company is dealing in its own stock, losses never are recognized. What would otherwise be considered a loss is recorded as a reduction in stockholders' equity. The exact nature of the transaction in this case is unknown because of the lack of detail.
2. b (L.O. 7) Treasury stock is stock that has been issued. For the purpose of cash dividends, however, treasury stock is not considered to be outstanding.
3. c (L.O. 3) The number of authorized shares is the maximum number of shares a corporation can issue. Until such time as shares are issued, they are considered unissued. Outstanding shares are those shares that are issued and in the hands of stockholders (as opposed to in the treasury of the corporation). Treasury stock is considered to be issued.
4. d (L.O. 5) Because the preferred stock is noncumulative, there are no dividends in arrears.

Answers: Chapter 12

The current dividend declared will be distributed to preferred stockholders based on 7% of the par value of $100. Of the declaration, therefore, $7,000 will be distributed to the preferred stockholders (.07 × $100 × 1,000 shares). The remaining $33,000 will be distributed, pro rata, to the common stockholders.

5. d (L.O. 1) The stockholders of a corporation are protected from unlimited liability. Under most circumstances, their liability (or potential for loss) is limited to the amount of their investment.

6. d (L.O. 4) The declaration of a cash dividend requires a journal entry to record the liability and to reduce retained earnings by the amount of the declared dividend. On the date of payment of the dividend, a journal entry is required to record the elimination of the liability created on the date of declaration and the reduction in cash as a result of the payment. The date of record is the data-gathering date, and no journal entry is required.

7. b (L.O. 4) If stock is purchased after the date of record, the new owner has no rights to the dividends not yet distributed.

8. d (L.O. 5) The call feature on stock specifies an amount for which the corporation can buy back the stock. It is binding to the stockholder and to the issuing corporation in spite of possible differences between the call price and the market value at the time the stock is called.

Exercises

1. (L.O. 2, 4, 6, 8)

General Journal

Date		Description	Debit	Credit

Jan.	1	Organization Costs
		    Cash
		        Paid legal and incorporation fees
			8,000	8,000

Feb.	9	Cash
		    Common Stock
		    Paid-in Capital in Excess of Par Value, Common
		        Issued 5,000 shares of $100 per value common stock
			575,000	500,000
				75,000

Apr.	12	Buildings
		    Preferred Stock
		    Paid-in Capital in Excess of Stated Value, Preferred
		        Issued 20,000 shares of preferred stock in exchange for a building
			240,000	200,000
				40,000

June	23	Cash Dividends Declared
		    Cash Dividends Payable
		        Declared a cash dividend on common stock
			20,000	20,000

July	8	Cash Dividends Payable
		    Cash
		        Paid cash dividend declared on June 23
			20,000	20,000

Dec.	20	Cash
		    Common Stock
		    Paid-in Capital in Excess of Par Value, Common
		        To record exercise of stock option by president
			22,000	20,000
				2,000

	31	Amortization Expense, Organization Costs
		    Organization Costs
		        To amortize organization costs for the year
			1,600	1,600

2. (L.O. 7)

\multicolumn{5}{c}{General Journal}
\multicolumn{2}{c}{Date}	Description	Debit	Credit

Jan	12	Treasury Stock, Common
		    Cash
		        To record purchase of treasury stock
			300,000	300,000

	20	Cash
		    Treasury Stock, Common
		    Paid-in Capital, Treasury Stock
		        To record reissue of treasury stock
			130,000	120,000
				10,000

	27	Cash
		Paid-in Capital, Treasury Stock
		    Treasury Stock, Common
		        To record reissue of treasury stock
			116,000
			4,000
				120,000

	31	Common Stock
		Paid-in Capital in Excess of Par Value, Common
		Retained Earnings
		    Treasury Stock, Common
		        To record retirement of treasury stock
			10,000
			40,000
			10,000
				60,000

3. (L.O. 5)
   a. $18,000 (1,000 × $100 × 6% × 3 years)
   b. $33,000 ($51,000 − $18,000)

Answers: Chapter 12

Chapter 13

Matching

1. j	6. b	11. p	16. h
2. c	7. n	12. d	17. f
3. r	8. g	13. o	18. q
4. s	9. i	14. a	19. e
5. m	10. l	15. k	20. t

Short Answer

1. (L.O. 1) Net loss from operations, cash dividend declaration, stock dividend declaration, certain prior period adjustments, and certain treasury stock transactions
2. (L.O. 2) A stock split changes the par or stated value of the stock; a stock dividend does not. Also, a stock dividend transfers retained earnings to contributed capital; a stock split does not.
3. (L.O. 8) It must be unusual in nature, and it must occur infrequently.
4. (L.O. 7, 8) Correct order: 5, 1, 4, 6, 3, 2

True-False

1. F (L.O. 7) The net of taxes amount is less than $20,000.
2. F (L.O. 3) Restricted Retained Earnings is not a cash account.
3. T (L.O. 5)
4. F (L.O. 2) Each stockholder owns the same percentage as before.
5. T (L.O. 2)
6. F (L.O. 2) Its main purpose is to increase marketability by causing a decrease in the market price. The decrease in par value is more a by-product of a stock split.
7. F (L.O. 8) It does not because it is not an unusual and infrequently occurring event.
8. F (L.O. 8) Extraordinary items appear on the income statement.
9. T (L.O. 8)
10. F (L.O. 2) It is part of contributed capital.
11. T (L.O. 9)
12. T (L.O. 7)
13. T (L.O. 1)
14. F (L.O. 9) Common stock equivalents always are included.
15. T (L.O. 2)

Multiple Choice

1. a (L.O. 1, 2) A stock split simply requires replacing the number of shares outstanding before the split with the number of shares outstanding after the split. There is no other adjustment to stockholders' equity.
2. c (L.O. 2) The firm distributed a stock dividend of 1,000 shares (10% of 10,000 shares). The 11,000 shares outstanding after the stock dividend then were split into 4 shares for each 1 share (11,000 × 4), resulting in total shares outstanding of 44,000.
3. d (L.O. 3) The restriction on retained earnings is simply an indication of the intended use of the balance. The restricted amount remains in the stockholders' equity section of the balance sheet but should be identified separately to identify the amount that is not available for dividends.
4. c (L.O. 2) On the date of distribution of a stock dividend, Common Stock is credited and Common Stock Distributable is debited. Retained Earnings will be reduced at the end of the accounting period when Stock Dividends Declared is closed to Retained Earnings.
5. a (L.O. 8) Extraordinary items appear on the income statement to indicate the overall economic impact of the financial event on the company. Extraordinary items are presented after income (loss) from continuing operations and after income (loss) from discontinued operations.
6. c (L.O. 9) For EPS calculations, 40,000 shares were outstanding for the entire year. An additional 20,000 shares were outstanding for 9/12 of the year. 20,000 × 9/12 = 15,000 shares.

40,000 shares + 15,000 shares is 55,000 average shares outstanding for the year.
7. b (L.O. 1) There was a $30,000 increase in retained earnings during the year, even after a $15,000 cash dividend. Therefore, net income for the year must have been $45,000 ($30,000 + $15,000).
8. c (L.O. 4, 8) Extraordinary gains and losses are shown in the income statement.
9. b (L.O. 5) If a corporation has just one type of stock, it would be common stock. Book value per share would be calculated by dividing total stockholders' equity (retained earnings and contributed capital) by the number of shares issued. The current year's dividends already would have reduced total stockholders' equity. Dividend information would be irrelevant to finding book value per share.
10. c (L.O. 1) Retained earnings accumulate over time as a result of undistributed income. Each accounting period that earnings are not entirely distributed to the stockholders through dividends, retained earnings increase. Accounting periods in which losses occur result in a reduction in retained earnings. Dividends declared are taken from retained earnings.

Exercises

1. (L.O. 2)

General Journal

Date		Description	Debit	Credit

Sept.	1	Cash
		    Common Stock
		    Paid-in Capital in Excess of Par Value, Common
		        To record issuance of stock
			1,200,000	1,000,000
				200,000

Mar.	7	Stock Dividends Declared
		    Common Stock Distributable
		    Paid-in Capital in Excess of Par Value, Common
		        To record declaration of stock dividend
			65,000	50,000
				15,000

	30	No entry		

Apr.	13	Common Stock Distributable
		    Common Stock
		        To record distribution of stock dividend
			50,000	50,000

2. (L.O. 6)

Operating Income Before Taxes		$100,000
Less Income Taxes Expense		40,000
Income Before Extraordinary Item		$ 60,000
Extraordinary Lightning Loss	$ 30,000	
Less Applicable Taxes	12,000	18,000
Net Income		$ 42,000

3. (L.O. 7)

\multicolumn{4}{c	}{General Journal}
Date	Description	Debit	Credit

19x1	Income Taxes Expense
	   Income Taxes Payable
	   Deferred Income Taxes
	     To record income taxes for 19x1
		24,000	16,000
			8,000

19x2	Income Taxes Expense
	Deferred Income Taxes
	   Income Taxes Payable
	     To record income taxes for 19x2
		12,000
		4,000
			16,000

19x3	Income Taxes Expense
	Deferred Income Taxes
	   Income Taxes Payable
	     To record income taxes for 19x3
		28,000
		4,000
			32,000

4. (L.O. 5)

Total stockholders' equity		$680,000
Less:		
Par value of outstanding preferred stock	$200,000	
Dividends in arrears	28,000	
Equity allocated to preferred shareholders		228,000
Equity pertaining to common shareholders		$452,000

Book value per share:

Preferred stock = $228,000/4,000 shares = $57.00 per share
Common stock = $452,000/30,000 shares = $15.07 per share

Solution to Crossword Puzzle

(Chapters 12 and 13)

```
                              ¹S        ²U        ³D
        ⁴A  ⁵C  O  M  P  R  E  H  E  N  S  I  V  E
            G   O              A         E         F
            E   M     ⁶P    ⁷A  R  R  E  A  R  S    I
        ⁸N  O   P  A  R      P     E               C
            C   L     I      P     ⁹S  P  L  I  T  I
            Y   E     O      R                     T
              ¹⁰E  X  T  R  A  O  R  D  I  N  A  R  Y
                              P
        ¹¹M  ¹²C    ¹³P  A  R    ¹⁴D ¹⁵I  L  U  T  E  D
          A    A         I         S
        ¹⁶R  E  S  I  D  U  A  L   ¹⁷S  T  A  T  E  D
          K    H         T           U
          E          ¹⁸R  E  D  E  E  M  A  B  L  E
        ¹⁹T  A  X  E  S      D
```

292   Answers: Chapter 13

Chapter 14

Matching

1. f	3. i	5. e	7. h	9. d
2. j	4. g	6. a	8. c	10. b

Short Answer

1. (L.O. 3) Issuing capital stock to retire long-term debt and purchasing a long-term asset by incurring long-term debt
2. (L.O. 4) Because they represent noncash expenses that have been legitimately deducted in arriving at net income. Adding them back effectively cancels out the deduction.
3. (L.O. 6) Cash Flows from Investing Activities, Cash Flows from Financing Activities, and Schedule of Noncash Investing and Financing Transactions
4. (L.O. 1) Money market accounts, commercial paper (short-term notes), and U.S. Treasury bills

True-False

1. T (L.O. 1)
2. F (L.O. 3) It is considered an operating activity.
3. T (L.O. 5)
4. T (L.O. 4)
5. T (L.O. 4)
6. F (L.O. 3, 4) Depreciation, depletion, and amortization would be found in the operating activities section.
7. F (S.O. 8) The reverse is true.
8. T (S.O. 8)
9. F (L.O. 7) It implies that the business is generally contracting.
10. T (L.O. 5)
11. F (L.O. 4) It would be added to net income.
12. F (L.O. 4) Depreciation must be *deducted* from operating expenses in this case.
13. T (L.O. 5)
14. T (L.O. 3, 5)
15. F (L.O. 6) A change in methods does not produce a different net-change-in-cash figure.
16. F (L.O. 7) Dividends are deducted because in the long run they must be paid to retain stockholder interest.

Multiple Choice

1. a (L.O. 4) Cash receipts from sales, interest, and dividends are used to calculate cash inflows from operating activities. Under the indirect method, they are simply components of the net income figure presented.
2. b (L.O. 4) Net income in the operating activities section of the statement of cash flows includes the gain on sale of investments. That amount needs to be backed out of the operating activities section to avoid duplication of cash inflow data.
3. a. (L.O. 4) An increase in accounts payable indicates an increase in cash available to the firm. To reflect the absence of that cash outflow, the amount by which the payables have increased is added to the Cash Flows from Operating Activities section under the indirect method of preparing a statement of cash flows.
4. e (L.O. 3) The purchase of a building by incurring a mortgage payable does not involve any cash inflow or outflow. The investing and financing activity is disclosed in the schedule of noncash investing and financing transactions.
5. d (L.O. 5) The payment of dividends is a cash outflow and would be disclosed in the financing activities section of the statement of cash flows. Investments made in a corporation by the stockholders through the purchase of stock are considered a source of financing by the corporation.
6. a (L.O. 4) Interest paid is a component of operating activities and would be recorded as a cash outflow.
7. b (L.O. 4) The increase in inventories represents a cash outflow and would be deducted from net income in the operating activities section of the statement of cash flows. The counterentry is the adjustment for changing levels of accounts payable.
8. c (L.O. 5) Cash payments from the issuance of stock are a cash inflow from financing activities. No adjustment to net income is required because the sale of stock is not recorded as a revenue and is not presented on the income statement.
9. d (S.O. 8) In the analysis of transactions for the preparation of the statement of cash flows, each operating, investing, and financing activity of the period is reconstructed. Net income results in an increase in Retained Earnings, and the analysis begins with a credit entry to that account.
10. b (L.O. 4) Total sales were $100,000. Of that amount, $14,000 was diverted by an increase in accounts receivable. $100,000 less $14,000 equals $86,000 in cash receipts from cash sales and accounts receivable.
11. c (L.O. 7) The numerator for all three calculations is net cash flows from operating activities.

Exercises

1. (L.O. 4)
   a. $57,000 ($70,000 operating expenses + $1,000 increase in Prepaid Expenses + $6,000 decrease in Accrued Liabilities – $20,000 in Depreciation Expense)
   b. $360,000 ($350,000 Sales + $10,000 decrease in Accounts Receivable)
   c. $31,000 ($33,000 Income Taxes Expense – $2,000 increase in Income Taxes Payable)
   d. $221,000 ($240,000 Cost of Goods Sold – $12,000 decrease in Inventory – $7,000 increase in Accounts Payable)
   e. $51,000 (b – d – a – c above)

2. (L.O. 7)
   a. 2.0 times
   b. 13.3%
   c. 15%
   d. $55,000

3. (S.O. 8)

Webb Corporation
Work Sheet for Statement of Cash Flows
For the Year Ended December 31, 19x9

Description	Account Balances 12/31/x8	Analysis of Transactions for 19x9 Debit	Analysis of Transactions for 19x9 Credit	Account Balances 12/31/x9
Debits				
Cash	35,000		(x) 6,000	29,000
Accounts Receivable	18,000	(b) 3,000		21,000
Inventory	83,000		(c) 11,000	72,000
Plant Assets	200,000	(f) 62,000	(e) 30,000	232,000
Total Debits	336,000			354,000
Credits				
Accumulated Depreciation	40,000	(e) 10,000	(g) 26,000	56,000
Accounts Payable	27,000	(d) 8,000		19,000
Bonds Payable	100,000	(h) 10,000		90,000
Common Stock	150,000		(h) 10,000	160,000
Retained Earnings	19,000	(i) 12,000	(a) 22,000	29,000
Total Credits	336,000	105,000	105,000	354,000
Cash Flows from Operating Activities				
Net Income		(a) 22,000		
Increase in Accounts Receivable			(b) 3,000	
Decrease in Inventory		(c) 11,000		
Decrease in Accounts Payable			(d) 8,000	
Gain on Sale of Plant Assets			(e) 4,000	
Depreciation Expense		(g) 26,000		
Cash Flows from Investing Activities				
Sale of Plant Assets		(e) 24,000		
Purchase of Plant Assets			(f) 62,000	
Cash Flows from Financing Activities				
Dividends Paid			(i) 12,000	
		83,000	89,000	
Net Decrease in Cash		(x) 6,000		
		89,000	89,000	

Chapter 15

Matching

1. g
2. b
3. l
4. e
5. j
6. f
7. h
8. i
9. k
10. d
11. m
12. a
13. c

Short Answer

1. (L.O. 6) Profit margin, asset turnover, return on assets, and return on equity.
2. (L.O. 5) Horizontal analysis presents absolute and percentage changes in specific financial statement items from one year to the next. Vertical analysis, on the other hand, presents the percentage relationship of individual items on the statement to a total within the statement.
3. (L.O. 2) Rule-of-thumb measures, analysis of past performance of the company, and comparison with industry norms
4. (L.O. 1) The risk of total loss is far less with several investments than with one investment because only a rare set of economic circumstances could cause several different investments to suffer large losses all at once.
5. (L.O. 6) Cash flow yield, cash flows to sales, cash flows to assets, and free cash flow

True-False

1. T (L.O. 5)
2. F (L.O. 5) Common-size financial statements show relationships between items in terms of percentages, not dollars.
3. F (L.O. 6) The current ratio will increase.
4. T (L.O. 6)
5. F (L.O. 6) It equals the cost of goods sold divided by average inventory.
6. F (L.O. 6) The reverse is true because the price/earnings ratio depends on the earnings per share amount.
7. F (L.O. 6) Interest is not added back.
8. T (L.O. 6)
9. F (L.O. 6) The higher the debt to equity ratio, the greater the risk.
10. F (L.O. 6) Receivable turnover measures how many times, on average, the receivables were converted into cash during the period.
11. T (L.O. 6)
12. T (L.O. 6)
13. F (L.O. 6) It is a market strength ratio.
14. F (L.O. 5) Sales would be labeled 100 percent.
15. T (L.O. 3)
16. T (L.O. 3)
17. T (L.O. 6)
18. T (L.O. 4)

Answers: Chapter 15

Multiple Choice

1. **b** (L.O. 6) Interest coverage is a measure of security that a creditor can use to gauge a company's ability to cover interest payments on loans extended to the firm.
2. **d** (L.O. 6) The quick ratio measures a company's ability to cover immediate cash requirements for operating expenses and short-term payables.
3. **c** (L.O. 6) Asset turnover is calculated using sales as the numerator and average total assets as the denominator. It is a measure of the efficient use of a company's assets.
4. **a** (L.O. 6) A high price/earnings ratio indicates optimism about a company's future. That positive outlook may be due to anticipated increases in earnings and growth of the company.
5. **a** (L.O. 5) Index numbers are calculated to reflect percentage changes over consecutive periods of time. The base year is assigned the value of 100%; then changes from that base are assigned a percentage so that adjustments to subsequent amounts can be compared with base amounts. This method is used to identify trends, eliminating differences resulting from universal changes, such as inflation.
6. **b** (L.O. 1) Management uses financial statements to make decisions about the future of the company. Management also uses financial statements to analyze variances between actual results and budgeted results of operations. By using financial statements, management is better able to plan and control major functions of management. Each of the other choices listed is an external user of financial statements.
7. **d** (L.O. 2) Each of the factors listed in choices *a* through *c* contributes to the complications of comparing a company with the industry in which it operates.
8. **c** (L.O. 6) The turnover of receivables is the number of times receivables are collected in relation to sales in an accounting period. If the number is low, average accounts receivable balances are presumed to be high and credit policy is presumed to be weak.
9. **b** (L.O. 5) Net income is given a percentage in relation to sales, as are all other components of the income statement. Sales equal 100%.
10. **c** (L.O. 6) The commitments free cash flow allows for are dividends and net capital expenditures.

Exercises

1. (L.O. 5)

	19x1	19x2	Increase (Decrease) Amount	Percentage
Sales	$200,000	$250,000	$50,000	25.0
Cost of goods sold	120,000	144,000	24,000	20.0
Gross margin	$ 80,000	$106,000	26,000	32.5
Operating expenses	50,000	62,000	12,000	24.0
Income before income taxes	$ 30,000	$ 44,000	14,000	46.7
Income taxes	8,000	16,000	8,000	100.0
Net income	$ 22,000	$ 28,000	6,000	27.3

2. (L.O. 6)
   a. 2.0 ($500,000/$250,000)
   b. 1.3 $\left(\dfrac{\$500,000 - \$180,000}{250,000}\right)$
   c. 1.9 times ($350,000/$180,000)
   d. 192.1 days (365/1.9)
   e. 12.0% ($106,000/$880,000)
   f. 22.1% ($106,000/$480,000)
   g. 6.0 ($600,000/$100,000)
   h. 60.8 days (365/6.0)
   i. 17.7% ($106,000/$600,000)
   j. 0.7 times ($75,000/$106,000)
   k. 12.5% ($75,000/$600,000)
   l. 8.5% ($75,000/$880,000)
   m. .68 times ($600,000/$880,000)
   n. 8 times $\left(\dfrac{\$40}{\$106,000/\$21,200}\right)$

Answers: Chapter 15

Chapter 16

Matching

1. b	**5.** j	**9.** l	**13.** e
2. f	**6.** d	**10.** n	**14.** m
3. i	**7.** k	**11.** h	**15.** a
4. g	**8.** p	**12.** o	**16.** c

Short Answer

1. (L.O. 4)

Classification	Method
Noninfluential and noncontrolling	Cost adjusted to market
Influential but noncontrolling	Equity
Controlling	Equity (also, consolidate)

2. (L.O. 4) Under the cost adjusted to market method, Dividend Income is recorded when dividends are received. Dividend Income is credited. Under the equity method, the Investment account is credited (decreased).

3. (L.O. 6) When the cost exceeds the book value of the net assets purchased, any excess that is not assigned to specific assets and liabilities should be recorded as goodwill.

4. (L.O. 5) Intercompany items are eliminated to avoid misleading consolidated financial statements. For example, if intercompany receivables and payables were (incorrectly) included in consolidated financial statements, that portion would represent the amount that the combined companies owed themselves.

5. (L.O. 1) When the exchange rate changes between the transaction date and the payment date, and foreign currency is involved, the domestic company would record an exchange gain or loss.

True-False

1. T (L.O. 4)
2. F (L.O. 4) The investor would do that under the equity method.
3. F (L.O. 4) Over 50 percent is the requirement for consolidated financial statements.
4. T (L.O. 6)
5. F (L.O. 5) The subsidiary's earnings are included from the date of acquisition only.
6. T (L.O. 4)
7. F (L.O. 6) A minority interest should be reported in the stockholders' equity section.
8. T (L.O. 6)
9. T (L.O. 1)
10. T (L.O. 1)
11. T (L.O. 1)
12. T (L.O. 1)
13. F (L.O. 7) Purchases of goods and services from outsiders should not be eliminated.
14. T (L.O. 6)

Multiple Choice

1. **b** (L.O. 4) Under the cost adjusted to market method of accounting for investments, dividends received are recorded as a source of income. The dividends are not used to adjust the value of the investment.

2. **d** (L.O. 6) The book value of each long-term asset will be reduced in proportion to the value of each asset relative to the whole. Each asset will maintain its value relative to the other assets, but the total book value will be reduced to the purchase price.

3. **a** (L.O. 6) The investment in the subsidiary company will be credited in making eliminations to prepare consolidated financial statements of the parent and subsidiary companies.

4. **b** (L.O. 6) Goodwill is used as a plug figure on the consolidation of the parent and subsidiary companies. Goodwill does not appear on the unconsolidated financial statements of the parent company.

5. **d** (L.O. 7) Profit on goods sold by the subsidiary to outsiders is an income item that is part of the total income of the parent and subsidiary upon consolidation. It will not be eliminated during consolidation.

6. **d** (L.O. 4) The adjustment required to recognize a loss on long-term investments includes a debit to Unrealized Loss on Long-Term Investments and a credit to Allowance to Adjust Long-Term Investments to Market. Since the market value of the investment is $35,000 below the cost, and since the allowance account has a credit balance of $10,000, the adjustment for the current period will be an additional $25,000 credit.

7. **d** (L.O. 4) So that the users of financial statements will get a fair picture of the value of the company, Unrealized Loss on Long-Term Investments appears as a reduction in stockholders' equity. The corresponding allowance account is a contra-asset account and is used to revalue the investment account to the lower market. Upon disposal of the long-term investment, the unrealized loss may be realized and appear on the income statement.

8. **c** (L.O. 1) Since fewer dollars were required to satisfy the payment for the asset, the company has experienced a gain in reporting the transaction in dollars. At the payment date, more francs were received per dollar.

Exercises

1. (L.O. 6)

Account Debited	Amount	Account Credited	Amount
Commont Stock (Carter)	$60,000	Investment in Carter Corporation	165,000
Retained Earnings (Carter)	90,000	Minority Interest	30,000
Building	10,000		
Goodwill	35,000		

2. (L.O. 4)

General Journal				
Date		Description	Debit	Credit
		Cash	12,000	
		Dividend Income		12,000
		To record cash dividend from Andrews*		
		Cash	15,000	
		Investment in Wilkins Company		15,000
		To record cash dividend from Wilkins		
		Investment in Wilkins Company	19,500	
		Income, Wilkins Company Investment		19,500
		To recognize 30% of income reported by Wilkins Company		

*Andrews' earnings of $110,000 are irrelevant, since Fairfax is using the cost adjusted to market method to account for the investment.

3. (L.O. 1)

General Journal				
Date		Description	Debit	Credit

		Accounts Receivable, Mexican Company
		   Sales
		      To record sale of merchandise
			5,000	5,000

		Cash
		Exchange Gain or Loss
		   Accounts Receivable, Mexican Company
		      To record receipt of payment
			4,500
			500
				5,000

Solution to Crossword Puzzle

(Chapters 14, 15, and 16)

	1 L	2 P	R	I	C	E	E	A	R	N	3 I	N	G	S	
	E	O									N				
	4 V	E	R	T	I	C	A	L			T		5 Y		
	E	T					6 I	N	T	E	R	I	M		
	R	7 F	L	O	W	S					E		E		
	A	O									E		L		
	G	L		8 A	N	A	L	Y	S	I	S		D		
	E	I									T				
		9 C	O	M	M	O	N	S	10 I	Z	E		11 C		
		U							N			12 D	O		
	13 T	R	E	N	D				D		14 R	I	N		
		R							E		A	R	T		
		15 E	Q	U	I	T	Y		X		T	E	R		
		N									I	C	O		
		16 T	A	X		17 H	O	R	I	Z	O	N	T	A	L

Answers: Chapter 16   303

Appendix B

Exercises

1. (L.O. 1)

Mammoth Mart, Inc.
Work Sheet
For the Month Ended March 31, 19xx

Account Name	Trial Balance Debit	Trial Balance Credit	Adjustments Debit	Adjustments Credit	Adjusted Trial Balance Debit	Adjusted Trial Balance Credit	Income Statement Debit	Income Statement Credit	Balance Sheet Debit	Balance Sheet Credit
Cash	1,000				1,000				1,000	
Accounts Receivable	700				700				700	
Merchandise Inventory	400				400				620	
Prepaid Rent	750			(a) 250	500				500	
Equipment	4,200				4,200				4,200	
Accounts Payable		900				900				900
Common Stock		3,000				3,000				3,000
Retained Earnings		1,200				1,200				1,200
Sales		9,800				9,800		9,800		
Sales Discounts	300				300		300			
Purchases	3,700				3,700		3,700			
Purchases Returns and Allowances		150				150		150		
Freight In	400				400		400			
Salaries Expense	3,000		(b) 500		3,500		3,500			
Advertising Expense	600				600		600			
	15,050	15,050								
Rent Expense			(a) 250		250		250			
Salaries Payable				(b) 500		500				500
Depreciation Expense			(c) 375		375		375			
Accumulated Depreciation, Equipment				(c) 375		375				375
Income Taxes Expense			(e) 180		180		180			
Income Taxes Payable				(e) 180		180				180
			1,305	1,305	16,105	16,105	9,705	10,570	7,020	6,155
Net Income							865			865
							10,570	10,570	7,020	7,020

2. (L.O. 2)

	General Journal		
Date	Description	Debit	Credit
	Income Summary	131,900	
	Sales Returns and Allowances		5,300
	Cost of Goods Sold		52,700
	Freight In		3,200
	Selling Expenses		39,400
	General and Administrative Expenses		24,800
	Income Taxes Expense		6,500
	Sales	244,100	
	Income Summary		244,100
	Income Summary	112,200	
	Retained Earnings		112,200
	Retained Earnings	50,000	
	Dividends		50,000

Appendix C

Matching

1. a
2. d
3. c
4. e
5. b

Exercises

1. (L.O. 2)
a. J	d. CP	g. J	j. CP
b. CR	e. S	h. J	k. CR
c. P	f. CP	i. J	

2. (L.O. 2)

Cash Receipts Journal								
			Debits			Credits		
Date		Account Debited/ Credited	Post. Ref.	Cash	Sales Disc.	Other Accts.	Accts. Receiv.	Sales	Other Accts.
Feb.	3	Frank Simpson	✓	490	10		500		
	9	Equipment	135	8,000					8,000
	14	Common Stock	311	10,000					10,000
	23	Stanley Hall	✓	150			150		
	28	Sales		25,000				25,000	
				43,640	10		650	25,000	18,000
				(111)	(412)		(114)	(411)	(✓)

3. (L.O. 2)
   a. Cash payments journal
   b. The "Other Accounts" total should have a check (not an account number) below it to signify that it is not posted at the end of the month.
   c. May 1 Paid Vincennes Supply Co. for $800 of supplies previously purchased. Paid within the discount period, receiving a $16 discount.
   May 7 Purchased for cash $2,000 of office equipment from Jeppson Business Equipment.
   May 13 Paid for ad placed in the *Daily Planet*.
   May 19 Paid Olsen Motors for $420 of items previously purchased. Did not pay within the discount period (or no discount allowed).
   d. 1. The amounts in the Accounts Payable column were posted to the accounts payable subsidiary accounts (Vincennes Supply and Olsen Motors).
   2. The amounts in the Other Accounts column were posted to the general ledger accounts (Office Equipment and Advertising Expense).
   3. The 315 is an error, as already explained. The other numbers refer to the postings of column totals to the general ledger accounts.

Appendix D

Matching

1. e   5. b   8. h
2. f   6. c   9. a
3. j   7. g   10. d
4. i

Exercises

1. (L.O. 4)
    a. A = $14,500 (10,000 + 3,000 + 1,500)
        B = $13,000 (10,000 + 2,000 + 1,000)
        C = $13,000 (10,000 + 2,500 + 500)
    b. A = $7,000 (10,000 + 3,000 − 6,000)
        B = $8,000 (10,000 + 2,000 − 4,000)
        C = $10,500 (10,000 + 2,500 − 2,000)
    c. A = ($8,000) (10,000 + 3,000 − 21,000)
        B = ($2,000) (10,000 + 2,000 − 14,000)
        C = $5,500 (10,000 + 2,500 − 7,000)

2. (L.O. 5)

\multicolumn{5}{c}{General Journal}
Date		Description	Debit	Credit
a.		Cash	12,000	
		G, Capital	800	
		H, Capital	800	
		I, Capital	400	
		J, Capital		14,000
		To record purchase of one-third interest by J		
b.		Cash	15,000	
		J, Capital		15,000
		To record purchase of one-third interest by J		
c.		Cash	21,000	
		G, Capital		1,600
		H, Capital		1,600
		I, Capital		800
		J, Capital		17,000
		To record purchase of one-third interest by J		

Appendix E

Matching

1. j
2. q
3. c
4. m
5. g
6. s
7. b
8. a
9. n
10. e
11. l
12. p
13. h
14. o
15. f
16. d
17. r
18. i
19. k

Exercises

1. (L.O. 3)

\multicolumn{4}{c	}{General Journal}		
Date		Description	Debit	Credit

Jan.	1	Estimated Revenues
		    Appropriations
		    Fund Balance
			950,000	935,000
				15,000

Mar.	15	Property Taxes Receivable
		    Revenue
		    Estimated Uncollectible Property Taxes
			900,000	891,000
				9,000

	25	Encumbrances Reserve for Encumbrances	50,000	50,000
May	9	Expenditures Cash	30,000	30,000
June	15	Cash Estimated Uncollectible Property Taxes Property Taxes Receivable	893,000 7,000	900,000
	27	Reserve for Encumbrances Encumbrances	50,000	50,000
	27	Expenditures Vouchers Payable	51,000	51,000
July	5	Vouchers Payable Cash	51,000	51,000

Dec.	31	Revenues
		    Estimated Revenues
		    Fund Balance
			955,000	950,000
				5,000

	31	Appropriations Fund Balance Expenditures	935,000 12,000	947,000

Appendix F

Exercises

1. (L.O. 1–3)

\multicolumn{5}{c}{**General Journal**}
Date		Description	Debit	Credit

Mar.	1	Investment in Bonds
		Interest Income
		  Cash
		    To record purchase of bonds
			9,600.00
			140.00
				
				9,740.00

July	1	Cash
		Investment in Bonds ($288 − 280)
		  Interest Income
		    To record semiannual interest and amortization of discount
			420.00
			8.00
				
				428.00

Dec.	31	Accrued Interest Receivable
		Investment in Bonds
		  Interest Income
		    To record accrued interest and amortization of discount
			420.00
			12.36
				
				432.36

Jan.	1	Cash
		  Accrued Interest Receivable
		    To record receipt of interest
			420.00	
				420.00

Mar.	1	Investment in Bonds*
		  Interest Income
		    To amortize 2 months' interest
			4.31	
				4.31

	1	Cash ($9500 − 200 + 140)
		Loss on Sale of Investments
		  Investment in Bonds
		  Interest Income
		    To record sale of bonds
		
		    *$9,620.36 × 9% × 1/6 = $144.31
		     10,000 × 8.4% × 1/6 = 140.00
		                                   $ 4.31
			9,440.00
			324.67
				
				9,624.67
				140.00